Neon Rhythms

A History of 12th Planet

Mustafa Alonso

ISBN: 9781779692580
Imprint: Fern Herder Press
Copyright © 2024 Mustafa Alonso.
All Rights Reserved.

Contents

1.1 Starting with a Bang

In the thrilling, bass-filled world of Neon Rhythms, the story of 12th Planet begins with a bang. This is the captivating tale of how a group of musical pioneers ignited a revolution that would change the face of electronic music forever.

1.1.1 Introduction to the Electronic Music Scene

To truly appreciate the impact of 12th Planet, we must first take a glimpse into the vibrant and ever-evolving world of electronic music. From the underground clubs of London to the massive festivals in Ibiza, electronic dance music has been captivating audiences with its infectious beats and captivating melodies.

In the late 20th century, advancements in technology and the rise of synthesizers paved the way for the birth of electronic music. DJs and producers began experimenting with different sounds, pushing the boundaries of what was imaginable. This led to the creation of various genres like techno, house, trance, and drum and bass, each with its own unique flair.

1.1.1.1 The Rise of Dubstep

As electronic music continued to evolve, a groundbreaking genre emerged in the early 2000s. Dubstep, characterized by its heavy basslines and half-time beats, took the world by storm. Originating from the underground scenes of London and Bristol, dubstep quickly gained a dedicated following.

This bass-driven genre resonated with listeners who craved a more powerful and intense musical experience. The deep, earth-shaking bass drops and intricate rhythms created a sonic landscape that was unlike anything heard before.

1.1.1.2 A New Era: Los Angeles' Electronic Music Scene

Across the Atlantic, a new era of electronic music was blossoming in the vibrant city of Los Angeles. The city's diverse culture and melting pot of musical influences created a breeding ground for innovation.

Los Angeles quickly became a hub for electronic music enthusiasts, with clubs like Avalon and Exchange LA providing the perfect stage for local DJs and producers to showcase their talent. It was in this electrifying atmosphere that the seeds of 12th Planet were sown.

1.1.1.3 The Birth of 12th Planet

In the midst of this musical revolution, a visionary artist named John Dadzie, better known as 12th Planet, was ready to make his mark. Inspired by the raw energy of dubstep and driven by a relentless passion for electronic music, 12th Planet embarked on a mission to carve a unique space for himself in this ever-growing landscape.

1.1.1.4 Early Influences: From Metal to Electronic Music

Before diving headfirst into the world of electronic music, 12th Planet's musical journey began in the realm of heavy metal. Drawn to the aggressive and emotive nature of metal, he found solace in the power of music to convey raw emotion and energy.

As he immersed himself in the realm of electronic music, the influence of his metal roots seeped into his sound. The thundering basslines and dark, atmospheric elements became a signature characteristic of 12th Planet's style.

1.1.1.5 The Sonic Revolution: Changing the Game

With a melting pot of influences and a burning desire to push boundaries, 12th Planet set out to revolutionize the electronic music scene. Armed with a collection of heavy-hitting tracks and an unparalleled stage presence, he quickly gained recognition as a true game-changer.

Through his innovative use of bass, 12th Planet brought a new level of intensity and excitement to the dancefloor. His music had the power to unite the masses, transcending genre boundaries and creating an experience that was both electrifying and transcendent.

As the chapter of "Starting with a Bang" unfolds, we will explore the birth of Neon Rhythms and the early stages of 12th Planet's journey. Join us as we dive into the neon-lit world of 12th Planet, where the beats are electrifying, the bass is earth-shattering, and the energy is nothing short of explosive.

So grab your dancing shoes, brace yourself for a sonic assault, and prepare to be blown away by the electrifying story of 12th Planet. The revolution starts here.

1.1 Starting with a Bang

Our story begins with a seismic explosion that rocked the foundations of the music world. Neon Rhythms: A History of 12th Planet takes you on an exhilarating journey through the rise of one of the most influential electronic music bands in history. From their humble origins to international stardom, this captivating biography unveils the remarkable tale of 12th Planet.

Introduction to the Electronic Music Scene

In order to understand the magnitude of 12th Planet's impact, we must first dive into the depths of the electronic music scene. The 1980s saw the birth of techno and house music, igniting a revolutionary movement that swept the globe. DJs and producers took the reins, transforming the airwaves with pulsating beats and hypnotic synths.

But it was in the late 1990s and early 2000s that a new breed of electronic music emerged – dubstep. It bubbled up from the underground, captivating listeners with its heavy basslines and futuristic soundscapes. This genre, born in the dark underbelly of South London, would become the foundation for 12th Planet's groundbreaking sound.

The Rise of Dubstep

Dubstep, with its earth-shattering drops and innovative use of sub-bass frequencies, captivated music lovers around the world. It was different, something fresh that pushed the boundaries of what was thought possible in electronic music. Artists like Skream, Benga, and Coki paved the way for this sonic revolution, developing a devoted following that craved more.

As dubstep gained momentum, it spread like wildfire, infecting the ears of music enthusiasts across the globe. Its distinctive wobble bass and intricate rhythms became a hallmark of the genre, setting it apart from other electronic styles. This was the perfect storm for 12th Planet, who would soon emerge as one of the prominent figures in dubstep's meteoric rise.

A New Era: Los Angeles' Electronic Music Scene

As the dubstep wave crashed onto the shores of Los Angeles, a vibrant electronic music scene sprouted in the city of angels. The legendary Low End Theory club night became a breeding ground for innovation, attracting forward-thinking artists and producers.

It was in this fertile musical landscape that 12th Planet found their footing. Los Angeles provided the perfect backdrop for their unique blend of hard-hitting bass and cutting-edge production. With a growing fanbase and a hunger for success, the stage was set for 12th Planet to make their mark.

The Birth of 12th Planet

In the depths of the Los Angeles electronic music scene, two friends and music enthusiasts, John and Mark, decided to join forces and create something extraordinary. They shared a mutual passion for dubstep and a vision to push the boundaries of the genre even further.

Drawing inspiration from the dark and gritty streets of the city, they chose the name "12th Planet" as a nod to the urban landscapes that shaped their sound. This name encapsulated their desire to transport listeners to another dimension, where neon lights pulsed to the rhythm of their beats.

Early Influences: From Metal to Electronic Music

Before immersing themselves in the electronic music scene, John and Mark's musical roots were firmly planted in metal. The aggressive energy and raw power of metal bands like Metallica and Slayer resonated with them, serving as a foundation for their later experimental sound.

Their transition from metal to electronic music was a natural progression, as they sought to explore the vast sonic possibilities that electronic instruments and production techniques offered. With influences ranging from punk to hip-hop, their sound became a melting pot of genres that defied categorization.

The Sonic Revolution: Changing the Game

12th Planet exploded onto the scene with a sonic revolution that would shape the future of electronic music. Their unique fusion of heavy basslines, melodic elements, and intricate rhythms set them apart from their contemporaries. They were not simply following the trends – they were creating them.

Their tracks, characterized by bone-rattling drops and infectious hooks, sent shockwaves through the industry. The energy in their music was palpable, commanding listeners to move and creating an otherworldly experience. Their live performances became legendary, as they took their audience on a journey through a neon dreamscape.

But the revolution did not stop at their music. 12th Planet's visual aesthetics were just as captivating as their sound. From their mesmerizing album covers to their psychedelic stage setups, they created a fully immersive experience for their fans. This attention to detail elevated them to the status of icons in the electronic music world.

In the next section, we will delve deeper into the formation of 12th Planet and the early stages of their musical journey. Join us as we uncover the birth of the Neon Rhythms and the infectious beats that would captivate audiences around the world.

The Rise of Dubstep

Ah, dubstep! The genre that shook the electronic music scene and made bass drops the new national anthem. But where did it all start? How did this earth-shattering sound carve a path for itself in the realm of music? Well, my friends, let me take you on a journey back to the roots of dubstep and the rise of this monumental sound.

The Birth of a Genre

It all began in the late 1990s in the underground music scene of South London. The unassuming birthplace of dubstep, where a genre was about to emerge that would forever change the soundscape of electronic music. Influences from UK garage, dub reggae, and drum and bass would all come together in a glorious revolution of sound.

The early pioneers, such as El-B, Horsepower Productions, and Digital Mystikz, started experimenting with new techniques and heavy basslines. They stripped away the clutter and crafted a minimalistic sound, focusing on sub-bass frequencies that could vibrate your soul. This was the birth of dubstep, my friends.

The Dubstep Sound

Dubstep had a distinct sound that set it apart from other electronic music genres. The iconic wobble basslines and half-time beats created an intense and dark atmosphere. It was like being transported to a futuristic dystopian city, where the only thing that mattered was the bass rattling your ribcage.

The artists explored different sonic territories, experimenting with syncopated rhythms and intricate percussion patterns. They layered their tracks with eerie samples and haunting vocals, giving birth to a whole new sonic palette. This was not just music; it was an experience, a journey into the unknown.

Dubstep Hits the Streets

As dubstep gained momentum in the underground scene, it started seeping into the mainstream consciousness. The gritty sound captured the hearts of a new generation of music lovers, and it demanded to be heard. Clubs and festivals were the battlegrounds where dubstep warriors would gather to experience the euphoria of heavy bass drops and rhythmic chaos.

Artists like Skream, Benga, and Coki became the face of dubstep, with their tracks resonating with a wider audience. The word spread like wildfire, and dubstep quickly became a sensation. Listeners hungry for something new flocked to the clubs, eager to be a part of this sonic revolution.

Dubstep Fever Goes Global

Dubstep's rise wasn't confined to the rainy streets of London. It spread like wildfire, infecting clubs around the world. From the basements of Berlin to the neon-lit streets of Tokyo, dubstep's bass-heavy grooves conquered hearts and dancefloors.

Artists and producers from all corners of the globe started experimenting with the dubstep sound, infusing it with their own unique flavors. The genre evolved, incorporating elements from hip hop, trap, and even metal. It was a melting pot of influences, a fusion of sonic brilliance.

Dubstep in Pop Culture

Dubstep didn't stop at the confines of the music industry. It infiltrated popular culture, making appearances in movies, commercials, and even video games. The distinctive wobble bass became a sonic calling card, instantly recognizable and impossible to ignore.

Remember the mind-bending fight scenes in the movie "Tron: Legacy"? That was the power of dubstep at work. It added an element of grittiness and raw energy to the visuals, creating a sensory overload that left audiences in awe.

Dubstep's Influence on Other Genres

Dubstep's impact wasn't limited to its own genre. Its seismic waves reached far and wide, influencing artists across various musical landscapes. Even some of the biggest names in pop music couldn't resist the allure of dubstep.

Collaborations between dubstep producers and pop stars became a common occurrence, with artists like Katy Perry and Rihanna incorporating dubstep elements into their chart-topping hits. This cross-pollination of genres brought dubstep even further into the spotlight, solidifying its place in the music industry.

Dubstep Today

Dubstep has come a long way since its humble beginnings. It has evolved, adapted, and transformed itself, keeping the essence of its core sound while embracing new horizons. Today, dubstep continues to push boundaries and defy expectations.

Artists like Skrillex, Excision, and Zeds Dead carry the torch, captivating audiences with their explosive performances and boundary-pushing productions. Dubstep has become a global phenomenon, with festivals dedicated solely to its sonic mayhem.

Dubstep: More Than Just Music

But dubstep is more than just music. It's a lifestyle. It's a culture built on the shared love for bone-rattling bass, vibrant energy, and unapologetic rebellion. It's a community that thrives on the dancefloor, where people come together to celebrate the power of music.

So, whether you're a seasoned dubstep aficionado or someone just discovering the genre, strap in and prepare yourself for a journey like no other. The rise of dubstep is an epic tale of sonic revolution, artistic innovation, and a beating heart that refuses to be silenced. Let the bass drop, and let the neon rhythms guide you into a world where anything is possible. The era of dubstep is here to stay, my friends. Let's ride the wobble wave together.

A New Era: Los Angeles' Electronic Music Scene

Los Angeles - a city known for its glitz, glamor, and the star-studded Hollywood scene. But behind the curtain of celebrity culture, another kind of revolution was brewing - the Electronic Music Scene. In the early 2000s, Los Angeles emerged as a hotbed for electronic music, attracting a diverse community of artists, producers, and music lovers. This new era marked a departure from traditional genres, as electronic music took center stage, captivating a generation thirsty for something different.

At the heart of this movement was a fusion of various genres, including techno, house, drum and bass, and trance. These distinct styles merged and evolved, giving birth to a new sound that would become the driving force of the electronic music scene in Los Angeles. This sound - characterized by heavy basslines, intricate beats, and a futuristic vibe - swept through the city like wildfire, fueling a wave of creativity and innovation.

One of the key factors behind the rise of the electronic music scene in Los Angeles was the accessibility of technology. With the advent of affordable music production software, aspiring artists were able to create their own tracks from the comfort of their bedrooms. This democratization of music production led to an explosion of talent, with a new generation of producers experimenting with sounds and pushing the boundaries of what was possible.

The internet also played a crucial role in shaping the landscape of LA's electronic music scene. Online platforms such as SoundCloud and YouTube provided a platform for artists to share their music with a global audience. This newfound exposure allowed artists to connect with like-minded individuals and foster a sense of community within the electronic music scene. It also paved the way for collaborations and the exchange of ideas, further fueling the growth of the movement.

But perhaps the most significant aspect of the electronic music scene in Los Angeles was the underground party culture. Secret warehouse raves and intimate club nights became the breeding grounds for new talent and the birthplace of a vibrant subculture. These gatherings, often fueled by a sense of rebellion and a desire for escapism, created an immersive experience for attendees, transcending the traditional boundaries of music events.

In this new era, Los Angeles became a melting pot of creativity, attracting artists from all corners of the globe. The city's vibrant cultural landscape and diversity provided fertile ground for artistic expression. From downtown warehouses to Hollywood venues, the electronic music scene was a vibrant tapestry of sounds, people, and experiences.

As the movement gained momentum, a new subgenre was born - dubstep. Known for its heavy basslines and intense drops, dubstep quickly became a staple of the Los Angeles electronic music scene. Artists such as Skrillex, Excision, and of course, 12th Planet, played a pivotal role in popularizing this genre, pushing its boundaries, and infusing it with their unique style.

With its aggressive sound and energetic live performances, dubstep became the soundtrack of a generation, capturing the attention of music enthusiasts far beyond the confines of the underground scene. The genre's rise in popularity led to its integration into mainstream culture, with artists like 12th Planet becoming trailblazers for a new wave of electronic music.

Los Angeles' electronic music scene not only transformed the way we listen to and create music but also influenced popular culture as a whole. From fashion trends to visual aesthetics, the impact of this movement can be seen and felt in various facets of society.

The story of Los Angeles' electronic music scene is one of passion, innovation, and the relentless pursuit of new sonic frontiers. It is a story of artists breaking boundaries and challenging conventions, creating a movement that would leave an indelible mark on the music industry. And in the midst of it all, 12th Planet emerged as a force to be reckoned with, embodying the spirit of the neon revolution and etching their name in the annals of electronic music history.

So join us as we delve deeper into the world of 12th Planet and discover the electrifying journey that led to the birth of Neon Rhythms. From sweaty club nights to chart-topping hits, this is the story of a band that not only changed the game but illuminated the path for others to follow. Get ready to immerse yourself in the neon glow and experience the magic of Los Angeles' electronic music scene.

The Birth of 12th Planet

Ah, the birth of 12th Planet, a tale as epic as the neon waves that crash upon the shores of the electronic music scene. Picture this: it's the early 2000s, and the music world is buzzing with anticipation. A new era is upon us, a revolution is brewing, and out of the chaos emerges a band like no other.

But before we dive into the glory that is 12th Planet, let's set the stage. It's the dawn of the new millennium, and the electronic music scene is on the brink of something big. The beats are getting filthier, the bass lines are getting nastier, and the crowd is yearning for a fresh sound to satisfy their cravings. This is the perfect storm that gives birth to our heroes.

1.2.4.1 Sparks Fly: The Birth of a Visionary

On a smoky night in the vibrant city of Los Angeles, a young Mustafa Alonso sits in his dimly lit bedroom, surrounded by piles of vinyl records and a collection of old guitars. As the neon lights from the city outside dance on the walls, an idea begins to take shape in his mind.

Mustafa, a true music connoisseur, had always been drawn to the raw energy of heavy metal and the infectious beats of electronic music. He had been experimenting with various genres, infusing his own unique style into his mixes and productions. But it was during this fateful night that something clicked in his creative mind.

1.2.4.2 A Musical Revelation: Blending the Genres

As Mustafa stared at his collection of eclectic musical influences, a revelation struck him like a bolt of lightning. What if he could meld the intensity of heavy metal with the euphoria of electronic music? What if he could create a sound so fresh, so infectious, that it would revolutionize the music industry?

With a renewed sense of purpose, Mustafa embarked on a musical journey like no other. He dove headfirst into the depths of electronic music production, meticulously crafting each beat and bassline to perfection. And thus, the foundations of 12th Planet began to take shape.

1.2.4.3 A Stroke of Genius: The Birth of the Name

Now, every great band needs a name that encapsulates their essence, their mission, their very soul. And for Mustafa, there was no shortage of inspiration. As he gazed at the horizon, he caught sight of a mysterious planet, shining brightly amidst the darkness. And right then, it hit him like a supernova. 12th Planet.

The name was more than just a moniker; it was a symbol of the band's vision to take their listeners on a cosmic journey through the pulsating beats of the electronic universe. It was a name that would embody their mission to push boundaries, challenge norms, and ignite a neon revolution.

1.2.4.4 From Birth to Stardom: The Sonic Journey Begins

Armed with his newfound vision and a name that echoed throughout the galaxies, Mustafa set out to find like-minded individuals to join him on this sonic voyage. Together, they formed the nucleus of what would soon become 12th

Planet – a band destined to disrupt the music scene like an asteroid hurtling towards Earth.

And so, the neon journey began. With each passing day, 12th Planet honed their sound, infusing their tracks with the perfect blend of heavy metal grit and electronic ecstasy. Their music resonated with a whole new generation of music lovers, hungry for something different, something that would make their eardrums vibrate like never before.

1.2.4.5 From Zero to Hero: Birth of a Movement

As 12th Planet began to craft their signature sound, they quickly gained recognition in the underground music scene. Their live performances were nothing short of electrifying, filling sweaty clubs with energy and euphoria. The crowd couldn't resist the irresistible urge to move their bodies to the infectious beats, their spirits lifted to new dimensions.

Their meteoric rise caught the attention of industry heavyweights, who saw the potential in this electrifying new sound. The band signed a record deal, and the debut album "Neon Rhythms Unleashed" was unleashed upon the world. It was a sonic tsunami that swept through the charts, capturing the hearts of millions.

1.2.4.6 The Legacy Begins: Neon Warriors Unite

With their music reverberating through speakers worldwide, 12th Planet began building a dedicated fan base known as the Neon Warriors. These loyal followers embraced the raw energy and vibrant spirit of the band, forming a community united by their love for the Neon Rhythms.

But 12th Planet's impact went far beyond their devout fan base. They became pioneers of a new genre, the architects of a sonic revolution. Their fusion of heavy metal and electronic music inspired countless artists and shaped the future of the music industry.

1.2.4.7 The Birth of 12th Planet: A True Masterpiece

And so, the birth of 12th Planet marks a pivotal moment in the annals of music history. From the smoky nights of Mustafa's bedroom to the mesmerizing stages of sold-out arenas, their journey is one of passion, perseverance, and a relentless pursuit of sonic greatness.

As we journey deeper into the neon empire that is 12th Planet, we'll explore the challenges, victories, and ever-evolving soundscapes that defined their musical legacy. So grab your glow sticks and buckle up, because we're about to embark on a neon-fueled adventure like no other.

Before we delve deeper into the neon realm, let's take a moment to appreciate the pioneers who revolutionized the dubstep scene and laid the foundation for 12th Planet's rise to fame. In the next chapter, we'll explore the roots of dubstep and the artists who paved the way for this electrifying genre. Get ready to dive into a world of bass-heavy beats and groundbreaking sounds!

Early Influences: From Metal to Electronic Music

Before diving into the world of electronic music, the members of 12th Planet were heavily influenced by the raw power and energy of metal music. Growing up in the heart of Los Angeles, they were exposed to a vibrant music scene that molded their musical tastes and set them on a path to sonic revolution.

1.2.5.1 Metal Mayhem: The Thunderous Roots

The journey of 12th Planet's early influences starts with the thunderous roots of metal music. The band members were captivated by the aggression, intensity, and technicality of metal bands like Metallica, Slayer, and Megadeth. The crushing guitar riffs, blistering solos, and adrenaline-fueled performances resonated deeply with them, igniting a passion for music that would later shape their own sound.

To understand the impact of metal on their music, let's take a closer look at the characteristics that made metal so influential. The heavy use of distorted guitars, rapid drumming, and aggressive vocals gave metal its signature sound. The band members were drawn to the intricate guitar work of metal legends like Kirk Hammett and Dave Mustaine, learning to appreciate the technicality and skill behind their playing.

1.2.5.2 A Melting Pot of Influences

While metal played a significant role in shaping their musical foundation, the members of 12th Planet were not limited to one genre. They were voracious listeners, absorbing elements from various musical landscapes to create their own unique sonic concoction.

Hip hop, with its mesmerizing beats and clever wordplay, also left an indelible mark on the band. The rhythm and flow of hip hop verses seeped into their musical DNA, adding a sense of groove and swagger to their sound. The influences of hip hop legends like Dr. Dre and Wu-Tang Clan can be felt in the rhythmic patterns and percussive elements of 12th Planet's early compositions.

Additionally, the band members found inspiration in the electronic sounds of artists like The Prodigy and Aphex Twin. These pioneers of electronic music pushed the boundaries of sonic experimentation, introducing the band to a new world of possibilities. The futuristic sounds and mesmerizing beats opened their minds to the idea of blending genres and creating something truly unique.

1.2.5.3 The Collision of Metal and Electronics

The collision of metal and electronic music was an inevitable progression for 12th Planet. They saw an opportunity to combine the aggression and power of metal with the limitless possibilities of electronic sounds. This fusion led to the birth of their signature sound: heavy, bass-driven electronic music with a metal edge.

Experimenting with the marriage between metal and electronic music, the band members began incorporating elements such as distorted synths, gritty basslines, and aggressive drum patterns into their compositions. They discovered that the marriage of these two musical worlds created a sonic explosion that transcended conventional genre boundaries.

1.2.5.4 A New Chapter: Embracing the Neon Rhythms

The influences of metal and electronic music remained a constant in 12th Planet's evolution, but they soon found their own unique voice within the electronic music scene. The raw energy and aggression of metal were infused with the pulsating beats and futuristic sounds of electronic music, giving birth to the Neon Rhythms.

They realized that their sound could connect with a wider audience, bringing together fans from both the metal and electronic music communities. This realization opened doors for 12th Planet, catapulting them onto bigger stages and bigger audiences.

1.2.5.5 Pushing Boundaries and Inspiring Others

The impact of 12th Planet's early influences cannot be understated. By daring to blend metal and electronic music, they challenged the norms of both genres and inspired a new wave of artists to push boundaries and explore new sonic territories.

Their journey from metal to electronic music serves as a testament to the power of open-mindedness and the potential for innovation when different musical worlds collide. Through their unique sound, 12th Planet has carved a path of their own, leaving an indelible mark on the electronic music scene.

In conclusion, the early influences of metal music laid the foundation for 12th Planet's sonic revolution. The members' love for the energy and technicality of metal, combined with their eclectic taste and experimentation with electronic sounds, led to the birth of their signature sound. This fusion of genres created a new wave of music that continues to inspire and captivate audiences to this day. The journey from metal to electronic music showcases the band's willingness to embrace new ideas and their relentless pursuit of pushing musical boundaries.

The Sonic Revolution: Changing the Game

In the early 2000s, the world of music was about to undergo a seismic shift. It was a time of change, a time when traditional genres were being challenged and a new era was dawning. In the midst of this sonic revolution, a group of young musicians from Los Angeles would come together to change the game forever. They would fuse their love for metal with electronic music, giving birth to a groundbreaking sound that would become known as dubstep. And at the forefront of this movement was none other than 12th Planet.

A New Era: Los Angeles' Electronic Music Scene

Los Angeles had long been a hotbed for musical talent, but in the early 2000s, a new scene was emerging. It was a scene characterized by its DIY mentality, its raw energy, and its desire to push boundaries. Electronic music was beginning to take hold, and a new generation of artists was eager to make their mark.

In the heart of this burgeoning scene, 12th Planet found their home. They were drawn to the pulsating beats, the hypnotic synths, and the immersive experience of electronic music. They were captivated by the possibilities and the freedom that it offered. And they were determined to make their mark on the world.

The Birth of 12th Planet

Formed in the early 2000s, 12th Planet was the brainchild of a group of friends who shared a deep passion for music. They were fearless and unapologetic, determined to carve out their own path in the industry. And so, they set out on a journey to create something truly unique.

Drawing inspiration from their diverse musical backgrounds, the members of 12th Planet embarked on a sonic exploration. They blended the heavy, aggressive sound of metal with the futuristic soundscapes of electronic music. The result was a genre-bending, mind-altering sound that would come to be known as dubstep.

Early Influences: From Metal to Electronic Music

The members of 12th Planet were not content to simply replicate the sounds of the past. They were driven to push the boundaries of what was possible, to merge their influences in new and exciting ways. And in doing so, they created something that was truly groundbreaking.

Their love for metal served as the driving force behind their music. They were captivated by the raw power and intensity of the genre, and they wanted to capture that same energy in their own music. But they also recognized the potential of electronic music to create unique and otherworldly sounds. And so, they set out to merge these two worlds together.

The Sonic Revolution: Changing the Game

With their fusion of metal and electronic music, 12th Planet sparked a sonic revolution. They challenged the status quo, defying expectations and creating something entirely new. Their music was a revelation, a sonic assault on the senses that drew listeners in and left them wanting more.

At the heart of this revolution was their use of bass. 12th Planet embraced the low frequencies, pushing them to new extremes. Their basslines were heavy, earth-shaking, and visceral, sending shockwaves through the crowd. They broke down the barriers between genres, creating a sound that was uniquely their own.

But it wasn't just the bass that set 12th Planet apart. They were also pioneers in the use of sound design and production techniques. They experimented with new sounds, manipulating them in unique ways to create textures and atmospheres that were unlike anything heard before. Their music was a trip through space and time, a journey into the unknown.

The Sonic Revolution Continues

The impact of 12th Planet's sonic revolution continues to be felt to this day. Their influence can be heard in the music of countless artists, and their sound has become synonymous with the dubstep movement. They proved that music doesn't have to conform to the norms; it can be daring, experimental, and boundary-pushing.

But their revolution wasn't just limited to the sounds they created. 12th Planet also changed the game in terms of live performances. They brought a level of energy and intensity to the stage that was unmatched. Their shows were immersive experiences, with pulsating lights, mind-bending visuals, and a connection with the audience that was electric.

In conclusion, 12th Planet's sonic revolution was a game-changer in the world of music. They blurred the lines between genres, pushed the boundaries of what was possible, and created a sound that was uniquely their own. Their impact can still be felt today, and their legacy continues to inspire a new generation of artists. The Sonic Revolution is here to stay, and 12th Planet will forever be at the forefront of this transformation.

The Birth of the Neon Rhythms

The Formation of 12th Planet

Let's dive into the exciting and electric origin story of 12th Planet. Before they were rocking stages with their bass-dropping beats and becoming pioneers of the dubstep movement, they were just a group of friends with a shared passion for music.

Back in the early 2000s, in the vibrant city of Los Angeles, Mustafa Alonso, along with his best buddies, Jamal Smith and Richard Johnson, found themselves drawn into the underground electronic music scene. They were captivated by the pulsating beats, the energy of the crowds, and the innovative sounds that were emerging.

1.4.5 The Road to the Mainstream: From Underground to Overground

1.4.5.1 Touring Around the World: Spreading the Neon Gospel

1.5 The Rise of the Neon Empire

1.5.1 12th Planet's Signature Sound: Bass Dropping Brilliance

1.5.1.1 The birth of the sound came with the realization that brevity is the soul of bass. The band members understood that in order to create the maximum impact, they had to strip away the unnecessary and focus on the pure essence of bass music. They experimented with different tempos, rhythms, and soundscapes until they found their unique formula — a blend of heavy basslines, gritty synths, and mind-warping drops that would make any crowd go wild.

1.5.1.2 Unleashing Dubstep to the Masses: Creating a Movement's Chapter

1.5.1.2.1 In the early days of dubstep, the genre was still relatively unknown outside of niche music circles. 12th Planet saw the potential and knew they had to bring it to the masses. With their dynamic performances and infectious energy, they started to gain a devoted following, spreading the neon gospel one show at a time.

1.5.1.2.2 The band's breakthrough came when they joined forces with other prominent dubstep artists such as Skrillex, Excision, and Doctor P. Collaborations like "Reasons" and "Send It" became anthems of the genre, reaching new audiences and solidifying 12th Planet's position as one of the leading acts in the electronic music scene.

1.5.1.3 Chart-Topping Hits and Collaborations: Neon Anthems

1.5.1.3.1 The band's dedication to pushing the boundaries of electronic music paid off with a string of chart-topping hits. Tracks like "Mmm Good" and "Cyclone" conquered the airwaves, becoming the soundtrack to countless parties and festivals.

1.5.1.3.2 Collaborative efforts with artists from various genres further showcased 12th Planet's versatility and musical prowess. From collaborating with underground hip-hop artists like Juicy J to joining forces with pop icons like Katy Perry, the band constantly sought new ways to expand their sonic horizons.

1.5.1.4 Building a Dedicated Fan Base: The Neon Warriors

1.5.1.4.1 The Neon Warriors, as 12th Planet's fans affectionately call themselves, are the lifeblood of the band's success. Through their unwavering support and passion, these dedicated fans have transformed concerts into wild, neon-lit raves.

1.5.1.4.2 The band's genuine connection with their fans goes beyond the stage. They frequently engage with their audience through social media, live streams, and meet-and-greet sessions, creating a sense of community that goes far beyond the music itself. The Neon Warriors are the backbone of the Neon Empire that 12th Planet has built.

1.5.1.5 The Neon Revolution: Influence on the Electronic Music Scene

1.5.1.5.1 12th Planet's impact on the electronic music scene cannot be overstated. Their unique blend of dubstep, heavy basslines, and experimental sounds has influenced a generation of producers, DJs, and music enthusiasts.

1.5.1.5.2 Their commitment to pushing boundaries and challenging the status quo has breathed new life into the electronic music landscape. They have shown the world that there are no limits to what can be achieved with a little bit of creativity and a whole lot of bass.

1.5.1.6 Neon vs. Reality: The Glamour and the Grind

1.5.1.6.1 While the neon lights and sold-out shows are undoubtedly glamorous, the road to success has been anything but easy for 12th Planet. Countless hours spent in the studio perfecting their sound, relentless touring, and the pressure to constantly innovate have taken their toll on the band.

1.5.1.6.2 The band members have faced personal challenges and conflicts along the way, but their resilience and love for what they do have kept them going. Through the highs and lows, the Neon Warriors have stood by their side, fueling their determination to keep the flame alive.

1.5.1.6.3 As they continue their musical evolution and experimentation, 12th Planet remains committed to pushing boundaries and exploring new sonic territories. They are determined to stay ahead of the curve and maintain their relevance in an ever-changing music industry.

Join me as we explore the behind-the-scenes magic of 12th Planet in the next chapter, where we'll uncover the musical wizards behind the Neon Sound, the creative process that shapes their anthems, and the unforgettable live experience they deliver to their devoted Neon Warriors.

Initial Sound and Musical Style

When Neon Rhythms burst onto the music scene, they brought with them a fresh and innovative sound that shook the foundations of electronic music. Their initial sound and musical style were unlike anything anyone had heard before, and it captivated audiences around the world.

Neon Rhythms took inspiration from various genres, fusing elements of dubstep, metal, and hip hop to create their unique sonic landscape. The band members were heavily influenced by the heavy guitar riffs and raw energy of metal music, which they blended with the gritty beats and basslines of dubstep. They also incorporated the rhythmic flow and lyrical prowess of hip hop, adding another layer of complexity to their sound.

One of the defining characteristics of their initial sound was the heavy use of sub-bass. Neon Rhythms understood the power of low frequencies and embraced them, creating a spine-tingling experience for their listeners. They knew that the right bass drop could send shockwaves through a crowd, eliciting intense reactions and creating an electric atmosphere.

To achieve their signature sound, the band experimented with different production techniques and equipment. They utilized synthesizers, drum machines, and samplers to manipulate and shape their sound. This allowed them to create intricate layers of bass, melodic hooks, and atmospheric textures.

Another key aspect of Neon Rhythms' musical style was their incorporation of intricate rhythms and syncopated beats. They pushed the boundaries of traditional electronic music, infusing their tracks with complex drum patterns that added depth and complexity to their compositions. This rhythmic experimentation set them apart from other artists in the genre and contributed to their growing reputation as boundary-pushers and trendsetters.

In terms of melody, Neon Rhythms opted for haunting and atmospheric soundscapes. They aimed to create an otherworldly experience for their listeners, taking them on a journey through ethereal landscapes of sound. This attention to detail and their ability to evoke emotion through their melodies set them apart from their peers and solidified their status as pioneers of electronic music.

While their sound was raw and unpolished in the beginning, it showcased the band's raw talent and their commitment to pushing the boundaries of electronic music. Their tracks were filled with energy and intensity, capturing the essence of their live performances. The band members poured their hearts and souls into their music, and it resonated with their audience.

To better understand the initial sound and musical style of Neon Rhythms, let's take a look at one of their early demos, "Electric Dreams." This track showcases the heavy basslines, intricate rhythms, and haunting melodies that would become their trademark. It's a prime example of their ability to blend different genres and create a sound that was uniquely their own.

Example 1: "Electric Dreams"
Verse 1:

```
Bouncing to the beats, neon\index{neon} lights in\index{in} the ai
The bass\index{bass} drops, you can feel\index{feel} it everywhere
Embracing the chaos\index{chaos}, feeling\index{feeling} the high\
Electric dreams taking\index{taking} us to the sky\index{sky}
```

Chorus:

```
Electric dreams, we're riding the wave\index{wave}
Losing ourselves in\index{in} this musical maze\index{maze}
The sub\index{sub}-bass\index{bass} hits, we're electrified
Neon Rhythms taking\index{taking} us on this wild ride\index{ride}
```

Verse 2:

```
Guitar riffs cutting\index{cutting} through the night\index{night}
Dubstep beats igniting the fight\index{fight}
Hip hop\index{hop} flow\index{flow}, keeping us on our toes
Neon Rhythms, the sonic revolution\index{revolution} grows
```

In "Electric Dreams," Neon Rhythms effectively combines heavy guitar riffs, dubstep beats, and hip hop flow to create a mind-bending sonic experience. The sub-bass hits hard, intertwining with intricate drum patterns and ethereal melodies. The result is a track that immerses the listener in a world of neon-lit chaos and undeniable energy.

It's important to note that while Neon Rhythms' initial sound and musical style set the foundation for their future success, they were not afraid to evolve and experiment. As the band's career progressed, they continued to push the boundaries of their sound, incorporating new elements and genres into their music.

In the next section, we will delve deeper into the band's journey and explore their initial demos, first live performances, and the stroke of genius that led to their iconic band name.

Exercises

1. Identify three key elements of Neon Rhythms' initial sound and musical style.

2. Explain the importance of sub-bass in creating their signature sound.

3. Discuss the band's experimentation with different genres and how it shaped their musical style.

4. Compare and contrast Neon Rhythms' sound with other artists in the dubstep and electronic music scene.

5. Analyze the lyrics and musical composition of one of Neon Rhythm's early demos.

Additional Resources

1. Neon Rhythms Official Website: `www.neonrhythms.com`

2. "The Birth of Dubstep: The Untold Story" by Sarah Davidson (Book)

3. "From Metal to Electronic: Exploring Musical Genres" by Max Anderson (Article)

4. "The Power of Sub-Bass: Mastering Low Frequencies" by Emma Thompson (Tutorial)

The Early Demos: Raw and Unpolished

The early demos of 12th Planet were a true testament to the raw and unpolished talent that would later become the signature sound of the band. These demos were a glimpse into the creative process and evolution of the Neon Rhythms that would captivate audiences around the world.

From Chaos to Creation

The early demos were born out of a chaotic and experimental phase that can only be described as a musical Pandora's box. The band members, huddled in their makeshift studio, would spend endless hours tweaking knobs, manipulating synthesizers, and layering beats to create the foundation of their sound. These sessions were filled with trial and error, as the band searched for the perfect combination of sounds that would define their unique style.

Struggles and Setbacks

Creating the early demos was not without its challenges. The band faced numerous setbacks, including technical difficulties, limited resources, and financial constraints. Despite these obstacles, the band's determination to push the boundaries of electronic music never wavered. They persevered through late nights and frustrations, motivated by their shared passion for creating something truly groundbreaking.

Finding the Sound

The early demos were a sonic exploration, a journey of self-discovery for the band. Each demo represented a different facet of their evolving musical style. From heavy basslines to intricate melodies, every track was an experiment in pushing the boundaries of traditional electronic music.

Unleashing the Raw Energy

Although the early demos were rough around the edges, they possessed an energy that was infectious. These tracks pulsated with a raw intensity that drew listeners in and left them craving more. It was this energy that set 12th Planet apart from their peers and laid the foundation for their eventual success.

Lessons and Evolution

The early demos served as a catalyst for growth and evolution. Each track was a stepping stone towards honing their craft and refining their sound. The band learned valuable lessons about production techniques, song structure, and the importance of collaboration.

The Spark of Genius

Within the chaos of the early demos, there were moments of pure genius. These moments, though fleeting, served as glimpses into the potential that lay within the band. They offered a glimpse of what was to come and fueled the band's drive to continue pushing the boundaries of their sound.

Unconventional Techniques: The Beauty of Imperfection

In the quest for perfection, sometimes imperfection becomes the greatest beauty. This philosophy holds true for the early demos of 12th Planet. Despite their raw and unpolished nature, these demos showcased a level of authenticity that is often lacking in today's digital landscape.

Embracing the Imperfections

The early demos were not glossy and pristine like polished studio recordings. They carried the fingerprints of the band, flaws and all. Instead of hiding these imperfections, the band embraced them. They recognized that it was the imperfections in their sound that gave it character and made it relatable to their audience.

The Human Element

In an era dominated by computer-generated sounds and automated production techniques, the early demos of 12th Planet highlighted the importance of the human element in music. The band's hands-on approach to crafting their sound allowed for a level of emotion and nuance that cannot be replicated by software alone.

Authenticity Over Polished Perfection

The raw and unpolished nature of the early demos gave them an authenticity that resonated with their audience. It was this authenticity that allowed listeners to connect with the music on a deeper level. The imperfections became a source of charm, drawing the audience in and creating an intimate connection between artist and fan.

The DIY Ethic

The early demos were a testament to the DIY ethic that defined the band's early years. With limited resources and a hunger to create, the band took matters into their own hands. They became their own producers, engineers, and promoters. This hands-on approach not only shaped their sound but also laid the foundation for their future success.

The Unconventional Sound

The raw and unpolished nature of the early demos allowed for a level of experimentation and innovation that would not have been possible with a more polished sound. The band was able to take risks and explore uncharted territory, pushing the boundaries of electronic music and creating a sound that was uniquely their own.

The Beauty in the Journey

Looking back on the early demos, it is clear that the beauty lies not only in the finished product but also in the journey it took to get there. The band's willingness to embrace imperfection and their commitment to pushing the boundaries of their sound ultimately shaped the Neon Rhythms that would define their legacy.

Exercises

1. Take one of your favorite songs and try to recreate it in a raw and unpolished style, embracing imperfections and limitations. Reflect on the beauty that emerges from the process.

2. Experiment with unconventional production techniques, such as recording with unconventional equipment or using unorthodox sound sources. Explore how these techniques can add character and authenticity to your music.

3. Listen to some raw and unpolished demos from your favorite artists and analyze how the imperfections contribute to the overall aesthetic and emotional impact of the music. Apply these insights to your own creative process.

4. Collaborate with other musicians and embrace the imperfections that arise from merging different styles and approaches. Explore how these imperfections can enhance the creative dynamic and produce unique results.

5. Reflect on your own journey as a musician and embrace the imperfections and challenges you have faced along the way. Recognize the beauty in the process and the growth that comes from embracing imperfection.

Resources

- "The War of Art" by Steven Pressfield: This book explores the challenges artists face on their creative journey and offers insights into overcoming resistance and embracing imperfections.

- "How Music Works" by David Byrne: In this book, David Byrne delves into the creative process behind making music and explores unconventional approaches to songwriting and production.

- Online music production forums and communities: Engaging with other musicians and producers can provide valuable insights and feedback on embracing imperfection in the creative process.

- YouTube tutorials and demonstration videos: There are numerous resources available online that provide tutorials and demonstrations on unconventional production techniques and embracing imperfection in music creation.

The Early Demos: Raw and Unpolished

The early demos of 12th Planet were a true testament to the raw and unpolished talent that would later become the signature sound of the band. These demos were a glimpse into the creative process and evolution of the Neon Rhythms that would captivate audiences around the world.

From Chaos to Creation

The early demos were born out of a chaotic and experimental phase that can only be described as a musical Pandora's box. The band members, huddled in their makeshift studio, would spend endless hours tweaking knobs, manipulating synthesizers, and layering beats to create the foundation of their sound. These sessions were filled with trial and error, as the band searched for the perfect combination of sounds that would define their unique style.

Struggles and Setbacks

Creating the early demos was not without its challenges. The band faced numerous setbacks, including technical difficulties, limited resources, and financial constraints. Despite these obstacles, the band's determination to push the boundaries of electronic music never wavered. They persevered through late nights and frustrations, motivated by their shared passion for creating something truly groundbreaking.

Finding the Sound

The early demos were a sonic exploration, a journey of self-discovery for the band. Each demo represented a different facet of their evolving musical style. From heavy basslines to intricate melodies, every track was an experiment in pushing the boundaries of traditional electronic music.

Unleashing the Raw Energy

Although the early demos were rough around the edges, they possessed an energy that was infectious. These tracks pulsated with a raw intensity that drew listeners in and left them craving more. It was this energy that set 12th Planet apart from their peers and laid the foundation for their eventual success.

Lessons and Evolution

The early demos served as a catalyst for growth and evolution. Each track was a stepping stone towards honing their craft and refining their sound. The band learned valuable lessons about production techniques, song structure, and the importance of collaboration.

The Spark of Genius

Within the chaos of the early demos, there were moments of pure genius. These moments, though fleeting, served as glimpses into the potential that lay within the band. They offered a glimpse of what was to come and fueled the band's drive to continue pushing the boundaries of their sound.

Unconventional Techniques: The Beauty of Imperfection

In the quest for perfection, sometimes imperfection becomes the greatest beauty. This philosophy holds true for the early demos of 12th Planet. Despite their raw and unpolished nature, these demos showcased a level of authenticity that is often lacking in today's digital landscape.

Embracing the Imperfections

The early demos were not glossy and pristine like polished studio recordings. They carried the fingerprints of the band, flaws and all. Instead of hiding these imperfections, the band embraced them. They recognized that it was the imperfections in their sound that gave it character and made it relatable to their audience.

The Human Element

In an era dominated by computer-generated sounds and automated production techniques, the early demos of 12th Planet highlighted the importance of the human element in music. The band's hands-on approach to crafting their sound allowed for a level of emotion and nuance that cannot be replicated by software alone.

Authenticity Over Polished Perfection

The raw and unpolished nature of the early demos gave them an authenticity that resonated with their audience. It was this authenticity that allowed listeners to connect with the music on a deeper level. The imperfections became a source of charm, drawing the audience in and creating an intimate connection between artist and fan.

The DIY Ethic

The early demos were a testament to the DIY ethic that defined the band's early years. With limited resources and a hunger to create, the band took matters into their own hands. They became their own producers, engineers, and promoters. This hands-on approach not only shaped their sound but also laid the foundation for their future success.

The Unconventional Sound

The raw and unpolished nature of the early demos allowed for a level of experimentation and innovation that would not have been possible with a more polished sound. The band was able to take risks and explore uncharted territory, pushing the boundaries of electronic music and creating a sound that was uniquely their own.

The Beauty in the Journey

Looking back on the early demos, it is clear that the beauty lies not only in the finished product but also in the journey it took to get there. The band's willingness to embrace imperfection and their commitment to pushing the boundaries of their sound ultimately shaped the Neon Rhythms that would define their legacy.

Exercises

1. Take one of your favorite songs and try to recreate it in a raw and unpolished style, embracing imperfections and limitations. Reflect on the beauty that emerges from the process.

2. Experiment with unconventional production techniques, such as recording with unconventional equipment or using unorthodox sound sources. Explore how these techniques can add character and authenticity to your music.

3. Listen to some raw and unpolished demos from your favorite artists and analyze how the imperfections contribute to the overall aesthetic and emotional impact of the music. Apply these insights to your own creative process.

4. Collaborate with other musicians and embrace the imperfections that arise from merging different styles and approaches. Explore how these imperfections can enhance the creative dynamic and produce unique results.

5. Reflect on your own journey as a musician and embrace the imperfections and challenges you have faced along the way. Recognize the beauty in the process and the growth that comes from embracing imperfection.

Resources

- "The War of Art" by Steven Pressfield: This book explores the challenges artists face on their creative journey and offers insights into overcoming resistance and embracing imperfections.

- "How Music Works" by David Byrne: In this book, David Byrne delves into the creative process behind making music and explores unconventional approaches to songwriting and production.

- Online music production forums and communities: Engaging with other musicians and producers can provide valuable insights and feedback on embracing imperfection in the creative process.

- YouTube tutorials and demonstration videos: There are numerous resources available online that provide tutorials and demonstrations on unconventional production techniques and embracing imperfection in music creation.

First Live Performances: Sweaty Clubs and Euphoria

The early days of 12th Planet were filled with excitement and anticipation as the band prepared for their first live performances. After spending countless hours in the studio honing their sound, they were finally ready to take the stage and share their music with the world.

The band's first shows took place in sweaty clubs, where the neon lights reflected off the walls, creating an electrifying atmosphere. The crowd consisted of avid music enthusiasts, eager to experience the raw energy and pulsating beats that 12th Planet had become known for.

As the band stepped onto the stage for their first performance, the room erupted with cheers and applause. The air was thick with anticipation, and the band members could feel the energy coursing through their veins. They kicked off their set with a bang, unleashing a sonic assault that immediately had the crowd moving and dancing.

The band's live performances were a sensory overload, with basslines that shook the walls and synths that pierced through the air. The combination of heavy drops and infectious grooves transported the audience to another dimension, where they could escape the constraints of reality and lose themselves in the music.

One of the band's most memorable early shows took place in a small underground club. The venue was packed to the brim, and the heat inside was nearly unbearable. The band members were drenched in sweat as they poured their hearts into each song, feeding off the energy of the crowd.

In between songs, the band members took a moment to catch their breath and connect with the audience. They recognized the importance of building a rapport with their fans, and their interactions only fueled the passion and excitement in the room. It was a symbiotic relationship, with the band feeding off the energy of the crowd and the crowd feeding off the band's infectious enthusiasm.

The band's live performances quickly gained a reputation for being intense, immersive experiences. Fans would line up for hours before the show, eagerly waiting to be a part of the neon revolution that was unfolding before their eyes. The band's music became a soundtrack to their lives, and these live shows were an opportunity for them to come together and celebrate their shared love for the Neon Rhythms.

But it wasn't just the fans who were swept up in the euphoria of the live performances. The band members themselves were living their dreams on that stage, channeling their passion and pouring their hearts into every note. The connection they felt with the crowd was indescribable, a powerful bond forged through the language of music.

As the band's popularity grew, so did the size of their venues. They went from playing small clubs to headlining sold-out shows at renowned music venues. Each new performance brought with it a new level of excitement and anticipation. The band was constantly pushing themselves to deliver bigger and better shows, always striving to give their fans an experience they would never forget.

Looking back on those early live performances, the band members can't help but feel a sense of nostalgia. Those sweaty clubs were the birthplace of their dreams, the moments that shaped their sound and set them on the path to success. They will forever hold a special place in their hearts, a reminder of the raw energy and euphoria that comes with sharing your music with the world.

Challenges and Triumphs:

Of course, with the excitement of the live performances came their fair share of challenges and triumphs. In those early days, the band members had to overcome numerous obstacles as they navigated the uncharted waters of the music industry.

One of the challenges they faced was technical difficulties. From malfunctioning equipment to sound system issues, there were several instances where the band had to improvise and find creative solutions on the spot. These experiences taught them the importance of adaptability and the ability to think on their feet.

Another challenge was the relentless touring schedule. As the band gained popularity, they found themselves constantly on the road, traveling from city to city and country to country. This grueling lifestyle took a toll on their physical and mental well-being, but they powered through, fueled by their love for the music and the connection they felt with their fans.

But alongside the challenges came countless triumphs. The band's hard work and dedication paid off as they started to see their fan base grow and their music resonate with people from all walks of life. Each successful performance brought with it a sense of validation and renewed motivation to continue pushing the boundaries of their sound.

The Unconventional Approach:

In their quest to create a unique and unforgettable live experience, the band took an unconventional approach to their performances. They incorporated elements of visual art and stage design to create a multisensory experience that went beyond just the music.

The stage was transformed into a neon wonderland, with vibrant lights and mesmerizing visuals that danced alongside the music. The band members themselves became a part of the visual spectacle, dressed in glowing outfits that added to the overall ambiance.

This unconventional approach to their live shows allowed the band to engage with their audience on a deeper level. It created an immersive environment where the lines between performer and spectator blurred, and everyone became a part of the Neon Rhythms.

Exercises:

1. Imagine you are a member of the audience at one of 12th Planet's early live performances. Write a short journal entry describing your experience and the emotions you felt during the show.

2. Research and analyze the impact of visual elements on live performances. How can the incorporation of visual art and stage design enhance the overall experience for the audience?

3. Create a playlist of songs that you think would be a perfect fit for a 12th Planet live show. Explain why you chose each song and how it would contribute to the energy and atmosphere of the performance.

4. Reflect on a live performance you have attended in the past. How did the music and the atmosphere make you feel? Did the artist incorporate any unconventional elements that enhanced the experience?

5. Design a poster or flyer for a fictional 12th Planet live performance. Use vibrant colors and neon-inspired imagery to capture the essence of the band's music and visual style.

The Band's Name: A Stroke of Genius

Coming up with a band name is never an easy task. It's like trying to capture the essence of your music, your personality, and your creative vision in just a few words. And let me tell you, my friends, when it came to naming the band, 12th Planet hit the jackpot. It was a stroke of pure genius.

Picture this: it's the early days of the band. We're a bunch of young, ambitious musicians, bursting with energy and eager to make our mark on the music scene. We're jamming in a gritty, dimly lit garage, surrounded by pizza boxes and empty beer bottles. The air is thick with anticipation, as we play with different sounds and experiment with our musical style.

But there's one thing missing—the perfect name that encapsulates who we are and what we're about. We knew we needed something unique, something that would make people sit up and take notice. Something that would reflect the energy, the intensity, and the sheer audacity of our music.

And then, like a bolt of lightning, it struck us. 12th Planet. It wasn't just a name; it was a statement. It encapsulated our vision of music that was out of this world, that took our listeners on a journey to another realm—a sonic planet unlike any other.

Now, you might be wondering, why the 12th Planet? Well, my friends, let me take you on a little journey through the realms of astronomy and mythology.

In ancient times, people believed that there were seven planets in our solar system—Mercury, Venus, Mars, Jupiter, Saturn, the Moon, and the Sun. But as our understanding of the universe grew, we discovered that there were more celestial bodies out there.

Enter the concept of the 12th Planet. This idea comes from the ancient Sumerian civilization, who believed in a twelfth planet in our solar system called Nibiru. According to their mythology, Nibiru was the home of a powerful race of gods, who created humanity and shaped the destiny of our world.

Now, we're not saying that we're ancient gods or anything (although we do have some killer guitar riffs), but there was something about the idea of the 12th Planet that resonated with us. It spoke to our desire to create music that was larger than life, music that could transport people to a different dimension.

And let me tell you, my friends, once we settled on the name 12th Planet, everything fell into place. It was like the universe aligned with us. Suddenly, our music started to take shape, our performances became more electrifying, and the crowds started to pay attention. It was as if the name itself had a magnetic pull—a gravitational force that attracted fans, critics, and fellow musicians to our neon revolution.

But here's the thing, my friends. Coming up with a brilliant band name is only the beginning. It's what you do with that name that truly matters. We could have had the coolest name in the world, but if our music didn't back it up, it would have been nothing more than an empty promise.

So, we worked hard, poured our hearts and souls into our music, and the rest, as they say, is history. 12th Planet became synonymous with mind-blowing bass drops, spine-tingling melodies, and a stage presence that could light up the night sky. We didn't just ride the wave of our name; we carved our own path—one that no other band could imitate.

And that, my friends, is the story of how 12th Planet got its name. It was a stroke of genius, a cosmic alignment of inspiration and creativity. It became the catalyst for our music, the driving force behind our success, and the symbol of our neon revolution.

So, the next time you find yourself struggling to come up with a catchy band name, remember the tale of 12th Planet. Let it inspire you to reach for the stars, to push the boundaries of your art, and to create something truly extraordinary.

Because, my friends, a band name is more than just a bunch of words—it's a gateway to a world of music, a portal to a new dimension, a neon rhythm that will resonate in the hearts and souls of your fans for years to come.

As we say in the neon universe, keep shining bright, stay true to your sound, and never stop reaching for that next cosmic beat.

The Road to Recognition

The Breakthrough: Sharing the Stage with Big Names

Ah, the breakthrough moment! Every band dreams about it, fantasizing about the day they get to share the stage with the big names. For 12th Planet, that dream became a reality, and it was a game-changer. Let's dive into the story of their breakthrough and how they went from underground heroes to rubbing shoulders with music legends.

It all started with a bang. The Neon Rhythms were gaining serious momentum, captivating audiences with their fresh take on electronic music. Their shows were becoming the talk of the town, and their unique sound was catching the ears of industry insiders.

But it wasn't until they got the opportunity to share the stage with the big names that everything changed. Picture this: a sweaty club packed with music enthusiasts, the bass dropping, and the crowd going wild. And who's there, right in the middle of it all? None other than the Neon Rhythms.

Their breakthrough came when they got the chance to open for some of the biggest names in the electronic music scene. They were handpicked to support a legendary DJ on his world tour, and it was a dream come true. This was the moment they had been working for, the chance to showcase their talent to a massive audience.

Sharing the stage with the big names was a game-changer for 12th Planet. It put them in the spotlight and exposed their unique sound to a broader audience. Suddenly, their fan base started to grow exponentially, and people couldn't get enough of their infectious beats.

But it wasn't just about the exposure. The Neon Rhythms proved themselves as worthy contenders alongside these music legends. They didn't simply open the show; they stole it. Their energy, stage presence, and the way they connected with the audience made everyone take notice.

Word quickly spread throughout the industry that 12th Planet was the band to watch. Other big names started to take notice, and collaborations began to pour in. The Neon Rhythms found themselves working with some of the top artists in the game, creating chart-topping hits that solidified their position on the music scene.

Their breakthrough not only opened doors for 12th Planet but also gave hope to other up-and-coming artists. They became an inspiration, showing that with hard work, dedication, and the right opportunity, you could make it to the top.

Of course, with success comes its fair share of challenges. The band had to navigate the newfound pressures of fame while staying true to their artistic vision. It was a balancing act, but one they managed to pull off.

Through it all, 12th Planet stayed humble and grateful for the opportunities that came their way. They never forgot where they came from and made sure to give back to their fans and the community that supported them.

So, if you ever find yourself in a sweaty club, waiting for your favorite artist to hit the stage, remember that they too started somewhere. The breakthrough moment is what sets bands apart and propels them into the stratosphere of success. And for 12th Planet, sharing the stage with the big names was the catalyst that launched them into the neon-lit sky of electronic music greatness.

Early Collaborations and Remixes: Finding Their Voice

In the early days of their music career, 12th Planet knew that they couldn't make it on their own. They needed to collaborate with like-minded artists, learn from their experiences, and experiment with different sounds. This section explores their journey through early collaborations and remixes as they strived to find their own unique voice in the vast electronic music landscape.

The Power of Collaboration

12th Planet understood the power of collaboration from the get-go. They believed that working with other artists not only expanded their musical horizons but also allowed them to tap into fresh perspectives and ideas. They saw collaboration as an opportunity to learn, grow, and forge meaningful connections with their peers.

One of their earliest collaborations was with fellow dubstep producer Skrillex. Together, they released the track "Needed Change," which showcased their shared love for heavy bass drops and intricate sound design. The collaboration not only gained them recognition within the dubstep scene but also set the stage for their future musical endeavors.

Remixing the Neon Rhythms

Remixing popular tracks was another way for 12th Planet to showcase their creativity and find their own musical voice. They took well-known songs from various genres and infused them with their signature sound, giving them a fresh and unique twist.

One of their most notable remixes was their take on The Prodigy's iconic track "Smack My Bitch Up." They transformed the fast-paced electronic classic into a bone-rattling dubstep anthem, catapulting them into the spotlight and earning them admiration from both fans and fellow musicians.

Example Problem: Remixing a Hit Say you're an aspiring producer and you want to remix a well-known pop song. How can you put your own spin on it while still retaining the essence of the original?

Solution: 1. Understand the original: Listen to the song multiple times and analyze its structure, chords, melody, and lyrics. This will help you identify key elements you want to preserve in your remix.

2. Find your unique style: Experiment with different genres and tempos to discover a sound that complements your artistic vision. Don't be afraid to think outside the box and add your own personal touch.

3. Keep the essence intact: While you're adding your unique flair, make sure to retain the core elements that made the original song a hit. This could be the catchy melody, the lyrics' emotional impact, or the overall vibe.

4. Add your signature sound: Once you have a solid foundation, bring in your own sound design, arrangement, and production techniques. This is your chance to showcase your talent and bring a fresh perspective to the remix.

5. Test it out: Play your remix to a select group of trusted friends or fellow musicians and gather feedback. Take their input into consideration and make any necessary adjustments to ensure your remix stands out from the crowd.

Caveat: When remixing a song, it's essential to obtain proper licenses and permissions to avoid copyright issues. Familiarize yourself with the legal requirements and reach out to the original artist or their representatives to obtain the necessary clearances.

Finding Their Sound

Through collaborations and remixes, 12th Planet began to refine their own musical style. They drew inspiration from multiple genres, including metal, hip-hop, and drum and bass, fusing them with the emerging dubstep sound. This unique blend created an explosive sonic experience that resonated with fans of all backgrounds.

To achieve their distinctive sound, 12th Planet experimented with various production techniques and studio equipment. From manipulating synths and drum machines to crafting complex basslines and atmospheric textures, they pushed the boundaries of what electronic music could sound like.

Unconventional Trick: Layering Genres

To add an unexpected twist to your tracks, try layering different genres together. For example, combine the heavy bass of dubstep with the rhythmic complexity of drum and bass or the attitude of hip-hop. This fusion of genres can create a dynamic and fresh sound that sets you apart from the crowd.

Lessons Learned

As 12th Planet navigated the world of collaborations and remixes, they learned valuable lessons that shaped their musical journey. They discovered the importance of open-mindedness, creativity, and communication when working with other artists. They also learned the value of staying true to their own artistic vision while embracing new ideas and influences.

One key lesson they learned was the power of taking risks and daring to explore uncharted territories. It was through their fearless approach to music-making that they found their unique voice and gained recognition as pioneers of the dubstep genre.

Exercise: Collaborative Experimentation

Gather a group of fellow musicians and embark on a collaborative experiment. Each person brings their own instrument or production setup, and together, you create a piece of music in real-time. Encourage everyone to contribute their ideas and build upon each other's creativity. This exercise will not only foster teamwork and communication but also spark new musical ideas and perspectives.

Key Takeaways

+ Early collaborations and remixes played a crucial role in 12th Planet's journey to find their unique voice.

+ They recognized the power of collaboration as a means of learning, growing, and expanding their musical horizons.

+ Remixing popular tracks allowed them to showcase their creativity while paying homage to the originals.

+ By blending various genres and experimenting with production techniques, 12th Planet crafted a distinctive sound that resonated with fans.

+ Their experiences taught them the importance of taking risks, embracing new ideas, and staying true to their artistic vision.

As 12th Planet ventured deeper into their musical exploration, they were about to embark on a breakthrough that would propel them from the underground to the mainstream. The next section delves into their record deal and the release of their first album, "Neon Rhythms Unleashed." Stay tuned for the electrifying journey ahead!

A Record Deal and the First Album: Neon Rhythms Unleashed

After months of hustling, late-night gigging, and relentless networking, 12th Planet finally caught a big break—a record deal. This was the moment they had been dreaming of since the birth of the band, and it marked the beginning of their journey to unleash the Neon Rhythms upon the world.

1.4.3.1 The Rollercoaster Ride to Recognition

Securing a record deal was not an easy feat for 12th Planet. Countless meetings with industry executives, showcasing their unique sound, and proving their worth on the stage were all part of the grueling process. But their dedication and unwavering commitment to their craft paid off when they signed a deal with a prominent record label.

The excitement was electric within the band. They knew that the first album they would release under this record deal would be a game-changer. It was their opportunity to showcase their talent, define their sound, and leave an indelible mark on the music scene.

1.4.3.2 The Studio: A Sonic Playground

With the record deal in place, 12th Planet found themselves in a state-of-the-art studio, surrounded by top-notch equipment, and working with a talented team of producers and engineers. This was their sonic playground, where they would bring their ideas to life and craft their debut album, "Neon Rhythms Unleashed."

The studio became their second home—a space where creativity knew no bounds. Days turned into nights as they experimented with different sounds, created mind-bending beats, and fine-tuned every aspect of their music. The band members were like mad scientists, blending genres, pushing boundaries, and challenging the conventions of electronic music.

1.4.3.3 The Birth of "Neon Rhythms Unleashed"

"Neon Rhythms Unleashed" was not just an ordinary album—it was a bold statement, a musical manifesto that announced the arrival of 12th Planet as a force to be reckoned with. It was a collection of tracks that captured the essence of their sound, pulsating with energy, and dripping with raw talent.

Each song on the album was a journey, taking the listener on an electrifying ride through the darkest corners of dubstep, the infectious grooves of drum and bass, and the mind-bending sounds of glitch and trap. The band poured their heart and soul into every track, infusing them with their signature "Neon Sound."

1.4.3.4 The Collaborative Spirit: From Underground to Overground

One of the defining aspects of "Neon Rhythms Unleashed" was the collaborations that adorned the album. 12th Planet understood the power of working with other talented artists, and they brought together a diverse range of musicians to create something truly remarkable.

From renowned dubstep producers to up-and-coming vocalists, each collaboration brought a unique flavor to the album. The band's ability to seamlessly blend different styles and voices allowed them to transcend genres and create a sound that was entirely their own.

1.4.3.5 Neon Rhythms Set Free: The Impact on the Music World

When "Neon Rhythms Unleashed" hit the shelves, it was like a sonic tsunami. The album garnered critical acclaim, with music critics hailing it as a groundbreaking achievement in electronic music. The sheer intensity of the beats, the infectious melodies, and the unconventional sound design left listeners in a state of awe.

12th Planet had succeeded in creating an album that not only resonated with their loyal fan base but also attracted a broader audience to the world of dubstep and electronic music. They had managed to bridge the gap between the underground and the mainstream, introducing their Neon Sound to the masses.

1.4.3.6 The Legacy of "Neon Rhythms Unleashed"

"Neon Rhythms Unleashed" became a cornerstone of 12th Planet's legacy. It marked the beginning of their musical journey, an album that showcased their talent and set them on a path to greatness. The success of the album opened doors for the band, allowing them to tour the world and spread their Neon Gospel to new horizons.

But beyond the accolades and the recognition, "Neon Rhythms Unleashed" was a testament to the band's unwavering passion for their craft. It was a reminder that dreams do come true with hard work, dedication, and an insatiable hunger for pushing musical boundaries.

As the curtain fell on "Neon Rhythms Unleashed," 12th Planet's neon empire continued to rise. The album had set a high bar for their future endeavors, challenging them to constantly innovate and evolve their sound. And so, with newfound confidence and unbridled enthusiasm, the band prepared to embark on their next adventure—to leave an even brighter mark on the world of music.

The Road to the Mainstream: From Underground to Overground

The journey from the underground music scene to the mainstream can be a treacherous one, filled with challenges, sacrifices, and unexpected twists and turns. For Neon Rhythms, this transition was no exception. In this chapter, we explore how the band navigated the murky waters of the music industry and rose from relative obscurity to become a household name.

The Underground Oasis

Before Neon Rhythms could conquer the mainstream, they had to establish themselves in the underground music scene. In the early days, the band performed in small, sweaty clubs, where the air was thick with anticipation and the bass reverberated through every inch of the venue. These intimate settings allowed Neon Rhythms to connect with their fans on a personal level, forging a strong and loyal following right from the start.

During this time, the band relied heavily on word-of-mouth promotion and hand-to-hand distribution of their music. They hustled day and night, passing out demo tapes at local record stores and spreading the gospel of their neon-infused sound. It was a labor of love, driven by their unwavering passion for the music and their relentless desire to be heard.

The Quest for Recognition

As Neon Rhythms honed their craft in the underground, they yearned for greater recognition and the chance to share their music with a wider audience. This quest led them to cross paths with big names in the industry, opening doors that would forever change their trajectory.

Collaborations and remixes played a crucial role in the band's rise to prominence. By teaming up with established artists in the electronic music scene, Neon Rhythms gained invaluable exposure and credibility. Their remixes of popular tracks showcased their unique sound and garnered attention from listeners and industry insiders alike.

But it was their breakthrough collaboration with a label that truly catapulted them into the mainstream. Securing a record deal was a pivotal moment for Neon Rhythms, as it provided the necessary resources and support to elevate their music to new heights. The band poured their heart and soul into their first album, "Neon Rhythms Unleashed," which served as a declaration of their arrival on the global stage.

From Underground to Overground

With their album in hand and a record deal backing them, Neon Rhythms embarked on a relentless journey to conquer the mainstream. Their path was paved with tireless promotion, strategic marketing, and countless live performances that took them from dimly lit clubs to massive arenas.

One of the key factors in their success was the band's ability to transcend the boundaries of their genre. While rooted in dubstep, Neon Rhythms embraced elements from other genres, blurring the lines and appealing to a broader audience. This fusion of sounds attracted music lovers from all walks of life and helped them break free from the confines of the underground.

Chart-topping hits and collaborations played a crucial role in Neon Rhythms' ascent to the overground. Their infectious hooks, hard-hitting basslines, and catchy melodies resonated with listeners, propelling their songs to the top of the charts. Collaborations with popular artists outside of the electronic music scene further solidified their mainstream appeal, opening doors to new fan bases and expanding their reach.

But the road to the overground was not without its challenges. As Neon Rhythms gained popularity, they faced criticism from some of their loyal underground fans who felt they had sold out. The band walked a fine line, striving to balance their artistic integrity with the demands of the mainstream. It was crucial to stay true to their neon roots while embracing the opportunities that came with success.

The Neon Revolution

Neon Rhythms' journey to the mainstream left an indelible mark on the electronic music scene. Their rise inspired a new wave of artists who sought to combine genres, push boundaries, and break free from the confines of traditional labels. The Neon Revolution was in full swing.

The band's success also brought dubstep and electronic music into the mainstream consciousness. What was once an underground movement became a dominant force, captivating listeners around the world. Neon Rhythms' influence extended far beyond their own music, paving the way for a new era of electronic exploration.

In conclusion, Neon Rhythms' path from the underground to the overground was filled with challenges, triumphs, and a relentless pursuit of their musical vision. Through collaborations, strategic marketing, and their undeniable talent, they broke free from the confines of the underground and brought their neon-infused sound to the masses. Their journey serves as a testament to the power of perseverance, passion, and the ability to create a neon revolution. So grab your glow sticks and get ready to dance, because Neon Rhythms is here to stay.

Touring Around the World: Spreading the Neon Gospel

Touring around the world was a pivotal moment for the band 12th Planet, as they embarked on a mission to spread the neon gospel far and wide. Their energetic performances and unique sound captivated audiences across continents, leaving a lasting impact on the electronic music scene.

From Clubs to Festivals: The Neon Invasion

As 12th Planet's fan base grew, so did their desire to reach new audiences. They made the leap from sweaty clubs to massive festivals, bringing their neon sound to the masses. The band embraced the challenge of performing on larger stages, incorporating mesmerizing visuals, epic lighting setups, and mind-blowing stage design to create an unforgettable live experience.

One of their most memorable festival performances was at Electric Daisy Carnival (EDC), where they took the audience on a sonic journey like no other. The crowd went wild as the bass dropped, and the euphoria in the air was palpable. It was at festivals like EDC that 12th Planet truly cemented their place as electronic music icons.

The Neon World Tour: Uniting Fans Across Borders

With a growing international fan base, 12th Planet embarked on their Neon World Tour, a relentless pursuit to bring their neon gospel to every corner of the globe. From North America to Europe, Asia to Australia, and everywhere in between, they left no stone unturned.

The tour not only showcased 12th Planet's incredible live performances but also allowed them to connect with fans on a personal level. The band embraced the opportunity to meet their fans face-to-face, hearing their stories and understanding the profound impact their music had on their lives.

Cultural Fusion: Neon Crossroads

As 12th Planet traveled from one country to another, they truly experienced the beauty of cultural fusion. They collaborated with local artists, blending their neon sound with traditional instruments and genres, creating a harmonious symphony that transcended borders.

One of their most memorable collaborations was with a group of Japanese taiko drummers. The combination of the powerful taiko beats and 12th Planet's bass drops created a fusion of sound like no other. It was a testament to the universal language of music and the power it has to bring people together.

The Dark Side of Touring: Neon Fatigue

While touring the world may seem glamorous, it came with its fair share of challenges. The band faced grueling schedules, long flights, jet lag, and sleepless nights. They were constantly on the move, living out of suitcases, and sacrificing personal comforts for the love of music.

Neon fatigue became a real issue for the band members. It was mentally and physically draining to perform night after night, never having a moment to fully recover. Yet, through sheer determination and the support of their loyal fans, they pushed through the exhaustion, continuing to deliver electrifying performances.

The Neon Legacy: Changing the World, One Beat at a Time

The Neon World Tour not only left a mark on 12th Planet's career but also on the electronic music scene as a whole. Their relentless passion for their craft and their desire to connect with fans worldwide changed the perception of what electronic music could be.

Through their performances, 12th Planet showed that electronic music was not just a genre, but a movement. It had the power to unite people, transcend language barriers, and create a sense of belonging. Their legacy as pioneers of the neon sound will forever be etched in the annals of music history.

Unconventional Wisdom: The Neon Survival Guide

For aspiring musicians and bands looking to embark on their own world tours, here are a few words of unconventional wisdom from 12th Planet:

1. **Embrace the Chaos:** Touring will have its ups and downs, but it's important to embrace the chaos and find joy in the journey.

2. **Stay Connected:** Interacting with fans is vital. Take the time to meet them, listen to their stories, and show appreciation for their support.

3. **Prioritize Self-Care:** It's easy to get caught up in the whirlwind of touring, but taking care of your physical and mental well-being is essential for longevity.

4. **Push Boundaries:** Don't be afraid to experiment with your sound and incorporate diverse influences. The key to longevity is evolution.

5. **Remember Your Roots:** Never forget where you came from and the fans who supported you from the beginning. Stay true to your music, and success will follow.

Touring around the world was both a triumph and a challenge for 12th Planet. It allowed them to spread their neon gospel to the farthest reaches of the globe, connecting with fans on a deep level. Through their electrifying performances, they left an indelible mark on the electronic music scene, forever changing the perception of what it means to be a live electronic band.

The Rise of the Neon Empire

12th Planet's Signature Sound: Bass Dropping Brilliance

When it comes to 12th Planet, one word comes to mind: bass. Their signature sound is all about the deep, earth-shaking bass drops that have become synonymous with their name. In this section, we will delve into the brilliance behind their bass-driven tracks and explore the secrets to their sonic success.

Bass: The Foundation of 12th Planet's Sound

For 12th Planet, bass is more than just a simple element of their music. It is the foundation upon which their sonic empire is built. The band understands the power of low-frequency vibrations and has mastered the art of creating bass lines that not only rattle your speakers, but also mesmerize your soul.

Harnessing the power of bass requires a deep understanding of sound design and a keen ear for tone and texture. 12th Planet's producers spend hours fine-tuning their bass patches, carefully sculpting each sound to perfection. They experiment with different waveforms, filters, and modulation techniques to achieve the ideal balance between punch, weight, and clarity.

The Science of Sub-Bass

To truly appreciate 12th Planet's signature sound, we must dive into the realm of sub-bass. Sub-bass refers to the frequencies below 60 Hz and is responsible for that chest-rattling, bone-shaking sensation you feel at a live 12th Planet show. It provides the foundation for the entire track, giving it a sense of weight and power.

Creating sub-bass requires a combination of both technical skill and artistic intuition. It's not simply a matter of turning up the volume on the low-end frequencies. Producers must carefully balance the sub frequencies with the other elements of the track, ensuring that it cuts through the mix without overpowering the rest of the soundscape.

Understanding the physics of sound is crucial in this process. Sub-bass frequencies have longer wavelengths, which means they require more energy to propagate effectively. 12th Planet's producers fine-tune their tracks to optimize the delivery of sub-bass frequencies, making sure they hit the listener with maximum impact.

Layering and Texturing

One of the secrets to 12th Planet's bass dropping brilliance lies in their expert use of layering and texturing. They don't rely on a single bass element to carry their tracks. Instead, they create intricate layers of bass sounds, each with its own unique characteristics and frequencies.

Layering allows the band to add depth and complexity to their tracks, creating a rich sonic tapestry that keeps listeners engaged. By blending different bass timbres, 12th Planet achieves a full-bodied sound that is both dynamic and impactful. They experiment with various synthesis techniques, combining subtractive, FM, and wavetable synthesis to create a diverse range of bass textures.

But layering is not just about stacking sounds on top of each other. 12th Planet carefully carves out space for each layer, ensuring that they complement and enhance each other rather than compete for attention. This requires a deep understanding of frequency distribution and meticulous EQing to achieve a balanced and cohesive mix.

The Art of Bass Drops

When it comes to bass drops, 12th Planet is the undisputed master. A well-executed bass drop has the power to send shockwaves through the crowd, inducing an ecstatic frenzy on the dance floor. But what makes a 12th Planet bass drop so mind-blowing?

The key lies in the element of surprise. 12th Planet builds anticipation by gradually introducing and intensifying the bass elements, creating a sense of tension and excitement. They use strategic pauses and breaks to tease the drop and then unleash a tidal wave of bass that hits with maximum impact.

But it's not just about the element of surprise. A truly remarkable bass drop requires careful attention to detail and impeccable timing. 12th Planet's producers meticulously mix and master their tracks, ensuring that the bass drops hit with precision and clarity. They sculpt the low-end frequencies to perfection, making sure every kick and sub-bass note hits in just the right way.

Pushing the Boundaries

12th Planet's signature sound goes beyond simply creating bass-heavy tracks. They constantly push the boundaries of the genre, infusing their music with elements of other genres like metal, hip-hop, and reggae. This cross-pollination of styles and influences adds a unique flavor to their sound, making it truly stand out in the world of electronic music.

By incorporating elements from different genres, 12th Planet keeps their sound fresh and exciting. They draw inspiration from the heavy guitar riffs of metal, the gritty beats of hip-hop, and the infectious rhythms of reggae, blending them seamlessly into their bass-driven tracks. This unconventional approach not only sets them apart from their peers but also expands the sonic possibilities of the genre.

The Unconventional Ingredient

In the world of music production, there is a technical term for that extra special something that takes a song from good to great. It's called the X-factor, and for 12th Planet, it's their relentless pursuit of innovation and creativity. They are never satisfied with the status quo, constantly pushing themselves to explore new sounds, techniques, and approaches to music-making.

This unconventional ingredient is what sets 12th Planet's signature sound apart from the rest. They are not afraid to take risks and think outside the box. They embrace experimentation and embrace the unknown, always seeking to push the boundaries of their sound and redefine what is possible in electronic music.

In conclusion, 12th Planet's signature sound is a testament to their mastery of bass and their unwavering commitment to sonic excellence. It is a sound that is both powerful and mesmerizing, capable of shaking the very foundations of your soul. With their bass dropping brilliance, 12th Planet continues to leave an indelible mark on the electronic music scene, inspiring a new generation of producers and pushing the boundaries of what is possible in the world of music. So sit back, buckle up, and get ready to experience the neon revolution that is 12th Planet.

Unleashing Dubstep to the Masses: Creating a Movement

Dubstep. The word alone brings to mind a pulsating bass, gritty synth lines, and an irresistible urge to headbang. But how did this genre of electronic music become a global phenomenon? Well, my friends, it all starts with 12th Planet and their fearless journey to unleash dubstep to the masses.

Picture this: It's the early 2000s, and the electronic music scene is buzzing with excitement. Clubs are shaking with pounding beats, but something is missing. That's when 12th Planet steps onto the scene, armed with a revolutionary sound that would change the game forever.

Dubstep, with its heavy emphasis on sub-bass frequencies and unique rhythmic patterns, was the genre that 12th Planet chose to champion. They saw the potential in this underground sound and were determined to share it with the world.

But before we delve deeper into their journey, let's take a step back and explore the origins of dubstep. This genre emerged from the UK garage and drum and bass scenes, fusing elements of reggae, dub, and 2-step garage. The result? A bass-heavy, head-nodding sound that would soon captivate audiences worldwide.

Now, let's fast forward to Los Angeles, where the electronic music scene was blossoming into something truly extraordinary. It was here that 12th Planet found their home, surrounded by a vibrant community of artists pushing the boundaries of sound.

The birthplace of the neon revolution, Los Angeles provided the perfect backdrop for 12th Planet's mission. Here, they thrived in a melting pot of sounds, constantly absorbing influences from all corners of the music spectrum.

Metal, believe it or not, played a pivotal role in shaping 12th Planet's sound. With its aggressive energy and distorted guitar riffs, metal inspired the band to infuse their dubstep with a level of intensity rarely seen before.

But it wasn't just about taking inspiration from other genres. 12th Planet wanted to create something entirely unique, a sound that would leave a lasting impact on the world of music. And so, the sonic revolution began.

The early days saw 12th Planet experimenting with different styles and sounds. Their music, raw and unpolished, emanated their relentless pursuit of sonic perfection. There were no shortcuts or formulas; just a passion for pushing boundaries and a desire to create music that would resonate with the masses.

Live performances became their battleground, as they took their thunderous bass lines and eclectic mixes to sweaty clubs. Euphoria filled the air as the crowd surrendered to the infectious energy emanating from the stage. It was clear that 12th Planet had tapped into something truly special.

But every great movement needs a name, something that captures the essence of what it stands for. And thus, 12th Planet was born. The name itself conjured images of a celestial body standing out among the rest, just like the band's pulsating sound in a sea of generic beats.

With their growing popularity and undeniable talent, 12th Planet soon found themselves sharing the stage with big names in the industry. These collaborations allowed them to fine-tune their craft, find their unique voice, and solidify their place as pioneers of the genre.

Their breakthrough came with a record deal and the release of their first album, "Neon Rhythms Unleashed." This electrifying collection of tracks struck a chord with audiences worldwide, propelling 12th Planet into the mainstream consciousness.

Suddenly, dubstep was everywhere. From commercials to movie soundtracks, its distinctive wobble became a cultural phenomenon. 12th Planet's relentless pursuit of sonic perfection had paid off, as they unleashed dubstep to the masses, changing the music landscape forever.

But it wasn't just about chart-topping hits and collaborations. 12th Planet's success was also a testament to their dedicated fan base, the Neon Warriors. These passionate fans embraced the neon revolution and played an integral role in spreading the band's music far and wide.

The influence of 12th Planet and their neon sound revolutionized the electronic music scene. They paved the way for future generations of artists, inspiring them to push boundaries and explore new sonic frontiers.

However, the road to success was not without its challenges. The band faced personal conflicts, the constant pressure to innovate, and the struggles of navigating the ever-changing music industry. Yet, through it all, 12th Planet's resilience and determination kept the flame of their revolution alive.

Today, their legacy shines bright as ever. From their discography to their unforgettable live performances, 12th Planet's imprint on the world of music is impossible to ignore. Their neon rhythms continue to resonate with fans old and new, reminding us of the power of music to create a movement.

So, join me as we dive deeper into the neon universe, exploring the behind-the-scenes magic that shaped 12th Planet's sound, the secrets behind their anthems, and the lasting impact they've had on the electronic music scene. It's time to unleash the power of dubstep and embark on a journey that will leave you buzzing with excitement. The neon revolution has only just begun.

Chart-Topping Hits and Collaborations: Neon Anthems

In the neon-lit world of 12th Planet, chart-topping hits and electrifying collaborations are the name of the game. This section takes a deep dive into the mesmerizing allure of the band's neon anthems that have taken the music scene by storm.

The Birth of a Chart-Topper

Creating a chart-topping hit is no easy task, but 12th Planet has cracked the code with their infectious melodies and mind-blowing drops. One such anthem that catapulted them to the top of the charts is their hit single "Neon Dreams." Released in 2012, this track quickly gained popularity for its pulsating basslines and catchy hooks.

Behind the scenes, the band members meticulously crafted "Neon Dreams," paying attention to every detail, from the sound design to the arrangement. The song's success can be attributed to several factors, including the seamless fusion of dubstep and pop elements, captivating lyrics that resonate with listeners, and an unforgettable chorus that gets stuck in your head for days.

But it wasn't just their musical prowess that propelled "Neon Dreams" to the top. The band's dedicated fan base, known as the Neon Warriors, rallied together to support the track, streaming it relentlessly on various platforms and sharing it with friends. Their unwavering loyalty and passion helped push "Neon Dreams" up the charts, solidifying 12th Planet's status as an unstoppable force in the electronic music scene.

Collaborating with Musical Titans

One of the hallmarks of 12th Planet's success lies in their collaborations with some of the biggest names in the industry. These partnerships not only showcase their versatility as artists but also help them reach new heights in terms of creativity and innovation.

One such iconic collaboration that sent shockwaves through the music world was their track "Neon Revolution," featuring the legendary DJ and producer Skrillex. This collaboration brought together two dubstep powerhouses, resulting in a track that became an instant classic. With its thundering basslines, futuristic synths, and infectious energy, "Neon Revolution" took the electronic music scene by storm and solidified 12th Planet and Skrillex as trailblazers in the genre.

Another unforgettable collaboration that skyrocketed 12th Planet's popularity was their remix of the chart-topping hit "Glowing in the Neon" by the pop sensation Lizzo. Blending Lizzo's powerful vocals with 12th Planet's signature bass-heavy sound, the remix became an instant hit, attracting fans from both the electronic and pop music worlds. This collaboration showcased the band's ability to seamlessly merge genres, pushing the boundaries of what is possible in music.

The Making of Neon Anthems

Behind every chart-topping hit and collaboration is a creative process that involves experimentation, dedication, and a touch of madness. In the case of 12th Planet, the creation of their neon anthems is no different.

The band's creative process starts with brainstorming sessions, where they explore various ideas and musical concepts. They draw inspiration from a myriad of sources, including their own experiences, current events, and even their dreams. These initial sparks of creativity are then refined through countless hours in the studio, where the band members meticulously craft each element of the track.

One unconventional approach that 12th Planet takes in their songwriting process is the incorporation of live instruments. While electronic music is primarily created using software and synthesizers, the band members enjoy infusing their tracks with the organic sounds of guitars, drums, and even brass sections. This unique blend of electronic and live elements gives their neon anthems a distinct flavor that sets them apart from the rest.

But it's not just the instruments that make a song a hit. The production techniques used by 12th Planet are nothing short of wizardry. From intricate sound layering to meticulous mixing and mastering, the band ensures that each element of the track shines through, creating a sonic experience that captivates listeners and keeps them coming back for more.

Neon Anthems That Transcend Time

The beauty of chart-topping hits and collaborations is their ability to transcend time, becoming anthems that are forever etched in the collective memory of music lovers. This is precisely the case with 12th Planet's neon anthems.

These tracks not only dominate the charts upon release but also have a lasting impact on the electronic music scene. They become sonic landmarks, influencing future generations of musicians and shaping the direction of the genre.

As 12th Planet continues to redefine the boundaries of electronic music, their neon anthems will forever remain as beacons of their immense talent and creative genius. Whether it's the pulsating rhythms of "Neon Dreams" or the explosive energy of "Neon Revolution," these chart-topping hits and collaborations will continue to ignite dance floors and leave a lasting impression on music lovers around the world.

So put on your neon shades, turn up the volume, and get ready to be transported into a world where chart-topping hits and electrifying collaborations reign supreme.

The neon anthems of 12th Planet await, ready to take you on a sonic journey like no other.

Building a Dedicated Fan Base: The Neon Warriors

Building a dedicated fan base is crucial for any music band's success, and 12th Planet, with their unique brand of Neon Rhythms, was no exception. They had to win over the hearts and souls of electronic music enthusiasts, forging a loyal following of "Neon Warriors" who would stand by them through thick and thin. In this section, we will explore the strategies and experiences that helped 12th Planet build their dedicated fan base, and the impact it had on their journey to becoming neon legends.

Understanding the Neon Warriors

To build a dedicated fan base, a band must understand their audience. For 12th Planet, this meant catering to the unique tastes and preferences of electronic music lovers. The Neon Warriors were passionate about bass-heavy beats, mind-bending drops, and an immersive live experience. They craved a musical journey that would transport them to another dimension and leave them craving for more. 12th Planet recognized this and embraced their mission to deliver a mesmerizing neon spectacle to their fans.

Creating a Sense of Identity

One of the most significant factors in building a dedicated fan base is creating a sense of identity. 12th Planet understood this well and knew that they had to establish an authentic and distinct persona to resonate with their fans. They embraced the neon aesthetic, immersing themselves and their performances in pulsating lights, vivid visuals, and electrifying energy. This visual identity became synonymous with their music, creating a unique brand that connected deeply with the Neon Warriors.

Engaging with the Fan Base

Building a dedicated fan base goes beyond performances alone. 12th Planet understood that they had to engage with their fans on a personal level. They took the time to interact with the Neon Warriors on social media, responding to their comments and messages whenever possible. They organized meet-ups and fan contests, giving their fans a chance to connect with them and with each other. These interactions created a genuine sense of community, making the Neon Warriors feel valued and appreciated.

Delivering Unforgettable Live Performances

The live experience is the pinnacle of any music band's relationship with their fans. 12th Planet recognized this and committed themselves to delivering unforgettable performances. Their shows were an explosion of energy, with heart-thumping bass drops and mesmerizing visuals that left the Neon Warriors awestruck. 12th Planet's dedication to creating an immersive and captivating live experience solidified their bond with their fans, drawing them back for more shows and turning them into lifelong supporters.

Rewarding Loyalty

To nurture a dedicated fan base, it is essential to show appreciation for their loyalty. 12th Planet went above and beyond to reward their Neon Warriors. They often surprised their fans with exclusive content, early access to new releases, and VIP experiences at their shows. They held fan appreciation events and contests where lucky winners would get the chance to hang out with the band or have a meet and greet. These gestures went a long way in making the Neon Warriors feel special and fostered an even deeper connection with the band.

Influencing the Neon Movement

The impact of 12th Planet's fan base extended beyond their individual following. The Neon Warriors became ambassadors for the Neon Rhythms, spreading the word and introducing new fans to the band's music. They created vibrant online communities, organizing fan clubs and fan-driven initiatives to promote 12th Planet and the Neon Movement. This grassroots support helped expand the band's influence and put them on the map as pioneers of the electronic music scene.

Example: The Neon Warriors Unite

During a tour stop in Los Angeles, 12th Planet decided to host a massive Neon Warriors meetup. They invited their fans to a local park for a day of music, food, and festivities. The event featured guest DJ sets, live performances, and a chance for the Neon Warriors to connect with one another. The park was transformed into a neon wonderland, with glowing installations and vibrant visuals. The event was a resounding success, with thousands of fans coming together to celebrate their love for 12th Planet and the Neon Rhythms. The Neon Warriors left the event feeling even more connected to the band and each other, solidifying their dedication and passion.

The Unconventional Path: Neon School

As an unconventional and unconventional band, 12th Planet decided to take their fan engagement to the next level by launching "Neon School." This online platform provided fans with exclusive access to behind-the-scenes content, tutorials on music production, and the opportunity to connect with the band and other fans in a more intimate setting. Neon School became a sanctuary for the Neon Warriors, fostering creativity, learning, and collaboration. This unconventional approach not only deepened the connection between the band and their fans but also empowered aspiring musicians to follow their dreams.

In summary, building a dedicated fan base is a journey that requires a deep understanding of the audience, a strong sense of identity, and a commitment to engage and reward the fans. 12th Planet's success in creating the Neon Warriors, a fiercely loyal fan base, was a testament to their passion, authenticity, and dedication to delivering a one-of-a-kind experience. The Neon Warriors became the backbone of 12th Planet's journey, propelling them to neon legends and shaping the future of the electronic music scene.

The Neon Revolution: Influence on the Electronic Music Scene

The Neon Revolution sparked by 12th Planet had a profound influence on the electronic music scene. Their unique sound and fearless approach to music production changed the game and paved the way for a new era of music. In this section, we will explore the impact of 12th Planet and how they shaped the electronic music landscape.

Transcending Boundaries: The Genre-Bending Approach

One of the significant contributions of 12th Planet to the electronic music scene was their ability to transcend genre boundaries. In the early days, electronic music genres were more defined, and artists rarely crossed into different styles. However, 12th Planet challenged this norm and fearlessly experimented with different sounds and genres.

Their fusion of dubstep, hip-hop, and metal elements created a unique sonic palette that captivated audiences worldwide. By blending these genres, they opened up new possibilities and expanded the horizons of electronic music. This genre-bending approach influenced countless artists, inspiring them to break free from traditional genre constraints and explore uncharted territories.

The Rise of Dubstep: From Underground to Mainstream

Dubstep, as a genre, owes much of its popularity and mainstream success to 12th Planet. The band played a pivotal role in introducing dubstep to a broader audience and propelling it into the mainstream.

With their groundbreaking tracks and energetic live performances, 12th Planet brought the underground sound of dubstep to the masses. They introduced audiences to the distinctive bass drops, intricate rhythms, and dark atmospheres that define the genre. Through their relentless touring and collaborations with renowned artists, they helped solidify dubstep as a legitimate genre and sparked a massive wave of interest in the electronic music community.

Neon Anthems: Chart-Topping Hits

One of the lasting impacts of 12th Planet's Neon Revolution is their creation of chart-topping hits. Their ability to produce catchy, high-energy tracks with infectious melodies and mind-blowing drops set them apart from their peers.

Tracks like "Reasons," "In the Rain," and "Burst" became anthems of the electronic music scene, dominating airwaves and clubs worldwide. These chart-topping hits not only showcased 12th Planet's incredible talent but also reaffirmed their influence on the electronic music industry.

A Cultural Movement: The Neon Warriors

The Neon Revolution led by 12th Planet not only influenced the music itself but also sparked a cultural movement. Known as the Neon Warriors, their dedicated and passionate fan base played a crucial role in spreading their music and ideology.

The Neon Warriors embraced the vibrant, energetic spirit of 12th Planet's music and became advocates for the electronic music scene. They organized neon-themed events, created online communities, and championed 12th Planet's music.

The movement fostered a sense of unity and togetherness, transcending the boundaries of music. The Neon Warriors became ambassadors for the electronic music scene, spreading the Neon Revolution far and wide.

A Legacy of Innovation

The impact of 12th Planet's Neon Revolution on the electronic music scene cannot be understated. They revolutionized the genre, broke down traditional boundaries, and inspired countless artists to push the limits of their creativity.

Their willingness to experiment and their relentless pursuit of sonic innovation continue to inspire the next generation of electronic musicians. They showed the world that electronic music can be more than just beats and drops—it can be a platform for artistic expression and cultural revolution.

As the Neon Revolution rages on, 12th Planet's legacy will forever be imprinted on the electronic music landscape. They not only influenced the industry but also created a movement that continues to evolve and thrive. The Neon Revolution is alive and well, and its impact will be felt for generations to come.

Key Takeaways

- 12th Planet's genre-bending approach transcended traditional boundaries in electronic music. - They played a crucial role in popularizing dubstep and bringing it into the mainstream. - Chart-topping hits like "Reasons" and "Burst" solidified their influence on the electronic music scene. - The Neon Warriors, their dedicated fan base, contributed to spreading their music and ideology. - 12th Planet's legacy of innovation continues to inspire the next generation of electronic musicians.

Neon vs Reality: The Glamour and the Grind

The Struggles of Success: Challenges on the Road

The path to success is never easy, and 12th Planet's journey was no exception. As they skyrocketed to fame, they faced numerous challenges that tested their resilience, both as individuals and as a band. In this chapter, we'll explore the struggles they encountered along the way and how they overcame them.

Finding Balance: Juggling Fame and Personal Life

One of the most significant challenges for any successful artist is finding a balance between their professional and personal lives. As 12th Planet's popularity grew, so did the demands on their time and energy. They faced the never-ending pressure of touring, recording, and promoting their music, leaving little time for themselves.

Members of the band found themselves constantly torn between their passion for music and their need for rest and personal connections. Late-night gigs and grueling tour schedules took a toll on their physical and mental well-being. The constant travel and time away from loved ones made it difficult to maintain lasting relationships.

To cope with these challenges, 12th Planet developed strategies to prioritize self-care and mental health. They recognized the importance of taking breaks and setting boundaries, even when their schedule seemed packed. Regular exercise, meditation, and spending quality time with friends and family became vital components of their routine.

The Dark Side of Fame: Neon Pressure

With fame comes great responsibility, but it also brings intense scrutiny and pressure. 12th Planet experienced the weight of public expectations as their popularity soared. They faced critical reviews, relentless speculation about their personal lives, and the constant pressure to produce hit after hit.

The band members struggled with the fear of disappointing their fans and losing their relevance in a rapidly evolving music landscape. The spotlight magnified their insecurities and heightened their self-doubt. They constantly questioned whether they were living up to the expectations placed upon them.

However, instead of letting the pressure consume them, 12th Planet turned it into fuel for their creativity. They channeled their struggles into their music, using it as an outlet to express their fears and insecurities. This vulnerability resonated with their fans and helped them to build a deeper connection with their audience.

Navigating the Music Industry: The Neon Rollercoaster

The music industry can be a cutthroat and unpredictable landscape. 12th Planet faced their fair share of challenges when it came to navigating contracts, record labels, and industry politics. They had to learn the ins and outs of the business while staying true to their artistic vision.

Like many artists, they endured setbacks and faced rejection throughout their career. Deals fell through, collaborations didn't pan out, and expectations were sometimes crushed. However, with each setback, they grew more determined and persevered through the ups and downs of the industry.

To overcome these obstacles, 12th Planet developed a strong support network of mentors and industry professionals who believed in their talent and vision. They sought guidance from those who had walked the path before them, learning from their experiences and applying those lessons to their own journey.

The Burden of Creativity: Constant Innovation

Success in the fast-paced music industry is often fleeting, as trends come and go. Artists constantly feel the pressure to innovate and stay ahead of the curve. 12th

Planet faced the challenge of maintaining their unique identity while also pushing the boundaries of their sound.

They strived to bring something fresh to the table with each new release, experimenting with different genres and production techniques. This constant evolution was not without its risks, as there was always the possibility of alienating their fan base or failing to resonate with new listeners.

To overcome this challenge, 12th Planet embraced their artistic courage and trusted their instincts. They embraced collaboration and sought inspiration from other genres, constantly seeking ways to infuse their signature sound with new elements. This willingness to take risks ultimately became one of their greatest strengths, setting them apart from their peers.

Lessons Learned: The Neon Resilience

Despite the many challenges they faced, 12th Planet emerged stronger and more resilient than ever. Their struggles taught them valuable lessons about perseverance, self-care, and staying true to their artistic vision. They discovered the importance of surrounding themselves with a supportive network and finding balance in the face of fame.

The band's journey serves as a reminder that success is not without its hurdles. It takes unwavering determination, adaptability, and the willingness to embrace both the highs and lows of the industry. 12th Planet's story is a testament to the power of resilience and the enduring spirit of the Neon Rhythms.

The Unconventional Approach: Embracing the Unexpected

In the face of challenges, it's often helpful to approach them from an unconventional angle. One unconventional yet effective strategy adopted by 12th Planet was the use of humor and laughter as a coping mechanism. They found that taking a lighthearted approach to difficult situations helped to ease their stress and maintain a positive mindset.

Whether it was cracking jokes during long tour bus rides or engaging in friendly banter on stage, 12th Planet used humor as a way to bond with their bandmates and keep their spirits high. This unorthodox approach not only helped them navigate the tough times but also added an extra layer of authenticity to their live performances.

So, the next time you find yourself faced with a daunting challenge, try injecting a dose of humor into the situation. You may be surprised by the positive impact it can have on your mindset and your ability to overcome obstacles.

With every challenge they overcame, 12th Planet grew stronger, both individually and as a band. Their struggles fueled their creativity, pushed them to innovate, and deepened their connection with their fans. And while the road was not without its bumps, they emerged victorious, leaving an indelible mark on the world of electronic music.

Personal Challenges and Conflicts: Surviving the Chaos

Life on the road can be exhilarating and glamorous, but it also comes with its fair share of personal challenges and conflicts. For the members of 12th Planet, surviving the chaos of the music industry and maintaining their sanity amidst the constant pressure was no easy feat.

One of the most significant challenges they faced was the toll that fame and success took on their personal lives. As they rose to prominence, their schedules became packed with back-to-back shows, interviews, and appearances. They found themselves constantly on the go, away from their loved ones and the comforts of home. It was a whirlwind of late nights, early mornings, and non-stop travel.

The mental and emotional strain of this lifestyle weighed heavily on their shoulders. They often found themselves homesick and feeling disconnected from the world outside of music. The constant pressure to deliver hit tracks and maintain their relevance in the ever-evolving electronic music scene only added to their stress. It was a rollercoaster of emotions that required a delicate balance to navigate.

Moreover, the band members had to deal with their own personal conflicts and struggles. Each member had their own unique journey and demons to face. Whether it was battling substance abuse, relationship issues, or navigating the ups and downs of the music industry, they were tested on multiple fronts.

To survive the chaos, they had to rely on each other. Communication was key, and they made a conscious effort to be open and honest with one another. They leaned on their bandmates for support and often sought solace in their shared experiences. This sense of camaraderie became their anchor, keeping them grounded amidst the chaos.

They also sought professional help when needed. They recognized the importance of mental health and sought therapy and counseling to help them navigate their personal challenges. They learned coping mechanisms and strategies to deal with the pressures they faced, and these tools became invaluable in their journey.

In order to maintain their sanity and recharge their batteries, they also made a point of taking time for themselves. Whether it was taking a break from touring to spend time with family and friends, indulging in hobbies outside of music, or simply taking a day off to rest, self-care was a top priority.

Through it all, they learned the importance of resilience and perseverance. They understood that setbacks were inevitable, but it was their ability to pick themselves up and keep going that truly defined their success. They embraced the chaos, learning to find beauty in the midst of it all.

Their personal challenges and conflicts became the fuel for their music, driving them to create music that resonated with their fans on a deeper level. They channeled their struggles into their art, using it as an outlet for expression and healing. The chaos became a source of inspiration, and they embraced it as an integral part of their journey.

In conclusion, surviving the chaos of the music industry is no small feat. For 12th Planet, personal challenges and conflicts tested them both mentally and emotionally. But through open communication, seeking help when needed, and prioritizing self-care, they managed to navigate the chaos and emerge stronger than ever. It is their resilience and ability to find beauty in the chaos that has secured their place as influential figures in the electronic music scene.

Overcoming Obstacles: The Band's Resilience

Life on the road can be a wild ride, filled with highs and lows, triumphs and setbacks. For the members of 12th Planet, their journey has been no different. In this section, we explore the obstacles they faced along the way and the resilience that kept them going.

The Demands of the Industry

Being in a band is not just about making music and touring. It also involves navigating the complex landscape of the music industry. From negotiating contracts to dealing with record labels and promoters, it can be a daunting task. 12th Planet faced their fair share of challenges in this regard.

One major obstacle they encountered was the pressure to conform to industry standards. As their popularity grew, there was a temptation to dilute their unique sound and cater to mainstream trends. However, the band remained steadfast in their commitment to pushing boundaries and staying true to their artistic vision.

Another challenge was the constant demand for new material. In an industry that thrives on novelty, the pressure to continually produce fresh, groundbreaking music can be overwhelming. The band members had to find a balance between maintaining their signature sound while exploring new sonic territories.

Financial Struggles

Like many up-and-coming musicians, 12th Planet faced financial challenges early on in their career. Touring, recording, and promoting their music required substantial monetary investment. The band members often had to rely on their own savings or take odd jobs to make ends meet.

As they gained recognition and began playing larger venues, the financial strain eased, but it was still a constant battle. The costs of equipment, insurance, travel, and crew members added up quickly. To overcome these obstacles, the band members became savvy entrepreneurs, seeking out sponsorships and exploring opportunities for merchandise sales.

Creative Conflicts

With multiple creative minds working together, clashes and differences of opinion are bound to occur. The members of 12th Planet were no exception. As they experimented with different sounds and musical styles, disagreements arose about the direction the band should take.

These creative conflicts were not easy to navigate, but they ultimately led to a stronger, more cohesive unit. The band members learned the importance of compromise and open communication. They realized that embracing different perspectives could lead to exciting musical breakthroughs.

Personal Sacrifices

Behind the scenes, the members of 12th Planet made numerous personal sacrifices for their music. Late nights in the studio meant sacrificing sleep and social activities. Endless hours on the road meant being away from loved ones and missing important milestones.

The band's relentless touring schedule took a toll on their physical and mental well-being. Long stretches of travel and irregular sleeping patterns can be physically exhausting. It was essential for the members to prioritize self-care and find ways to maintain their health and overall well-being.

Resilience in the Face of Adversity

Despite facing various obstacles, the band's resilience was unwavering. They embraced the challenges as opportunities for growth and viewed setbacks as stepping stones to success. The band members drew strength from their passion for music and their unwavering belief in their artistic vision.

To overcome financial struggles, they developed a strong work ethic, honed their entrepreneurial skills, and sought out alternative revenue streams. They diversified their income through merchandise sales, sponsorships, and licensing opportunities.

In the face of creative conflicts, the band learned the value of compromise and collaboration. They recognized that their individual strengths complemented each other, and by embracing their differences, they were able to create music that was greater than the sum of its parts.

Personal sacrifices became a testament to their dedication and love for their craft. They managed their physical and mental well-being by adopting healthy habits on the road, including regular exercise, healthy eating, and finding time for relaxation and self-reflection.

Through it all, the band's resilience shone through. Their ability to adapt to challenges, learn from mistakes, and persevere in the face of adversity became a driving force in their success.

The Power of Resilience

The story of 12th Planet's resilience serves as an inspiration to aspiring musicians and creative individuals alike. It reminds us that success is not always linear and that setbacks are an integral part of the journey.

Resilience is not just about bouncing back from failures; it's about using those failures as fuel for growth. It's about finding the strength to persevere in the face of adversity and staying true to yourself and your vision.

As we continue to explore the band's journey, we delve deeper into the creative process that defined their sound and the impact they had on the electronic music scene. But before we do that, let's take a moment to appreciate the hurdles they overcame and the resilience that propelled them forward.

Remember, success is not solely determined by talent, but by the ability to overcome obstacles with unyielding determination and passion. The story of 12th Planet is a testament to the power of resilience and the rewards that come from never giving up.

Musical Evolution and Experimentation: Pushing Boundaries

In the ever-evolving landscape of music, it's crucial for artists to constantly push the boundaries and evolve their sound. 12th Planet understands this like no other, and their journey of musical evolution and experimentation is a testament to their dedication to pushing the limits of their craft.

Embracing Change: A Musical Revolution

As 12th Planet began their musical journey, they quickly realized that in order to stand out in the crowded electronic music scene, they needed to embrace change and pursue a musical revolution. They understood that sticking to the status quo would only lead to blending in with the sea of other artists.

To kickstart their musical evolution, 12th Planet took inspiration from a wide range of genres, including metal, hip hop, and even classical music. By infusing these diverse influences into their music, they were able to carve out a unique sonic identity that would set them apart from the rest.

The Power of Experimentation

Experimentation became the backbone of 12th Planet's musical evolution. They were not afraid to take risks and try out new ideas, even if it meant deviating from their established sound. By pushing the boundaries of their comfort zone, they were able to tap into new realms of creativity and unlock their true potential as artists.

One of the ways 12th Planet embraced experimentation was by collaborating with artists from different genres and backgrounds. These collaborations allowed them to explore new soundscapes and borrow elements from other musical styles. They understood that true innovation lay in the uncharted territories of musical fusion.

The Science of Sound

Behind every great musician lies a deep understanding of the science of sound. 12th Planet spent countless hours honing their craft and learning the technical aspects of music production. They delved into the intricacies of sound waves, frequencies, and mixing techniques, constantly seeking to improve the quality of their music.

Their dedication to the craft led them to experiment with new production techniques and equipment. They tirelessly explored the sonic possibilities of synthesizers, drum machines, and audio effects, always in pursuit of that unique sound that would captivate their audience.

From Drops to Grooves

As 12th Planet's musical evolution progressed, they realized that there was more to their sound than just bass drops. While their early tracks were known for their heavy, aggressive drops, they sought to add depth and complexity to their music.

They began focusing on the grooves and rhythms that underpinned their tracks. By incorporating elements of funk, jazz, and soul, they transformed their music into a multidimensional experience that went beyond just the drop. Their evolution into groove-driven beats showcased their versatility as artists and garnered them a wider audience.

Redefining Boundaries

12th Planet's musical evolution wasn't just about experimentation within the realm of electronic music. They were determined to redefine the boundaries of their genre and break away from the conventional norms.

By infusing elements of dubstep with hip hop, trap, and even rock, they challenged the expectations of their listeners and expanded the sonic possibilities of electronic music. This fearless approach to genre-blending allowed them to create a sound that was truly unique and distinctly theirs.

The Unorthodox Path

In their quest for musical evolution, 12th Planet took an unorthodox path. They didn't follow trends or conform to industry expectations. Instead, they remained true to their artistic vision and pursued the sounds that resonated with them.

This unconventional approach meant that not every experiment would be a success. They faced setbacks and encountered tracks that didn't quite hit the mark. However, they saw these failures as learning opportunities and used them to refine their sound and grow as artists.

The Ever-Evolving Journey

Even after achieving success and recognition, 12th Planet didn't rest on their laurels. They understood that the key to staying relevant in the music industry was to continually evolve and adapt.

They kept their finger on the pulse of music trends, always on the lookout for new sounds and genres to explore. This constant evolution ensured that their music remained fresh and exciting, drawing in new fans while keeping their loyal audience engaged.

The Sonic Revolution Continues

As the musical journey of 12th Planet continues, one thing remains clear: they are unafraid to push the boundaries and experiment with their sound. Their dedication to musical evolution has solidified their place among the greats of electronic music and inspired countless artists to follow in their footsteps.

As fans, we can only wait in eager anticipation to see where the Neon Rhythms will take us next. Will they continue to redefine genres? Will they pioneer new sonic territories? Only time will tell, but one thing is for certain: the sonic revolution of 12th Planet is far from over.

Keeping the Flame Alive: Continuing Success and Relevance

In the ever-changing landscape of the music industry, it takes more than just talent to maintain longevity and relevance. For 12th Planet, the key to keeping the flame alive lies in their unwavering commitment to evolving their sound, staying connected with their fan base, and continuously pushing the boundaries of electronic music. In this section, we dive into the strategies and practices that have allowed 12th Planet to thrive, adapt, and remain iconic in the neon-drenched world of music.

Staying Ahead of the Curve: Embracing Innovation

To keep the flame burning bright, 12th Planet is constantly on the lookout for new trends and cutting-edge sounds. They understand that the music industry is in a constant state of evolution, with emerging genres and technologies shaping the sonic landscape. Rather than resting on their laurels and sticking to a formula, the band actively seeks out innovative ways to incorporate fresh elements into their music.

One way 12th Planet accomplishes this is through collaborations with up-and-coming artists and producers. By joining forces with these rising stars, they gain access to groundbreaking approaches and novel ideas that keep their sound relevant. This collaborative spirit not only breathes new life into their own music but also propels the artists they work with to new heights.

Example: When dubstep began to fade from the mainstream, 12th Planet recognized the rise of trap music and embraced its fusion with electronic sounds. By collaborating with trap producers and incorporating trap elements into their music, they remained at the forefront of the evolving electronic music scene, attracting new fans and maintaining their relevance.

The Power of Authenticity: Staying True to Yourself

In a world where trends come and go, authenticity is a rare and invaluable commodity. 12th Planet understands the importance of staying true to their roots while still embracing change. Their unique blend of heavy bass, hard-hitting beats, and melodic undertones is a testament to their unwavering artistic vision.

Rather than chasing after fleeting trends, 12th Planet focuses on honing their craft and deepening their connection with their fan base. They recognize that their music resonates with a specific audience who values their individuality and authenticity. By staying true to themselves, they create music that not only speaks to their fans but also attracts new listeners who are tired of manufactured pop hits.

Example: Despite the commercial success of their early releases, 12th Planet resisted pressure to dilute their sound for mainstream appeal. Instead, they doubled down on their unique combination of heavy basslines and atmospheric melodies, becoming a central figure in the underground electronic music scene and inspiring a legion of devoted fans.

Adapting to Changing Landscapes: Harnessing the Power of Technology

As technology continues to reshape the music industry, 12th Planet understands the importance of harnessing its power to connect and engage with their audience. They embrace social media platforms, streaming services, and digital marketing strategies to stay relevant in an increasingly digital world.

By actively engaging with their fans on social media, 12th Planet creates a sense of community and fosters a loyal fan base. They understand that the bond between artist and audience goes beyond the music itself, and they leverage technology to bridge that gap. Through live streams, behind-the-scenes footage, and interactive experiences, they ensure that their fans feel involved and invested in their journey.

Example: During the COVID-19 pandemic, when live concerts were canceled, 12th Planet embraced the power of live streaming. They organized virtual concerts, complete with high-quality production value and interactive chat rooms, allowing fans from around the world to come together and experience the magic of their music from the comfort of their homes. This not only kept their flame alive but also expanded their reach and introduced their music to new audiences.

Embracing the Neon Warriors: Cultivating a Dedicated Fan Base

The neon warriors, as 12th Planet affectionately calls their fan base, are the lifeblood of the band. To keep the flame alive, 12th Planet recognizes the importance of nurturing these dedicated fans and creating an immersive experience that goes beyond the music.

By organizing exclusive events, fan meet-ups, and special VIP experiences, 12th Planet fosters a genuine connection with their fans. They understand that these interactions go a long way in creating a sense of loyalty and community. Additionally, they actively listen to their fans, incorporating their feedback and suggestions into their music and live performances.

Example: 12th Planet's annual "Neon Fest" is a prime example of their dedication to their fan base. This multi-day festival brings together music, art, and interactive experiences, creating a vibrant celebration of the neon revolution. With themed stages, live art installations, and surprise guest performances, Neon Fest allows fans to fully immerse themselves in the neon world while forging lifelong memories.

Keeping the Neon Flame Burning Bright: A Lasting Legacy

To ensure their flame continues to burn brightly even after their time in the spotlight, 12th Planet is dedicated to leaving a lasting legacy. They understand that their impact goes beyond their own music and actively invest in the next generation of artists and producers.

By mentoring emerging musicians, curating record labels, and organizing workshops, 12th Planet provides aspiring artists with the tools and guidance to succeed. They believe that supporting and nurturing talent not only pays homage to their own influences but also creates a ripple effect that fuels the future of electronic music.

Example: As part of their commitment to fostering talent, 12th Planet launched a music scholarship program aimed at assisting aspiring producers with limited access to resources. By providing financial support, mentorship, and networking opportunities, they opened doors for talented individuals who may otherwise have faced countless barriers.

The Unconventional Path: Embracing Risk and Unpredictability

In the pursuit of continuing success and relevance, 12th Planet understands that taking risks and embracing unpredictability is essential. They recognize that innovation often lies in uncharted territory and are unafraid to step outside their comfort zone.

By experimenting with new genres, collaborating with artists from diverse backgrounds, and exploring unconventional production techniques, 12th Planet keeps their music fresh and exciting. They know that staying comfortable breeds stagnation, and they are willing to embrace the unknown to keep their flame burning with intensity.

Example: In a bold move, 12th Planet released an album that defied genre conventions, incorporating elements of jazz, funk, and classical music into their signature sound. This unexpected fusion not only surprised their fan base but also attracted a new audience eager to explore the boundaries of electronic music.

Conclusion

12th Planet's journey has been one of continuous growth, adaptability, and fearless exploration. By embracing innovation, staying true to their sound, leveraging technology, cultivating a dedicated fan base, and investing in the future of electronic music, they have successfully kept the flame alive. Their relentless pursuit of pushing boundaries and leaving a lasting legacy ensures that the neon rhythms they pioneered will continue to reverberate for years to come.

Chapter 2 Behind the Beats

Chapter 2 Behind the Beats

Chapter 2: Behind the Beats

In this chapter, we will dive deep into the inner workings of the band 12th Planet, exploring the individuals behind the neon sound and the creative process that brings their music to life. From the founding members to their secret ingredients, we will uncover the magic that fuels the Neon Rhythms and makes them a force to be reckoned with in the electronic music scene.

The Musical Wizards: Masters of the Neon Sound

The band 12th Planet is composed of a group of incredibly talented individuals, each bringing their unique skills and musical background to the table. Let's take a closer look at the founding members and how their origins have shaped the distinctive Neon sound.

The Founding Members: Origins and Background   The origins of 12th Planet can be traced back to Los Angeles, where a group of childhood friends came together with a shared love for music. Mustafa Alonso, the driving force behind the band, discovered his passion for music at an early age.   Growing up in a neighborhood vibrant with diverse sounds, Alonso was exposed to a melting pot of musical influences, setting the stage for the eclectic Neon sound that would later emerge.

Joining forces with other talented musicians, including DJ X and MC Y, 12th Planet was born.   DJ X, a master of beats and rhythm, brought his extensive knowledge of electronic music to the mix, while MC Y, with his captivating lyrical prowess, added a dynamic element to the group's performances.   Together, they formed a powerful trio ready to take on the world with their Neon Rhythms.

Musical Roles and Contributions: A Harmonious Symphony   The members of 12th Planet each play a vital role in crafting the band's distinctive sound. Mustafa Alonso, as the lead producer, is the creative genius behind the Neon beats. With a keen ear for melodies and an innate ability to mix genres seamlessly, Alonso brings a unique perspective to electronic music.

DJ X, as the band's resident DJ, is responsible for igniting the dance floor with his infectious mixes and impeccable timing. His ability to read the crowd, anticipate their energy, and blend tracks flawlessly transforms the band's live performances into euphoric experiences.

MC Y, on the other hand, acts as the voice of 12th Planet, adding layers of depth and emotion to their tracks with his captivating lyrics and powerful delivery. His ability to connect with the audience through his words brings an intimate touch to the Neon experience.

The Chemistry Between Band Members: Sparking Creativity   What sets 12th Planet apart from other bands is the undeniable chemistry between its members. The shared history and deep-rooted friendship create an atmosphere of trust and freedom, where ideas flow effortlessly and creativity thrives.

When the trio comes together in the studio, their chemistry sparks a creative fire. Mustafa Alonso's ability to push boundaries and experiment with new sounds is met with DJ X and MC Y's unwavering support and enthusiasm. This collaboration of ideas and constant feedback allows the band to refine their sound and deliver exceptional music to their fans.

The Secret Ingredient: Creative Process and Inspiration   The creative process behind 12th Planet's music is a carefully crafted alchemy, blending inspiration from various sources with the band's unique vision. Mustafa Alonso draws inspiration from everyday life, finding musical motifs in the most unexpected places. Whether it's the hum of a city street or the chirping of birds outside his window, Alonso's ability to extract beauty from the mundane is a testament to his musical genius.

The band's artistic process involves hours of experimentation and exploration in the studio. They harness the power of technology, utilizing cutting-edge equipment and production techniques to manipulate sounds and create their signature Neon sound. From precisely timed bass drops to mesmerizing melodies, every element of their music is a result of their meticulous attention to detail.

Collaborations and Musical Connections: Neon Fusion   While the founding members of 12th Planet are the driving force behind the band's creative process, they also value the power of collaboration. Throughout their career, they have collaborated with artists from various genres, fusing their Neon sound with elements of hip hop, rock, and beyond.

These musical connections have allowed 12th Planet to push the boundaries of electronic music and explore new sonic territories. The band's openness to collaboration has not only expanded their creative palette but also introduced them to new audiences and helped them leave a lasting mark on the music industry.

Crafting the Neon Sound

In this section, we will delve into the evolution of 12th Planet's sound, exploring the influences, studio secrets, and experimentation that have shaped the band's signature Neon sound. From their roots in dubstep to their genre-bending evolution, we will uncover the secrets behind the beats that keep the Neon Rhythms pulsating.

The Evolution of 12th Planet's Sound: From Drops to Grooves The sound of 12th Planet has undergone a remarkable evolution since its inception. Beginning with a focus on bass-heavy drops synonymous with the dubstep genre, the band has since expanded their sonic landscape, incorporating diverse elements to create a more groove-oriented sound.

Through years of refining their style and pushing the boundaries of electronic music, 12th Planet has developed a sound that is both energetic and melodic. Their tracks seamlessly intertwine catchy hooks with heavy bass lines, giving their music an infectious quality that resonates with audiences around the world.

Influences from Various Genres: From Metal to Hip Hop The Neon sound of 12th Planet is a fusion of diverse musical influences. The band members' backgrounds in different genres have played a significant role in shaping their unique style.

Mustafa Alonso's love for metal music and its high-energy, aggressive nature has left an indelible mark on the Neon sound. The pulsating bass lines, intense drops, and raw power that define the band's music can be traced back to the influence of metal.

The band's exposure to hip hop and its rhythmic intricacies has also played a pivotal role in their sound. They draw inspiration from hip hop production techniques, incorporating complex drum patterns and intricate samples into their tracks. This infusion of hip hop elements adds a dynamic layer to the Neon beats, elevating their music to new heights.

Studio Secrets: Equipment and Production Techniques   At the heart of 12th Planet's sound lies their intricate production techniques and state-of-the-art equipment.   In the studio, they utilize a combination of analog and digital instruments to create their unique Neon sound.

From vintage synthesizers to cutting-edge software plugins, the band leverages a vast array of tools to shape their music. They meticulously tweak sounds, experimenting with different effects and textures to achieve the desired sonic palette.

Their attention to detail extends to their mixing and mastering process as well. The band utilizes advanced techniques to ensure that every element of their music shines through, striking the perfect balance between clarity and power.

Experimenting with New Sounds and Genres: Neon Chameleon   One of the hallmarks of 12th Planet's career has been their willingness to embrace new sounds and explore genres outside their comfort zone. Their ability to adapt and experiment has allowed them to evolve as artists and continually push the boundaries of their music.

From forays into drum and bass to collaborations with pop artists, 12th Planet has embraced their role as musical chameleons. They thrive on the challenge of incorporating different elements into their music, seamlessly blending genres to create a unique and captivating sonic experience.

Maintaining the Signature Sound: Consistency and Evolution   While 12th Planet is known for their ever-evolving sound, they have also mastered the art of maintaining a consistent signature style. Despite their genre-bending tendencies, their music retains a distinct Neon flair that sets them apart from their contemporaries.

The band achieves this balance between consistency and evolution by staying true to their artistic vision while embracing new ideas and influences. They constantly challenge themselves to push the boundaries of their sound without losing sight of the elements that make them who they are.

Through a meticulous understanding of their musical roots and a commitment to growth, 12th Planet has harnessed the power of consistency and evolution, solidifying their place as true masters of the Neon sound.

Creating Anthems: The Hits and Misses

In this section, we will uncover the stories and secrets behind 12th Planet's chart-topping hits, as well as the lessons learned from their musical explorations.

From the making of iconic tracks to the challenges of collaboration, we will dive into the highs and lows of the band's journey in creating musical anthems.

Chart-Topping Hits: Stories Behind the Success Throughout their career, 12th Planet has released a string of chart-topping hits that have captivated audiences worldwide. Each track has its own unique story, reflecting the band's evolution and growth as artists.

From the anthemic "Neon Dreams" to the infectious rhythms of "Electric Dreams," every chart-topper has been meticulously crafted to resonate with listeners at a profound level. The band's ability to capture the energy of their live performances and translate it into studio recordings is a testament to their musical prowess.

But behind each success lies hours of hard work, countless revisions, and a commitment to pushing the boundaries. The stories behind these hits not only serve as a celebration of the band's achievements but also provide valuable insights into their creative process.

The Making of Iconic Tracks: Behind the Studio Doors The creation of iconic tracks is often a journey filled with unexpected twists and turns. 12th Planet's music is no exception. Behind the scenes, the band has undergone the often grueling process of bringing their creative visions to life.

From the initial spark of an idea to the final mix, every step in the production process requires meticulous attention to detail. Finding the right melodies, layering the perfect synth sounds, and sculpting the bass lines to perfection are all part of the intricate puzzle that makes a track truly iconic.

In the studio, the band members immerse themselves in the creative process, experimenting with different sounds, tempos, and arrangements. They work tirelessly to capture the emotional essence of their music and ensure that it resonates with their audience.

Collaborative Successes and Challenges: Harmonizing with Others Collaborations have played a significant role in shaping 12th Planet's discography. Working with other artists not only expands their creative palette but also brings a fresh perspective to their music.

Collaborative success stories abound in the band's career, but they are not without their challenges. Bringing together different creative visions and finding a harmonious balance can be a delicate process. However, when the right synergy is found, the results can be extraordinary.

Through collaborations, the band has been able to explore new musical territories and fuse their distinct Neon sound with other genres. The challenges they encounter along the way serve as valuable lessons, helping them grow as artists and expand the boundaries of their music.

Hidden Gems and Unreleased Tracks: Neon Treasures Not all 12th Planet tracks that shine brightly in the studio see the light of day. Behind the scenes, there is a trove of hidden gems and unreleased tracks that have yet to grace the ears of their dedicated fans.

These hidden treasures serve as a testament to the band's constant exploration and willingness to take risks. While not every experimental track may find its footing in the mainstream, the process of creating and refining these hidden gems is an essential part of the band's creative journey.

Whether these tracks remain hidden forever or find their way into the spotlight, they represent the band's unyielding commitment to their craft and their constant search for the perfect Neon sound.

The Risks of Musical Exploration: The Misses and Lessons Learned Every artist faces the occasional miss on their creative journey, and 12th Planet is no exception. Stepping outside their comfort zone and exploring new genres and sounds comes with inherent risks.

Sometimes, musical explorations may fall short of expectations or fail to resonate with the intended audience. However, it is in these moments of perceived failure that crucial lessons are learned.

The misses and near-misses serve as fuel for growth, pushing the band to reassess their approach, refine their sound, and experiment with new ideas. They remind us that creativity is not always about hitting the mark on the first try but rather a continuous process of self-reflection and improvement.

The Live Experience: A Neon Spectacle

In this section, we will explore the breathtaking live performances of 12th Planet and the atmosphere they create on stage. From their energetic presence to the immersive visuals, we will uncover the secret ingredients that make a 12th Planet live show an unforgettable Neon spectacle.

The Band's Energetic Performances: Sweating on Stage When 12th Planet takes the stage, they bring an infectious energy that electrifies the crowd. The band's passion for their music is palpable, permeating the air and turning the atmosphere into a pulsating Neon dance floor.

From Mustafa Alonso's commanding presence behind the decks to DJ X's unmatched ability to read the room, the band members give their all during every performance. Sweat drips, hearts race, and bodies move in unison as the intense beats of their music provide a sonic backdrop for a collective euphoria.

The Evolution of 12th Planet's Live Shows: From Clubs to Arenas Throughout their career, 12th Planet has performed in a variety of venues, ranging from intimate clubs to expansive arenas. Their live shows have evolved alongside their music, incorporating larger-than-life production elements that elevate the Neon experience.

What started as humble performances in underground venues has transformed into an awe-inspiring multi-sensory journey. From intricate lighting setups to mesmerizing visuals, the band creates a captivating atmosphere that immerses the audience in the world of Neon Rhythms.

Creating a Unique Atmosphere: Lights, Visuals, and Stage Design To enhance the live experience, 12th Planet understands the importance of creating a unique atmosphere that complements their Neon sound. The band collaborates with talented lighting designers and visual artists to craft a visual spectacle that captivates the audience.

Vibrant neon lights dance in sync with the music, casting an otherworldly glow over the crowd. Mesmerizing visuals, seamlessly integrated with the performance, transport the audience to a surreal neon dreamscape. The stage design itself becomes an extension of the music, with intricate structures and pulsating LED screens.

This meticulous attention to detail ensures that every element of the live show contributes to the immersive experience, leaving the audience in a state of neon trance.

Touring Adventures and Mishaps: Stories from the Road Behind the glamour of touring lies a world filled with adventures, mishaps, and memorable moments. 12th Planet's journey on the road has been anything but ordinary, with countless stories to tell.

From missed flights and broken-down tour buses to unexpected encounters with fans, the band's touring adventures have shaped them as individuals and as a collective. These experiences, both humorous and challenging, have become the fabric of their journey and have helped forge unbreakable bonds between band members.

The road is filled with unexpected twists and turns, but it is also the place where unforgettable memories are made and shared, creating a community of fans and artists that extends beyond the music.

The Connection Between the Band and the Audience: Neon Unity   At the heart of every 12th Planet live show lies the undeniable connection between the band and their audience. The energy unleashed by the Neon sound creates an unbreakable bond, blurring the lines between the stage and the dance floor.

As the music pulsates through the venue, a sense of unity emerges. Strangers become friends, and individual experiences merge into a collective journey. The band feeds off the energy of the crowd, creating a feedback loop that fuels the performance and leaves both the band and the audience transformed.

This connection is a testament to the power of music to bring people together, to create a space where all are welcome, and to forge lasting memories that transcend time and place.

The Price of Fame: Neon Glitz and Grinding Gears

In this section, we will explore the realities of fame and the challenges that come with success. Behind the neon glitz lies the grit and determination required to survive in the music industry. From the balancing act of personal life and career to the constant pressure to innovate, we will uncover the stories of perseverance and resilience that have kept 12th Planet going.

Balancing Personal Life and Musical Career: Juggling Act   For the members of 12th Planet, the pursuit of a musical career has come with sacrifices and challenges. Balancing personal life with the demands of a touring schedule can be a delicate juggling act.

The band members navigate the complexities of maintaining relationships, nurturing friendships, and tending to their personal well-being while on the road. Long stretches away from home, sleepless nights, and constant travel can take a toll on both mental and physical health.

However, the band's unwavering dedication to their craft has taught them the importance of finding a balance. They have learned to prioritize self-care and surround themselves with a support system that understands the demands of their career.

The Mental and Emotional Toll of Fame: Neon Pressure   As 12th Planet's fame grows, so does the weight of expectations. The band members face the constant pressure to deliver groundbreaking music, exceed their previous successes, and live up to the Neon revolution they have sparked.

The mental and emotional toll of this pressure is something the band members openly acknowledge. They have learned to navigate the highs and lows of the industry, support one another during challenging times, and seek solace in their shared experiences.

Behind the neon glitz lies a resilient spirit that continues to push through the challenges, turning adversity into fuel for their creative fire.

The Ups and Downs of the Music Industry: Neon Rollercoaster   The music industry is no stranger to ups and downs, and 12th Planet has experienced its fair share of both. From the exhilarating highs of a chart-topping hit to the setbacks and disappointments that inevitably come with a creative career, the band has learned to weather the storm.

They understand that success is not a linear path but rather a rollercoaster ride filled with unexpected twists and turns. The key lies in resilience and a commitment to their artistic vision. Even in the face of adversity, they continue to evolve, grow, and push the boundaries of their sound.

The Constant Pressure to Innovate: Neon's Creative Burden   Innovation is the lifeblood of 12th Planet's music, but it also brings with it a burden. The constant pressure to innovate and push the boundaries of electronic music can be daunting.

The band members invest endless hours in the pursuit of sonic experimentation, unafraid to challenge conventions or explore uncharted territories. They feel a deep responsibility to their fans and to the music industry to continuously evolve and offer something new.

Yet, they also understand the importance of staying true to their artistic vision. Balancing the need to innovate with maintaining their core sound is a delicate dance, but one that ultimately fuels their creative fire and keeps them relevant in an ever-changing music landscape.

Navigating the Industry: Success, Setbacks, and Lessons Learned   The journey through the music industry is not without its setbacks, but 12th Planet has learned valuable lessons along the way.   From navigating record deals and contract negotiations to dealing with the ebbs and flows of popularity, they have gained a wealth of knowledge and experience.

They have found strength in the face of adversity, honing their talents and building a devoted fan base that supports them through thick and thin. Their journey serves as a reminder that success is not achieved overnight but rather through perseverance, dedication, and a willingness to overcome the obstacles that come their way.

Through their resilience and unwavering commitment to their music, 12th Planet continues to navigate the industry with grace and solidify their place as legends of the Neon sound.

Chapter 3: Neon Legends: Leaving a Mark

Introduction to Dubstep Pioneers: Groundbreakers and Game Changers

In this chapter, we will delve into the pioneering role of 12th Planet and other dubstep artists in revolutionizing the electronic music scene. From the origins of the genre to the impact of their music on the cultural landscape, we will explore the profound influence of dubstep pioneers and their enduring legacy.

The Roots of Dubstep: Early Influences and Artists   Dubstep, the genre that would forever transform electronic music, has its roots in the early electronic music scenes of London, UK. Drawing inspiration from various genres, including garage, dub reggae, and drum and bass, the pioneers of dubstep began shaping a sound that would captivate audiences around the world.

Artists like Skream, Benga, and Burial paved the way for the dubstep movement, infusing their music with deep bass lines, skittering beats, and haunting melodies. These early influences formed the foundation from which the neon sound would emerge.

The Creation of the Dubstep Sound: From Sub Bass to Wobble   At the heart of dubstep lies the iconic sub-bass, a fundamental element that distinguishes the genre from its electronic counterparts. The deep, rumbling bass lines, combined with syncopated rhythms, create a visceral listening experience that resonates with the core of one's being.

As the genre evolved, artists began experimenting with new production techniques, giving birth to the iconic dubstep wobble. The wobble, characterized by its distinctive modulation and oscillation, added a layer of complexity and intensity to the music, further solidifying dubstep's place in the electronic music landscape.

12th Planet's Role in the Dubstep Movement: Neon Flagbearer When discussing the pioneers of dubstep, it is impossible to overlook the role that 12th Planet played in the genre's ascension. As one of the early adopters of dubstep in the United States, 12th Planet became a torchbearer, introducing audiences to the powerful bass-driven sound that would revolutionize the electronic music scene.

The band's relentless dedication to their craft and their willingness to push boundaries helped propel them to the forefront of the dubstep movement. Their music became a rallying cry for a generation of music enthusiasts seeking a new sonic experience.

Collaborations with Dubstep Legends: Neon Alliances Throughout their journey, 12th Planet has had the opportunity to collaborate with some of the biggest names in dubstep. From Skream and Benga to Excision and Doctor P, these alliances have not only elevated the band's status but also solidified their place in the pantheon of dubstep legends.

These collaborations have been marked by a shared passion for pushing the boundaries of electronic music and a mutual desire to create sonic landscapes that captivate listeners. The coming together of these influential artists has sparked a creative fire, resulting in collaborative tracks that continue to reverberate through the electronic music scene.

Collaborations That Shaped the Neon Sound: A Fusion of Brilliance

In this section, we will explore the impact of collaborations on 12th Planet's music, delving into the fusion of brilliance that arises when artists come together. From cross-genre partnerships to the magic of collaborative creativity, we will uncover the stories behind some of the band's most powerful collaborative tracks.

Musical Partnerships Beyond Dubstep: Neon Cross-Pollination While dubstep may be the heart and soul of 12th Planet's music, the band has also ventured beyond the genre, seeking opportunities to collaborate with artists from diverse musical backgrounds.

These cross-genre partnerships have resulted in groundbreaking tracks that blend elements of dubstep with other genres, creating a sonic fusion that pushes the boundaries of what is possible in electronic music.

Whether it's teaming up with hip hop artists, rock bands, or pop sensations, 12th Planet's ability to seamlessly integrate their Neon sound with other genres demonstrates their versatility as artists and their commitment to pushing the envelope.

The Magic of Collaborative Creativity: Neon Alchemy   Collaborations are often driven by a shared desire to create something greater than the sum of its parts. In the case of 12th Planet, the magic of collaborative creativity lies in the alchemy that occurs when artists with distinct styles come together.

The band's ability to forge connections with collaborators and harness their collective creative energy is a testament to their vision and open-mindedness. Through a series of brainstorming sessions, experimentation, and mutual respect, they create tracks that capture the essence of both artists, resulting in a truly unique musical experience.

Breaking Boundaries: Cross-Genre Collaborations That Worked   When attempting cross-genre collaborations, one of the greatest challenges is finding a harmonious balance between the different musical styles. 12th Planet has managed to break through these barriers, creating collaborations that work by embracing the diversity of their partners' sounds.

Whether it's fusing dubstep with hip hop or introducing elements of rock into their music, the band's ability to find common ground and complement each other's strengths has resulted in collaborations that defy traditional genre boundaries.

By breaking down these barriers, 12th Planet has opened the door for a new wave of electronic music that seamlessly blends genres and challenges preconceived notions of what is possible.

Learning from Other Music Genres: Neon Inspiration   Collaborations not only allow artists to create innovative music but also provide an opportunity to learn from one another, gaining insight into different musical worlds.

12th Planet's collaborations with artists outside of dubstep have served as a source of inspiration, pushing them to experiment with new sounds and approaches. These forays into other genres have enriched their musical palette and helped shape the unique Neon sound that has captivated audiences around the world.

The band's ability to extract valuable lessons from each collaboration, whether it be a new production technique or a fresh perspective on music, has contributed to their growth as artists and their continued evolution.

The Impact of Collaboration on 12th Planet's Music: Neon Synergy   Collaboration is at the core of 12th Planet's musical journey. It has not only enriched their music but also helped shape the band's identity and sound.

The impact of collaboration extends beyond individual tracks; it permeates every aspect of the band's music and influences their creative process. The Neon synergy that arises from their collaborations pushes them to constantly evolve, experiment, and challenge themselves. It is through collaboration that the band finds a deeper understanding of their own creative potential and the limitless possibilities of electronic music.

Neon Innovators: Pushing the Boundaries of Sound

In this section, we will explore 12th Planet's innovative spirit and their role as pioneers of the Neon sound. From embracing the experimental and unconventional to their evolution from dubstep to hybrid genres, we will uncover the band's commitment to pushing the boundaries of electronic music.

Embracing the Experimental and the Unconventional: Neon Mavericks At the core of 12th Planet's ethos lies a thirst for experimentation and a willingness to embrace the unconventional. The band has never shied away from pushing the boundaries of electronic music, constantly seeking new sonic territories to explore.

Their artistic journey is marked by a series of bold choices and unorthodox approaches. They are not content with following trends or adhering to genre conventions; instead, they forge their own path, unafraid to challenge preconceived notions of what electronic music should be.

By embracing the experimental and the unconventional, 12th Planet has carved out a unique space in the music industry, where creativity knows no bounds and innovation takes center stage.

Evolving the Neon Sound: From Dubstep to Hybrid Genres While dubstep may have been the launching pad for 12th Planet's career, the band has continually evolved their sound, incorporating elements from various genres to create hybrid sonic landscapes.

Their music seamlessly combines the hard-hitting bass and energetic rhythms of dubstep with influences from hip hop, rock, and other genres. This evolution has allowed them to maintain their distinct Neon sound while also exploring new sonic territories and expanding their creative palette.

The band's ability to evolve without losing sight of their core sound is a testament to their versatility as artists and their commitment to constant growth and reinvention.

Blurring the Lines: Electronic Music and Pop Culture   12th Planet's impact on the music industry extends beyond the realm of electronic music. The band has played a pivotal role in blurring the lines between electronic music and pop culture, introducing the Neon sound to mainstream audiences.

Through their collaborations with pop artists and appearances in mainstream media, 12th Planet has managed to bridge the gap between the underground electronic scene and the mainstream music landscape. This crossover not only exposes new audiences to electronic music but also serves as a reminder of the genre's cultural relevance and its ability to shape popular culture.

Inspiring Future Generations of Electronic Musicians: A Neon Legacy   As pioneers of the Neon sound, 12th Planet has become a source of inspiration for future generations of electronic musicians. Their commitment to pushing the boundaries of electronic music and their relentless pursuit of innovation has left an indelible mark on the genre.

The band's legacy extends beyond their discography. It lies in the countless emerging artists and producers they have influenced and mentored along the way. Their willingness to share their knowledge and support others in their creative endeavors ensures that the Neon sound will continue to evolve and shape the future of electronic music.

The Legacy of 12th Planet: Shaping the Future of Music   12th Planet's legacy is one of innovation, resilience, and an unwavering commitment to their craft. Their journey has not only shaped the electronic music scene but also left an indelible mark on the cultural landscape.

Their pioneering role in the dubstep movement, their genre-bending sound, and their willingness to push the boundaries of electronic music have solidified their place as legends in the industry. The Neon sound they have cultivated continues to resonate with audiences, inspiring a new wave of artists to explore the limitless possibilities of electronic music.

As their legacy continues to unfold, 12th Planet remains committed to leaving a lasting impact on the music industry, a neon imprint that will forever illuminate the path for future generations of musicians.

Neon Beyond the Beats: Making a Difference

In this section, we will explore 12th Planet's impact and influence beyond the realm of music. From community involvement and activism to entrepreneurial ventures and philanthropy, we will uncover how the band's dedication to making a difference has extended beyond their Neon sound.

Community Involvement and Activism: Neon Hearts Beyond their musical pursuits, 12th Planet is deeply committed to making a positive impact on the communities they touch. Through their involvement in various charitable endeavors and activism, the band seeks to inspire change and promote social justice.

They use their platform to raise awareness about pressing issues, lend their support to grassroots movements, and encourage their fans to become agents of change. Their Neon sound becomes a powerful tool to unite people and effect social transformation.

Entrepreneurial Ventures and Philanthropy: Neon Business Minds In addition to their musical endeavors, 12th Planet has taken on various entrepreneurial ventures and philanthropic efforts. Their entrepreneurial spirit extends beyond the studio, as they explore business opportunities that align with their values and passions.

From music festivals to clothing lines, the band's entrepreneurial ventures not only diversify their creative portfolio but also provide platforms to support emerging artists and give back to the community. Their commitment to philanthropy ensures that their success is shared and that the Neon revolution extends beyond the realm of music.

Supporting Emerging Artists and Producers: Neon Mentorship As pioneers of the electronic music scene, 12th Planet understands the importance of nurturing and supporting emerging artists and producers. They have become mentors to a new generation of musicians, offering guidance, sharing their knowledge, and providing a platform for these artists to showcase their talent.

Through collaborations and mentorship programs, the band seeks to create a sense of community and support the growth of the next wave of electronic music pioneers. Their commitment to fostering talent ensures that the Neon legacy will continue to thrive and shape the future of music.

Exploring Other Artistic Endeavors: Neon Renaissance Beyond their music, 12th Planet's creative spirit extends to other artistic endeavors. From visual art to film and fashion, the band immerses themselves in a multidisciplinary approach, exploring new artistic territories and expanding their creative horizons.

Their exploration of other art forms not only feeds their creative inspiration but also adds new dimensions to their music and performances. By transcending the traditional boundaries of music, they embrace a Neon Renaissance, blurring the lines between art forms and creating a truly immersive artistic experience.

The Band's Impact and Influence Beyond the Music: Neon Cultural Shift   The impact of 12th Planet extends far beyond the realm of music. Their commitment to activism, entrepreneurial endeavors, mentorship, and exploration of other artistic disciplines has created a Neon cultural shift.

Their influence on the cultural landscape serves as a reminder of the transformative power of art. By harnessing the Neon sound and leveraging their platform, 12th Planet has sparked a cultural revolution, inspiring others to use their creativity to effect change and leave a lasting impact on the world.

The Neon Legacy: Forever Glowing

In this final section, we will reflect on 12th Planet's enduring legacy and the impact they have left on the music industry and beyond. From their discography and accomplishments to honoring the Neon legends that came before them, we will celebrate the lasting glow of the Neon revolution.

Looking Back: 12th Planet's Discography and Accomplishments   Reflecting on 12th Planet's discography is to behold a sonic journey filled with neon hues and bass-driven brilliance. From their early demos and breakthrough hits to their chart-topping anthems and collaborations, each track tells a story of evolution, innovation, and undeniable talent.

Their accomplishments, both within the music industry and beyond, serve as a testament to their unwavering commitment to their craft and their relentless pursuit of excellence. Awards, sold-out shows, and millions of streams are a testament to the enduring impact of the Neon revolution.

Honoring the Neon Legends: Paying Tribute to the Masters   As true pioneers of the Neon sound, 12th Planet recognizes the shoulders they stand upon. They pay homage to the dubstep legends who paved the way, acknowledging their contributions to the genre and the profound influence they have had on their own musical journey.

Through collaborations and shared performances, 12th Planet embodies the spirit of unity and respect that flows through the electronic music community.

They honor the Neon legends by carrying the torch and ensuring that the genre's rich history remains alive and vibrant.

Neon Rhythms: A Legacy Worth Remembering   Weaving its way through the beats and melodies of 12th Planet's music, the Neon rhythm has become a symbol of a cultural shift and a legacy worth remembering. The impact of their music reaches far beyond the dance floor, resonating with audiences around the world and inspiring future generations of musicians.

The Neon revolution sparked by 12th Planet will forever hold a special place in the annals of electronic music history. It represents the power of creativity, the joy of collaboration, and the ability of music to shape culture and ignite change.

Neon Retrospective: The Legacy Lives On   As we look back on 12th Planet's journey, we see a legacy that continues to thrive, captivating audiences with its undying glow. The band's impact on the music industry, their commitment to making a difference, and their unwavering dedication to their music ensure that the Neon sound will forever resonate in the hearts and souls of music lovers around the world.

Their ability to push the boundaries of electronic music, embrace collaboration, and transcend traditional genre limitations has forever left an indelible mark on the cultural landscape. The Neon revolution they sparked is a testament to the enduring power of music to inspire, connect, and shape the world we live in.

Remembering the Neon Revolution: The Lasting Impact of 12th Planet   As we close the chapter on 12th Planet's journey, we are reminded of the lasting impact they have had on the music industry and beyond. Their Neon sound, their commitment to artistic excellence, and their dedication to making a difference continue to reverberate through the collective consciousness of music enthusiasts around the world.

The Neon revolution they ignited serves as a beacon of creativity, innovation, and resilience. It is a reminder that art has the power to transcend boundaries, unite diverse communities, and inspire change.

As the neon glow fades into the distance, we are left with a legacy that will forever illuminate the path for future generations of musicians and dreamers. The impact of 12th Planet's music is imprinted in the cultural fabric of our time, a testament to the enduring power of the Neon Rhythms.

The Musical Wizards: Masters of the Neon Sound

The Founding Members: Origins and Background

The story of 12th Planet begins with four individuals who shared a passion for music and a burning desire to create something new and exciting. They hailed from different corners of the world, each bringing a unique set of skills, experiences, and influences to the table.

The Origins

Let's start with Mustafa Alonso, also known as Mustafa the Great, the mastermind behind the band. Mustafa was born in the vibrant city of Los Angeles, a melting pot of cultures and home to a thriving music scene. Growing up, he was exposed to a wide range of genres, from hip-hop and punk rock to reggae and metal. His love for music knew no bounds, and he always had a knack for discovering the most obscure and groundbreaking sounds.

On the other side of the world, we have Luna Hernandez, a prodigious guitarist hailing from Mexico. Luna's fiery guitar solos and intricate riffs would become the backbone of 12th Planet's sound. Luna's early exposure to Latin music and his undeniable talent on the guitar set him apart from the crowd. He was a force to be reckoned with, bringing a wild energy and blistering guitar skills to the band.

Next, we have Kai Chen, a bass prodigy from Shanghai, China. Kai's thunderous basslines and infectious grooves would become the heartbeat of 12th Planet. From a young age, Kai had an affinity for rhythm and a deep understanding of the intricacies of musical composition. He effortlessly blended his Chinese heritage with Western influences, creating a unique bass playing style that was both melodic and powerful.

Lastly, we have Alexei Ivanov, the enigmatic Russian keyboard virtuoso. Alexei's mastery of the keys and his uncanny ability to evoke emotion through music added a layer of depth and richness to the band's sound. With his classical training and a deep love for electronic music, Alexei brought a symphonic resonance to 12th Planet, elevating their music to a whole new level.

The Convergence

It was fate that brought these four musical prodigies together. Mustafa, Luna, Kai, and Alexei were all pursuing their individual musical careers when they crossed paths in the heart of Los Angeles. They instantly recognized the potential they held as a collective force, and 12th Planet was born.

Their backgrounds and influences coalesced into a sonic tapestry that defied categorization. Drawing inspiration from dubstep, metal, classical music, and everything in between, they forged a sound that was electrifying, dynamic, and utterly unique. The fusion of Luna's blistering guitar solos, Kai's thunderous basslines, Alexei's symphonic keys, and Mustafa's genre-bending vision created an explosive mixture that would captivate audiences around the world.

The Neon Bond

But it wasn't just their musical talents that brought the founding members of 12th Planet together. It was their shared love for the neon-lit streets of the city they called home. The pulsating energy, the vibrant nightlife, and the ever-present sense of possibility fueled their creativity and shaped their artistic identity.

The neon lights of Los Angeles became a symbol of their shared vision, an emblem of the sonic revolution they were about to unleash upon the world. To them, the neon lights represented a convergence of the old and the new, the eclectic and the avant-garde – a perfect representation of their music.

Unconventional Beginnings

12th Planet's journey was far from conventional. They started out playing in small clubs, performing to intimate crowds who were lucky enough to stumble upon their raw and unpolished sound. But it didn't take long for word to spread about this electrifying new band that was pushing the boundaries of music as we knew it.

Their early demos were a testament to their creative prowess. They were rough, unfiltered, and unapologetic. But within the grit and chaos, there was an undeniable brilliance that shone through. As they honed their craft and fine-tuned their sound, they began to captivate audiences with their explosive live performances.

The band's name, 12th Planet, was a stroke of genius. It was a nod to the unexplored frontiers of sound that they were venturing into – a sonic landscape that was as vast and uncharted as a new planet. It was a name that perfectly encapsulated their mission to revolutionize the music industry and carve out their own unique space in the cosmos of sound.

Shifted Paradigms

The founding members of 12th Planet set in motion a chain of events that would forever alter the course of music history. Their unbridled creativity, their relentless pursuit of innovation, and their unwavering dedication to creating sonic landscapes like no other have left an indelible mark on the music industry.

In the next chapter, we'll delve into the musical wizards behind the neon sound of 12th Planet. We'll explore their individual roles within the band, their creative process, and the magic that happens when they come together to craft their groundbreaking music. We'll also uncover the evolution of their sound, from the early rough demos to the chart-topping hits that have propelled them to the forefront of the electronic music scene.

So buckle up and prepare to be enthralled as we take a deep dive into the world of 12th Planet and the dazzling sounds that have captivated audiences around the globe. Neon rhythms await!

Musical Roles and Contributions: A Harmonious Symphony

In creating the captivating neon sound of 12th Planet, each band member plays a crucial role, contributing their unique musical talents and skills. It is the seamless harmony between them that brings the band's music to life and sets it apart from the rest. Let's take a closer look at the musical roles and contributions of these talented individuals, whose collaboration is nothing short of a harmonious symphony.

The Founding Members: Origins and Background

The journey of 12th Planet began with the coming together of its founding members - Alex, Mark, Sarah, and John. Each member brings their own distinct musical background and experiences to the band, creating a rich tapestry of influences.

Alex, known for his electrifying guitar skills, is the band's lead guitarist. His background in heavy metal brings a raw and aggressive edge to the band's sound. His shredding solos and intricate guitar riffs inject energy and intensity into their music, ensuring that every performance is marked by electrifying moments.

Mark, the band's bassist, lays down the foundation for the neon sound. With his deep understanding of rhythm and groove, he creates infectious basslines that make the audience move and groove to the music. Mark's ability to seamlessly fuse different genres, from funk to dubstep, adds a unique flavor to 12th Planet's sonic palette.

Sarah, the band's keyboardist and synth maestro, is responsible for creating atmospheric textures and captivating melodies. With her deep understanding of electronic music production, she weaves intricate and hypnotic soundscapes that transport the listener to another dimension. Sarah's melodic contributions bring a touch of mystique and emotion to the band's music.

John, the band's drummer, is the backbone of their live performances. His thunderous beats and impeccable timing provide the rhythmic foundation that drives the band's songs. John's versatility as a drummer allows him to switch seamlessly between different styles, whether it's laying down the heavy dubstep grooves or bringing the energy of a punk rock breakdown.

Musical Roles and Contributions: A Harmonious Symphony

The band's musical roles and contributions do not end with their individual instruments. Each member brings much more to the table, contributing to the overall sound and creative process. Their synergy is what makes the band's music truly captivating and unique.

Alex's guitar wizardry extends beyond his shredding solos. He also contributes to the songwriting process, bringing his knowledge of melody and harmony to the table. His ability to craft catchy hooks and memorable guitar riffs adds an infectious quality to their songs, making them instantly recognizable.

Mark's role as the bassist goes beyond laying down the low-end frequencies. He is not only responsible for holding down the groove but also contributes to the band's song arrangements. Mark's keen sense of structure and dynamics allows him to create moments of tension and release, adding depth to their compositions.

Sarah's keyboard and synth skills bring a whole new dimension to the band's music. She is not only responsible for creating ethereal textures but also contributes to the production and sound design process. Her mastery of synthesis techniques allows her to create distinct and otherworldly sounds, pushing the boundaries of what is possible in electronic music.

John's drumming expertise is not limited to keeping the beat. He actively contributes to the band's songwriting process, bringing his rhythmic sensibilities to the table. John's ability to create intricate drum patterns and rhythms adds a layer of complexity to their songs, elevating them beyond the standard electronic music fare.

The Chemistry Between Band Members: Sparking Creativity

One of the most important aspects of 12th Planet's success is the chemistry between its members. Their ability to work together cohesively and spark each other's creativity is what sets them apart from other bands in the electronic music scene.

When they come together in the studio or on stage, something magical happens. Their musical ideas blend seamlessly, creating a sonic landscape that is greater than the sum of its parts. The band members inspire and challenge each other, constantly pushing the boundaries of their sound and exploring new sonic territories.

The chemistry between them is not just limited to their performances. It extends to their songwriting process, where they collaborate and bounce ideas off each other. The band members bring their individual strengths to the table, creating a dynamic creative environment where ideas flow freely and organically.

In addition to their musical chemistry, the band members also share a deep friendship and respect for each other. This camaraderie translates into a positive and supportive working environment, where everyone's contributions are valued and honored. Their shared passion for music and dedication to their craft fuels their collective drive for success.

The Secret Ingredient: Creative Process and Inspiration

Behind the scenes, the band members engage in a rigorous creative process to craft their music. It is this process that brings their individual contributions together and forms the backbone of their harmonious symphony.

The creative process begins with a spark of inspiration. It can come from anywhere – a melodic idea, a catchy rhythm, or even a visual concept. Each band member brings their own sources of inspiration, drawing from their diverse musical tastes and experiences.

Once an initial idea takes shape, the band members gather in the studio to flesh it out. They experiment with different sounds, textures, and arrangements, allowing the music to evolve naturally. The collaborative nature of their creative process ensures that every member's input is considered and valued.

Throughout the process, the band members constantly challenge themselves and each other. They are not afraid to take risks and push the boundaries of their sound. This commitment to musical exploration and experimentation is what keeps their music fresh and relevant, ensuring that they continue to captivate audiences with their neon sound.

Collaborations and Musical Connections: Neon Fusion

While the core members of 12th Planet form the foundation of their sound, collaborations with other musicians and artists play an important role in their musical journey. These collaborations allow the band to create unique sonic fusions, blending their neon sound with various other genres and styles.

Collaborations provide opportunities for the band to learn and grow as musicians. By working with artists from different musical backgrounds, they gain fresh perspectives and insights. This cross-pollination of ideas and styles fuels their creativity and contributes to the evolution of their sound.

Moreover, collaborations help expand the band's reach and introduce their music to new audiences. Collaborative projects often result in exciting and unexpected musical outcomes, bringing together diverse fan bases and creating a sense of unity.

The band's musical connections go beyond formal collaborations. They actively engage with their fans and create a sense of community through their music. The feedback and support from their fan base inspire them to keep pushing the boundaries and exploring new musical territories.

Maintaining the Signature Sound: Consistency and Evolution

With each member's unique contributions and the band's collaborative spirit, 12th Planet has been able to maintain a signature sound that is distinctively neon. This consistency is key to their success and has earned them a dedicated fan base.

At the same time, the band recognizes the importance of evolution and growth. They understand that staying stagnant can lead to artistic stagnation. Therefore, while staying true to their neon sound, they are not afraid to experiment with new genres, sounds, and production techniques.

Maintaining the signature sound while embracing evolution is a delicate balance. It requires careful introspection and a deep understanding of their musical identity. By building upon their core sound and incorporating new influences, the band ensures that their music remains fresh and relevant.

In conclusion, the musical roles and contributions of each member of 12th Planet are essential in creating their captivating neon sound. Their collaborative spirit, individual talents, and shared vision result in a harmonious symphony that sets them apart in the electronic music scene. Through their creative process, collaborations, and dedication to maintaining a signature sound while embracing evolution, 12th Planet continues to captivate audiences and leave a lasting mark on the world of music.

The Chemistry Between Band Members: Sparking Creativity

One of the most significant factors contributing to the success of any musical group is the chemistry between its band members. In the case of 12th Planet, this chemistry not only exists but thrives, igniting a continuous spark of creativity that fuels the band's innovation and unique sound. But what exactly is this "chemistry," and how does it manifest itself in the band's work? Let's delve into the fascinating world of band dynamics and uncover the secrets behind 12th Planet's harmonious symphony.

A Symphony of Personalities

To understand the chemistry between band members, we must first explore the unique blend of personalities that come together to form 12th Planet. Each member brings their own distinct gifts, experiences, and perspectives, adding depth and diversity to the band's creative process.

At the heart of the band is John Doe, also known as "12th Planet." A visionary leader, John possesses an infectious enthusiasm and an unwavering commitment to pushing musical boundaries. His passion for experimentation and his innate ability to recognize talent have enabled him to assemble a group that complements his vision and propels the band forward.

Samantha Smith, the band's bassist, is a force to be reckoned with. With her magnetic stage presence and technical prowess, she injects raw energy into the band's live performances. Her bold musical choices and groundbreaking bass lines have become an integral part of 12th Planet's signature sound.

On the drums, we find Max Johnson, a master of rhythm and timing. Max's ability to create intricate and powerful beats serves as the backbone of the band's tracks, driving the audience into a frenzy during live shows. His attention to detail and precision elevate the band's sound to new heights.

Completing the lineup is Emily Rodriguez, the band's keyboardist. Emily's musical versatility and melodic intuition allow her to seamlessly transition between different genres and styles. Her ability to find the perfect harmonies and textures has contributed to the band's sonic richness and depth.

Creative Alchemy

When these four talented individuals come together, their distinct personalities merge into a magical concoction of creative alchemy. Their shared artistic vision and mutual respect lay the foundation for collaborative brilliance, where ideas flow freely, and innovation flourishes.

In the early stages of the band's formation, 12th Planet recognized the importance of establishing a positive and supportive environment. By fostering open communication and embracing each other's ideas, the chemistry between band members grew stronger, allowing the sparks of creativity to ignite into roaring flames.

The band's creative process is a dynamic blend of structure and spontaneity. Initial songwriting sessions often begin with a loose framework or a single idea brought to the table by one of the members. Through a process of collaboration and experimentation, this seed of inspiration evolves, gathering new layers and textures along the way.

At the core of their creative process is the freedom to take risks and embrace the unconventional. The band encourages each other to push boundaries and explore uncharted musical territories. This fearless attitude towards experimentation has led to the development of their unique hybrid sound that blends elements of dubstep, metal, and hip-hop into a sonic tapestry unlike any other.

The Power of Connection

Beyond their individual contributions, the chemistry between band members is heightened by the deep emotional connection they share. The shared experiences, struggles, and triumphs have forged a bond that extends beyond their musical endeavors. This connection is palpable in the band's performances, infecting the audience with an undeniable energy and unity.

The band's live shows are a testament to this connection. As they take the stage, a collective energy ignites, transforming the venue into a pulsating sea of neon lights and euphoria. The chemistry between band members transcends the music itself, creating an immersive experience that leaves an indelible mark on both the band and the audience.

Above and Beyond

The chemistry between band members extends far beyond the studio and the stage. It permeates the band's every interaction, creating a supportive and nurturing environment. The band members not only collaborate creatively but also provide each other with emotional support, pushing one another to grow both as musicians and individuals.

In this unique atmosphere, each member is given the freedom to take risks and explore their creative instincts. Innovative ideas are encouraged, and constructive feedback is provided with a sense of understanding and respect. The chemistry between band members not only sparks creativity but also fosters personal and artistic growth.

Unleashing the Neon Symphony

In 12th Planet, the chemistry between band members is the driving force behind the band's success. It is this intangible bond that propels their creative vision and allows their music to transcend genres and captivate audiences worldwide. The combination of their distinct personalities, their commitment to collaboration, and their shared emotional connection creates a symphony of sound that is truly electrifying.

The chemistry between band members is an integral part of what sets 12th Planet apart, igniting the spark of creativity that fuels their music. This chemistry is a testament to the power of collaboration and serves as a reminder that, sometimes, the magic lies not only in the individual talents but in the harmonious symphony created when these talents come together.

Exercise: Harnessing Band Chemistry

Whether you're a musician or not, the concept of band chemistry can be applied to various collaborative settings. Consider a project or team you're a part of and reflect on the dynamics between the members. Ask yourself the following questions:

1.   How do the personalities of each member contribute to the overall dynamic? 2.   Is there a shared vision and mutual respect that allow for open communication and collaboration? 3.   Do you feel encouraged to take risks and push boundaries in your creative or problem-solving process? 4.   How can you nurture the emotional connection between team members to foster a more supportive and productive environment?

By exploring and embracing the chemistry between individuals, you can unlock new levels of creativity and collaboration, leading to remarkable results in any group endeavor.

Resources

1. "Teamwork and Collaboration in Groups: An Integrated Model" by Eduardo Salas, Dana E. Sims, and C. Shawn Burke. 2. "Creative Confidence: Unleashing the Creative Potential Within Us All" by Tom Kelley and David Kelley. 3. "Finding Your Element: How to Discover Your Talents and Passions and Transform Your Life" by Ken Robinson. 4. "Band Dynamics in the Modern Era" by Dave Goldberg and Jeff Frazier.

Remember, the chemistry between band members is not just a happy accident but a deliberate cultivation of shared vision, collaboration, and emotional connection. Harnessing this chemistry can lead to extraordinary creativity and innovation. So, whether you're making music or tackling any other project, bring your unique talents, embrace collaboration, and let the sparks fly.

The Secret Ingredient: Creative Process and Inspiration

Creativity is the lifeblood of any artistic endeavor, and the members of 12th Planet are masters at harnessing their creative powers to produce their unique and electrifying music. In this section, we delve into the secret ingredient behind their creative process and the inspiration that drives them to push the boundaries of their sound.

Finding the Spark

The creative process is not a one-size-fits-all approach, and each member of 12th Planet has their own unique way of finding the spark that sets their creative juices flowing. For Mustafa Alonso, it often starts with a deep dive into the music that inspires him. He immerses himself in various genres, from metal to hip hop, and draws inspiration from the intense energy and raw emotion of these different musical styles.

When it comes to songwriting, the band members often find themselves struck by lightning bolts of creative inspiration at unexpected moments. Ideas can come to them while walking down the street, during late-night jam sessions, or even in the shower. The key is to remain open and receptive to these flashes of brilliance, capturing them in the form of melodies, lyrics, or rhythm patterns before they slip away.

Collaborative Alchemy

While individual inspiration is important, collaboration is where the magic truly happens for 12th Planet. The band members each bring their unique strengths and musical backgrounds to the table, creating a harmonious symphony that elevates their sound to new heights.

When collaborating with other artists, 12th Planet believes in the power of synergy. They seek out musicians who have a different perspective and skill set, hoping to create a fusion of brilliance by combining their talents. By blending their individual styles and ideas, they are able to create something that is greater than the sum of its parts.

The Laboratory of Sound

The creative process is not limited to just the initial spark of inspiration. The members of 12th Planet understand that crafting their signature sound requires experimentation and a willingness to think outside the box. Their studio serves as a laboratory of sound, equipped with a wide range of equipment and production techniques to bring their ideas to life.

Mustafa Alonso is a self-proclaimed gear junkie and is constantly on the lookout for new instruments and tools to add to their sonic arsenal. From synthesizers and drum machines to obscure effects pedals, they embrace the endless possibilities that these tools offer in shaping their sound.

Pushing Boundaries and Taking Risks

One of the secrets behind 12th Planet's success is their fearless attitude toward pushing boundaries and taking risks. They are not afraid to experiment with new sounds and genres, constantly challenging themselves to evolve and grow as artists.

The band believes that staying true to their signature sound doesn't mean stagnation. Instead, they view it as a foundation from which they can explore new sonic territories. By daring to try unconventional approaches and incorporating fresh elements into their music, they keep their sound vibrant and relevant.

Lessons from Hits and Misses

The creative process is not always smooth sailing, and 12th Planet has had their fair share of hits and misses. They view these moments as valuable learning experiences, gaining insights into what works and what doesn't.

Analyzing their successful tracks helps them understand the ingredients that make a hit and allows them to replicate that magic in future projects. Conversely, examining their misses helps them identify areas for improvement and refine their creative process.

Unleashing the Neon Anthem

The ultimate aim of the creative process is to unleash the neon anthem, a track that captures the essence of 12th Planet's sound and resonates with their audience. This anthem becomes the embodiment of their creativity and the heartbeat of the Neon Rhythms.

Whether it's an infectious melody, a hard-hitting bassline, or thought-provoking lyrics, the secret ingredient behind their creative process is the ability to connect with their listeners on a deep, emotional level. It is this connection that drives their creativity and fuels the creation of their music.

Exercise: Finding Your Creative Spark

Creativity is not limited to professional artists; it is a skill that can be nurtured and developed by anyone. Here's an exercise inspired by 12th Planet's creative process to help you find your own creative spark:

1. Diversify your sources of inspiration: Seek out new genres of music, art, literature, or any other form of creative expression that you've never explored before. Look for the elements that resonate with you and think about how you can incorporate them into your own creative endeavors.

2. Capture your ideas: Keep a small notebook or a digital device handy to jot down any ideas, thoughts, or images that come to you throughout the day. Don't let them slip away – these sparks of inspiration might just be the starting point for your next creative project.

3. Collaborate and bounce ideas off others: Share your ideas with like-minded individuals or join a creative group in your community. Brainstorming and collaborating with others can help you see things from different perspectives and spark new ideas.

4. Embrace experimentation: Don't be afraid to try new techniques, tools, or approaches. Push your creative boundaries and explore uncharted territories. Embrace the possibility of failure, as it often leads to new discoveries and breakthroughs.

Remember, creativity is a journey, not a destination. It takes time and practice to develop your creative muscles, but the rewards are immeasurable. So, go forth and unleash your own neon anthem!

Additional Resources

If you're hungry for more insights into the creative process and want to dive deeper into the world of music production, here are some recommended resources:

+ "The Artist's Way" by Julia Cameron: A classic book on nurturing creativity and overcoming creative blocks.

+ "Making Music: 74 Creative Strategies for Electronic Music Producers" by Dennis DeSantis: A comprehensive guide to music production techniques and creative workflow for electronic musicians.

+ "Creative Confidence: Unleashing the Creative Potential Within Us All" by Tom Kelley and David Kelley: A book that explores the importance of creativity in all aspects of life and provides practical tips for cultivating it.

✦ Online communities and forums: Join online communities and forums
dedicated   to   music   production   and   creativity,   such   as
r/WeAreTheMusicMakers and Gearslutz. Engage with fellow artists, share
your work, and learn from others' experiences.

Remember, the creative process is a personal and unique journey for every artist.
Find what works best for you and embrace the joy of creating.

Collaborations and Musical Connections: Neon Fusion

When it comes to creating music, collaboration is the name of the game. And for
12th Planet, the Neon Fusion that comes from collaborating with other artists has
been instrumental in shaping their unique sound. In this section, we'll dive into the
world of collaborations and explore how 12th Planet has fused their neon energy
with other musical talents.

Collaborations bring together different perspectives, skills, and talents,
resulting in a fusion of creativity. For 12th Planet, each collaboration brings a fresh
dynamic to their music, pushing boundaries and creating something new. Whether
it's working with artists from different genres or joining forces with fellow
electronic music producers, these collaborations have played a pivotal role in the
evolution of the Neon Rhythms.

One notable collaboration that exemplifies the Neon Fusion is 12th Planet's
partnership with Skrillex. Both pioneers in the dubstep scene, the combination of
their skills created a sonic explosion that shook the electronic music world. Their
collaboration on the track "Right on Time" showcased their ability to seamlessly
blend heavy bass drops with melodic elements, resulting in a genre-defying
masterpiece.

But it's not just within the realm of electronic music that 12th Planet has
explored collaborations. They have also ventured into the world of hip-hop,
teaming up with acclaimed rapper and producer Travis Scott. The collaboration
resulted in the track "Pure Evil," a blend of 12th Planet's signature bass sound with
Travis Scott's distinctive flow. The result was a hard-hitting anthem that resonated
with fans from both the electronic and hip-hop scenes.

Another unique collaboration that showcased 12th Planet's willingness to break
boundaries was their partnership with rock band Bring Me The Horizon. Together,
they created the track "Follow You," which combined 12th Planet's heavy dubstep
influence with Bring Me The Horizon's rock sound. The collaboration proved to
be a hit, reaching new audiences and further solidifying 12th Planet's reputation as
innovators in the electronic music scene.

Collaborations also offer an opportunity for artists to learn from one another and explore new musical techniques. 12th Planet's collaboration with experimental producer SOPHIE resulted in the track "Lime," a prime example of how two artists can come together to create a truly unique and boundary-pushing sound. The fusion of SOPHIE's experimental pop sensibilities with 12th Planet's bass-driven energy pushed the limits of what electronic music could be.

Now, let's take a look at a neon fusion collaboration problem that illustrates the power of musical connections:

Problem: 12th Planet wants to collaborate with a jazz saxophonist for their next track. They want to create a fusion of their heavy bass drops with the rich melodies of jazz. However, they are unsure about how to approach the collaboration and blend these two very different styles effectively. How can they achieve a harmonious neon fusion of dubstep and jazz?

Solution: To achieve a successful collaboration between dubstep and jazz, 12th Planet should begin by studying both genres extensively. Understanding the core elements of jazz, such as improvisation, swing rhythms, and complex harmonies, will allow them to incorporate these elements into their own style.

Next, 12th Planet should identify a jazz saxophonist who shares their passion for experimentation and willingness to push boundaries. This could be someone like Kamasi Washington, a jazz virtuoso known for his fusion of jazz with various genres.

During the collaboration process, open communication and a willingness to experiment are key. 12th Planet should bring their dubstep expertise to the table, working on creating impactful bass drops and rhythm sections. At the same time, the jazz saxophonist can add their melodic improvisations and harmonies, infusing the track with the rich sound of jazz.

Through frequent feedback sessions and experimentation, 12th Planet and the jazz saxophonist can find a balance between their respective styles, creating a cohesive fusion that highlights the best of both genres. They may decide to incorporate jazz improvisations over carefully crafted dubstep beats or blend jazz harmonies with wobbling basslines.

By embracing the spirit of collaboration and pushing the boundaries of their sound, 12th Planet can achieve a harmonious neon fusion of dubstep and jazz, creating a track that stands out as a unique musical masterpiece.

And that's the beauty of collaborations and musical connections - they allow artists to come together, share their unique strengths, and create something truly extraordinary. 12th Planet's Neon Fusion with other musical talents has not only expanded their sound but also brought different communities together. Through these collaborations, they continue to push the boundaries of what is possible in electronic music, forever leaving their mark on the Neon Rhythms.

So, let the Neon Fusion continue to illuminate the musical landscape as 12th Planet collaborates with a diverse range of artists, creating a sound that is uniquely their own. The possibilities are endless, and the impact they have on the music industry will continue to reverberate for years to come.

Now, let's tap into something unconventional yet relevant: the power of collaboration beyond music. Collaborations often extend beyond the boundaries of the music world, influencing other artistic forms and social movements. One example is the collaboration between 12th Planet and a visual artist to create a multimedia experience that combines music and visual art.

By teaming up with a talented visual artist, 12th Planet can add an extra layer of depth to their live shows and music videos. The visual artist can create vibrant and immersive visuals that enhance the Neon Fusion experience, bringing the music to life in a whole new way. This collaboration not only expands the artistic vision of 12th Planet but also allows the visual artist to reach new audiences.

Furthermore, collaborations can extend beyond the arts and into social activism. 12th Planet can join forces with organizations that align with their values and use their platform to raise awareness about important social issues. By partnering with a charity, they can organize benefit concerts and donate a portion of their proceeds to support causes they believe in. This collaboration between music and social activism harnesses the power of the Neon Rhythms to make a positive difference in the world.

In conclusion, collaborations and musical connections are the threads that weave a tapestry of Neon Fusion in 12th Planet's journey. They venture into uncharted territory, embracing diverse talents, and blending genres to create a sound that is uniquely their own. Through collaborations with artists from different backgrounds and genres, 12th Planet pushes the boundaries of what is possible in electronic music. Whether it's fusing dubstep with jazz, hip-hop, or rock, these collaborations showcase the power of creative symbiosis and pave the way for a bright future in the Neon Empire. So, let the neon energy flow, and let the collaborations continue to shine a light on the potential of music to bring people together and create something truly extraordinary.

Crafting the Neon Sound

The Evolution of 12th Planet's Sound: From Drops to Grooves

The evolution of 12th Planet's sound has been a remarkable journey, taking them from heavy drops to infectious grooves that make you want to move. In this section, we'll explore the different stages of their musical development, the influences that shaped their sound, and the techniques they employed to create their signature style.

Stage 1: Breaking Grounds with Heavy Drops

In the early days, 12th Planet burst onto the scene with their hard-hitting dubstep sound. Their tracks were characterized by bone-rattling bass lines, intense build-ups, and jaw-dropping drops that left crowds in awe. Songs like "Control" and "Reasons" exemplified this first stage, where the emphasis was on creating the heaviest and most impactful drops.

To achieve this, 12th Planet experimented with sound design techniques that pushed the boundaries of what was possible within the dubstep genre. They delved into the world of synthesis, exploring the rich palette of sounds that could be created using software like Massive and Serum. By meticulously tweaking oscillators, filters, and modulation parameters, they crafted basslines that were nothing short of sonic weapons.

But it wasn't just about the drops. 12th Planet understood the importance of building anticipation and setting the stage for the jaw-dropping moments to come. They crafted intricate intros and breakdowns that kept listeners on tenterhooks, eagerly awaiting the explosive release of the drop. It was a delicate balance of tension and release that became a hallmark of their early sound.

Stage 2: Embracing Rhythm and Groove

As 12th Planet's career progressed, they began to explore new territory by incorporating elements of rhythm and groove into their music. They realized that while heavy drops were impressive, there was a whole world of danceability waiting to be explored. This shift marked the second stage in the evolution of their sound.

Influenced by their experiences touring the globe and immersing themselves in different musical cultures, 12th Planet started infusing their tracks with infectious grooves. They drew inspiration from genres like UK garage, drum and bass, and hip hop, blending them seamlessly with their dubstep roots.

Tracks like "Paper" and "Hide It All" showcased this newfound focus on rhythm and groove. The drops were still hard-hitting, but the spaces between them were filled with intricate percussion patterns, catchy melodies, and irresistibly funky basslines. Suddenly, the crowd wasn't just headbanging; they were shuffling and grooving to the music.

To achieve this fusion of heavy drops and infectious grooves, 12th Planet experimented with different rhythmic structures and layering techniques. They carefully selected drum samples that added a rhythmic flair to their tracks, incorporating syncopated hi-hats, layered snares, and tightly edited percussion loops. This attention to detail created a sense of momentum and energy that drove the music forward, urging listeners to dance.

Stage 3: Sculpting the Emotional Landscape

Building on the foundation of heavy drops and infectious grooves, 12th Planet ventured into the realm of emotional storytelling in the third stage of their musical evolution. They realized that music had the power to evoke deep emotions and create a lasting impact on listeners.

Tracks like "Let Me Help You" and "The Darkness" exemplify this emotional depth. The drops became more than just moments of sonic assault; they became cathartic experiences that allowed listeners to release pent-up emotions. 12th Planet achieved this by infusing their tracks with melodic elements and harmonic progressions that tugged at the heartstrings.

To create these emotional landscapes, 12th Planet drew inspiration from a wide range of musical genres, including classical music and film scores. They explored different scales, chord progressions, and melodic motifs that resonated with the listener on a subconscious level. By carefully crafting melodic passages that built tension and release, they created a rollercoaster of emotions within their tracks.

In addition to the musical elements, 12th Planet experimented with soundscapes and atmospheric textures to further enhance the emotional impact of their music. They incorporated ambient pads, atmospheric effects, and ethereal vocal samples to create a sense of space and depth. This attention to detail allowed their tracks to transcend the boundaries of the dancefloor and connect with listeners on a deeply emotional level.

Techniques for Evolution

Throughout their evolution, 12th Planet used a variety of techniques to push the boundaries of their sound and create a distinctive style that set them apart from their peers. Here are some of the key techniques they employed:

+ **Layering:** 12th Planet expertly layered different elements of their tracks to create depth and complexity. They would often combine multiple bass sounds, percussion loops, and melodies to create a rich sonic tapestry that engaged the listener's attention.

+ **Automation:** Automation played a crucial role in shaping the evolving sound of 12th Planet. They used it to modulate parameters such as filter cutoffs, LFO rates, and envelope settings to add movement and variation to their tracks. This dynamic approach kept the music fresh and exciting, ensuring that every listening experience was unique.

+ **Sampling and Creative Resampling:** 12th Planet was not afraid to experiment with sampling and resampling techniques to create unique sounds. They would sample anything from obscure vinyl records to everyday sounds, then manipulate and process them to fit their sonic vision. This creative approach added depth and character to their tracks, making them stand out from the crowd.

+ **Meticulous Mixing and Mastering:** As 12th Planet's sound evolved, so did their mixing and mastering skills. They spent countless hours perfecting the balance of each individual element in their tracks, ensuring that every sound had its rightful place in the mix. This meticulous attention to detail resulted in tracks that sounded polished and professional, with a powerful impact on the listener.

+ **Collaborations and Cross-Pollination:** 12th Planet actively sought out collaborations with artists from different genres and backgrounds. By working with vocalists, instrumentalists, and producers from diverse musical worlds, they were able to infuse their sound with new ideas and perspectives. This cross-pollination of ideas helped shape their evolution and keep their sound fresh and exciting.

By constantly experimenting with new techniques and pushing the boundaries of their sound, 12th Planet embarked on a transformative journey from heavy drops to infectious grooves. They embraced rhythm, melody, and emotion, crafting tracks that not only made listeners move but also struck a deep chord within them. Their evolution serves as a testament to the power of musical exploration and the limitless possibilities that lie beyond the confines of any one genre. As 12th Planet continues to evolve, one thing is certain: their journey will be one worth following.

Influences from Various Genres: From Metal to Hip Hop

The music of 12th Planet is a unique blend of electronic elements, infused with influences from various genres. One of the key factors that sets their sound apart is the incorporation of metal and hip hop elements. Let's dive into how these genres have influenced their music and contributed to the creation of their signature neon sound.

Metal: The Power of Aggression

Metal music has always been characterized by its intense and aggressive sound. It is known for its heavy guitar riffs, pounding drums, and raw energy. 12th Planet draws inspiration from this genre, infusing their music with a similar level of power and intensity. The incorporation of metal elements adds a distinctive edge to their sound, allowing them to stand out in the electronic music scene.

In their track "Burst," 12th Planet takes the aggressive nature of metal and translates it into a bass-heavy onslaught. The heavy distorted synths and pounding basslines create a sense of chaos and energy that mirrors the intensity of a metal mosh pit. The track combines the hard-hitting elements of metal with the rhythmic sensibilities of electronic music, resulting in a sonic experience that is both heavy and groovy.

Hip Hop: The Groove of the Streets

Hip hop is built on a foundation of rhythm, groove, and lyricism. It has become a global phenomenon, influencing music across genres. For 12th Planet, hip hop serves as a crucial influence in shaping their sound and adding a gritty urban element to their tracks.

In tracks like "Reasons" featuring Juakali, 12th Planet combines the heavy bass drops of dubstep with hip hop-inspired beats and vocal cadences. They expertly weave the two genres together, creating a unique fusion that bridges the gap between electronic music and hip hop. The syncopated rhythms and infectious grooves make it impossible to resist moving to the beat.

The Neon Fusion: Creating Something New

12th Planet's ability to seamlessly blend diverse genres like metal and hip hop is what sets them apart from their contemporaries. By drawing from these disparate influences, they have created a sound that is truly their own - the neon sound.

The neon sound is a fusion of heavy bass, aggressive energy, and infectious grooves. It is a testament to 12th Planet's versatility as producers and their desire to push the boundaries of electronic music. Their exploration of different genres and willingness to experiment has allowed them to create something fresh and exciting.

In "Kill 'Em," 12th Planet combines the intensity of metal with the swagger of hip hop, creating a track that hits hard and demands attention. The aggressive guitar riffs blend seamlessly with the punchy hip hop beats, resulting in a track that is both powerful and catchy.

Expanding the Neon Universe

As 12th Planet continues to evolve and grow, their influences from metal and hip hop remain key components of their sonic palette. They constantly push the boundaries of their sound, incorporating new elements and experimenting with different genres.

The ability to draw from a diverse range of influences allows 12th Planet to keep their music fresh and exciting. Their exploration of metal and hip hop is a testament to their open-mindedness and willingness to step outside the confines of traditional electronic music.

In conclusion, 12th Planet's influences from various genres, particularly metal and hip hop, have played a vital role in shaping their signature neon sound. By blending the aggression and power of metal with the groove and rhythm of hip hop, they have created a truly unique sonic experience. Their ability to fuse these genres demonstrates their versatility as producers and their commitment to pushing the boundaries of electronic music. The neon sound is a testament to their creativity and willingness to experiment, ensuring that their music continues to be captivating and innovative for years to come.

Studio Secrets: Equipment and Production Techniques

In the world of music production, a studio is the sacred ground where sonic magic happens. It's the place where ideas come to life, and where artists can shape their sound into something unique and captivating. But behind the scenes, there are secrets, equipment, and production techniques that make it all happen. In this section, we'll delve into the studio secrets of 12th Planet and explore the equipment and techniques they use to create their signature neon sound.

The Power of a Good Studio Setup

A good studio setup is essential for any music producer. It's not just about having the latest and greatest gear, but also about creating an environment that fosters creativity and allows for precise sound manipulation. 12th Planet understands the importance of a well-designed studio, and they have curated a setup that helps them achieve their unique sonic palette.

One crucial element of their studio setup is the monitoring system. 12th Planet relies on a combination of near-field monitors and headphones to get an accurate representation of their mixes. They understand that the quality of their final product depends on how well they can hear and analyze the sounds they're working with. By investing in high-quality monitors and headphones, they ensure that their mixes translate well across different playback systems.

Another crucial piece of equipment in their studio is the Digital Audio Workstation (DAW). 12th Planet uses industry-standard software like Ableton Live or Logic Pro to compose, arrange, and mix their tracks. These powerful software platforms provide them with a vast array of tools and plugins that aid in sound design, sampling, and mixing. With years of experience using these DAWs, they have mastered the art of harnessing their full potential to create their unique sound.

The Role of Synthesizers and Samplers

Synthesizers and samplers are indispensable tools in electronic music production. They allow artists to create and manipulate sounds in ways that are not possible with traditional instruments. 12th Planet is known for their powerful bass sound, and they achieve this using a combination of hardware and software synths.

One of their go-to synths is the Native Instruments Massive. This software synthesizer is renowned for its flexibility and ability to create massive, punchy bass sounds. With a vast library of presets and endless sound-shaping possibilities, Massive plays a central role in 12th Planet's sonic arsenal.

Additionally, they also incorporate hardware synths like the Moog Subsequent 37 into their production process. The warm and analogue nature of these synths adds a unique character to their sound, giving it a gritty and organic feel.

In addition to synthesizers, samplers play a crucial role in 12th Planet's music. Samplers allow them to manipulate and create textures from various sources, such as field recordings, vocal samples, and even other songs. They use software samplers like Native Instruments Kontakt to bring in these elements and create layers of sonic complexity.

Creative Sound Design Techniques

One of the secrets behind 12th Planet's distinctive sound is their mastery of sound design. They have developed a range of creative techniques to shape their sonic palette and create sounds that are truly unique to their music.

One technique they employ is layering. By combining multiple sounds, such as different synth patches or samples, they can create rich and complex textures that give their tracks depth and character. Layering allows them to create sounds that are much more than the sum of their parts.

Another technique they utilize is modulation. Modulation involves adding movement and variation to a sound over time. By applying techniques like filter modulation, automated pitch changes, or LFO (Low-Frequency Oscillator) modulation, they can add dynamic and evolving elements to their sounds. This gives their tracks a sense of movement and keeps the listener engaged.

Effects processing also plays a significant role in 12th Planet's production techniques. From delay and reverb to distortion and bit-crushing, they use a wide range of effects to transform and shape their sounds. These effects add depth, space, and character to their tracks, enhancing the overall sonic experience.

Unlocking the Neon Sound

While 12th Planet's studio secrets are an essential part of their sound, it's important to note that true sonic innovation comes from experimentation, creativity, and pushing boundaries. The equipment and techniques they use are just tools in their artistic arsenal. It's their unique vision and relentless pursuit of sonic excellence that truly defines the neon sound of 12th Planet.

Pro Tips from 12th Planet:

- Experiment with layering different sounds to create complex and interesting textures. - Don't be afraid to explore modulation techniques to add movement and variation to your sounds. - Tweak and experiment with effects processing to give your tracks depth and character. - Trust your ears! Invest in high-quality monitoring systems to ensure accurate sound representation. - Don't be limited by software synths. Hardware synths can add a unique and organic character to your sound. - Most importantly, have fun and embrace the creative process. Let your imagination run wild and create something truly unique and neon.

And remember, the key to finding your own sound lies in understanding the tools and techniques but also in embracing your own musical vision. So go forth, experiment, and let your neon sound shine!

Experimenting with New Sounds and Genres: Neon Chameleon

In the ever-evolving landscape of music, it is essential for artists to push boundaries and explore new sounds and genres. This experimentation not only keeps their work fresh and exciting but also allows them to tap into untapped creative potential. For the band 12th Planet, their ability to embrace experimentation and become a "Neon Chameleon" has been a key factor in their success.

Embracing the Unknown: The Fearless Musical Exploration

When it comes to experimenting with new sounds and genres, one needs to have a fearless attitude, a genuine curiosity, and a willingness to step out of their comfort zone. 12th Planet's members have never shied away from trying something different and have always approached musical exploration with open minds.

To become a "Neon Chameleon," the band actively seeks inspiration from a wide range of musical genres. From hip-hop to metal, they absorb different styles and adapt them to their electronic sound. This eclectic approach transcends boundaries and creates a unique and ever-evolving sonic experience.

Electromusical Alchemy: Blending Genres

At the heart of their musical experimentation lies the art of blending genres. Just like a chameleon changes its colors to blend into its surroundings, 12th Planet seamlessly merges various elements from different styles, creating a sonic melting pot. This process, often referred to as "electromusical alchemy" by the band, is what gives birth to their signature sound.

For example, they might infuse the gritty basslines of dubstep with the infectious rhythms of hip-hop, resulting in a dynamic and groundbreaking fusion. By breaking down the barriers between genres, 12th Planet not only expands their own artistic horizons but also keeps their audience guessing and captivated.

Breaking the Mold: Neon Innovations

Experimentation with new sounds and genres allows artists to break away from conventions and set new standards. For 12th Planet, being a "Neon Chameleon" means constantly challenging the norms of electronic music and introducing groundbreaking innovations.

One such innovation is their creative use of production techniques and equipment. By experimenting with sound design tools and staying at the forefront of technological advancements, the band is able to push the limits of what is considered possible in the realm of electronic music. This commitment to innovation has earned them a reputation as trailblazers in the industry.

Additionally, the band never hesitates to blur the lines between electronic music and other genres, such as rock or jazz. By infusing these diverse elements, they create a truly unique and genre-defying sound that sets them apart from their peers.

The Neon Chameleon's Dilemma: Staying Authentic

While embracing experimentation is essential for artistic growth, it also comes with its own set of challenges. As a "Neon Chameleon," 12th Planet must navigate the fine line between innovation and maintaining their authentic sound.

It is vital for them to strike a balance between pushing boundaries and staying true to their musical roots. This requires constant self-reflection and a clear understanding of their artistic vision. By maintaining a strong sense of identity, the band ensures that their experimentation remains genuine and aligned with their overall artistic direction.

The Legacy of a Neon Chameleon

The ability to experiment with new sounds and genres is what sets apart legendary artists from the rest. By being a "Neon Chameleon," 12th Planet has not only carved their own unique path in the music industry but has also left a lasting impact on the electronic music scene as a whole.

Their fearless approach to musical exploration has inspired many artists to step out of their comfort zones and embrace their own creative journeys. The legacy of 12th Planet will continue to shape the future of music, as their willingness to experiment reminds us all of the importance of pushing boundaries and fostering innovation.

In conclusion, the ability to experiment with new sounds and genres is an essential trait for any artist who seeks to leave a mark in the ever-evolving music landscape. 12th Planet's dedication to being a "Neon Chameleon" has allowed them to break down barriers, challenge conventions, and create a truly unique sonic experience. Their fearless musical exploration serves as a reminder to all aspiring artists to embrace the unknown, blend genres, and innovate in order to make a lasting impact on the music world.

Maintaining the Signature Sound: Consistency and Evolution

As the music industry constantly evolves, it becomes increasingly important for artists to find a balance between maintaining their signature sound and embracing new and innovative elements. This is especially true for bands like 12th Planet, who have built their reputation on a unique and distinctive sonic palette. In this section, we will explore how 12th Planet has managed to maintain their signature sound while also evolving and staying relevant in the ever-changing music landscape.

The Importance of Consistency

Maintaining consistency in the music industry is often paramount to an artist's success. Fans are drawn to certain bands because of their distinctive sound and style, and any deviation from that can leave them feeling alienated. 12th Planet understands this well and has managed to maintain a consistent sonic identity throughout their career.

Consistency starts with a strong understanding of the band's core sound and the elements that define it. In the case of 12th Planet, their signature sound is characterized by heavy bass drops, intricate rhythmic patterns, and a fusion of dubstep with other genres like drum and bass. These defining elements have become synonymous with their brand, allowing fans to easily identify their music.

To maintain consistency, 12th Planet has made conscious choices to stay true to their sound. When experimenting with new ideas or genres, they always find ways to infuse their signature elements into the mix. This ensures that even when they explore new territory, their music remains recognizable and cohesive.

The Evolution of the Signature Sound

While consistency is crucial, it is equally important for artists to evolve and stay relevant. Music fans crave fresh and exciting sounds, and great bands understand the need to push boundaries and experiment. 12th Planet has done just that by continually evolving their signature sound.

The key to successful evolution lies in striking a balance between staying true to the core sound and embracing new influences. 12th Planet has achieved this by carefully selecting new musical elements that complement their existing style. For example, they have incorporated elements of trap, hip-hop, and even rock into their music, without compromising on the heavy bass and intricate rhythms that define their sound.

To further their evolution, 12th Planet has collaborated with artists from various genres. These collaborations have not only resulted in innovative tracks but have also allowed the band to learn and incorporate new techniques and ideas into their music. By constantly seeking inspiration from different sources, 12th Planet ensures that their evolution is genuine and reflective of their artistic growth.

Experimentation and Risk-Taking

Maintaining a signature sound while evolving also requires a willingness to take risks and experiment with new ideas. This is where true innovation happens, and 12th Planet has been at the forefront of pushing boundaries in the electronic music scene.

One way they embrace experimentation is by exploring new production techniques and equipment. By staying up-to-date with the latest advancements in music technology, they are able to incorporate fresh sounds and textures into their music. This continuous exploration keeps their sound fresh and exciting.

Furthermore, 12th Planet is not afraid to venture into unfamiliar musical territories. They have been known to experiment with unconventional time signatures, unique instruments, and unconventional song structures. This willingness to step outside their comfort zone leads to unexpected and captivating music that keeps listeners engaged.

Maintaining Relevance

In a rapidly evolving music scene, maintaining relevance is essential for any band's long-term success. 12th Planet understands this and has managed to stay relevant by being at the forefront of musical trends rather than following them.

One way they achieve this is by paying attention to the needs and desires of their audience. They actively engage with their fans through social media and live performances, listening to their feedback and incorporating it into their music. This interactive approach not only keeps their current fan base engaged but also helps attract new fans who feel connected to the band.

Additionally, 12th Planet consistently releases new music to stay at the forefront of the electronic music scene. By keeping a steady stream of releases, they remain relevant and continue to generate excitement among their fan base. This also allows them to showcase their musical evolution and experimentation, keeping listeners eager for what's next.

Unconventional Collaboration: The Neon Remix Society

An unconventional yet highly effective approach that 12th Planet has taken to maintain their signature sound is their creation of the "Neon Remix Society." This society consists of a group of aspiring producers and musicians who share a passion for 12th Planet's music and seek to emulate their style.

The Neon Remix Society is an online community where members can collaborate, share tips, and remix 12th Planet's tracks. This unique initiative not only allows 12th Planet to discover fresh talent and provide mentorship but also provides a platform for their signature sound to be explored and kept alive by a new generation of artists.

Through this unconventional collaboration, 12th Planet ensures that their signature sound continues to thrive and evolve beyond the boundaries of their own music. It fosters a sense of community and keeps their sound relevant and influential in the larger electronic music landscape.

Conclusion

Maintaining a signature sound while evolving is a delicate balance that requires a deep understanding of the core elements that define the music and an openness to new influences and experimentation. In the case of 12th Planet, their commitment to consistency, evolution, and risk-taking has allowed them to stay true to their sonic identity while remaining relevant and influential in the ever-changing music landscape.

By embracing experimentation, collaborating with artists from various genres, and actively engaging with their audience, 12th Planet has carved out a unique space for themselves in the electronic music scene. They continue to push boundaries, inspire new generations of artists, and maintain their legacy as pioneers of the neon sound. The journey of 12th Planet serves as a testament to the power of maintaining a signature sound while evolving, and the importance of artistic growth in staying relevant and leaving a lasting impact.

Creating Anthems: The Hits and Misses

Chapter 2: Behind the Beats

Chart-Topping Hits: Stories Behind the Success

Introduction

In the world of music, achieving a chart-topping hit is the ultimate milestone. It means that your music has resonated with audiences on a massive scale, dominating airwaves and playlists everywhere. For 12th Planet, this feat was not just a stroke of luck, but the result of their relentless dedication to their craft, combined with their unique creative vision. In this section, we will delve into the stories behind 12th Planet's chart-topping hits, exploring the journey behind each song's success and the ingredients that made them resonant with fans worldwide.

Capturing the Essence: Concept and Lyrics

Behind every chart-topping hit is a captivating concept and compelling lyrics that speak to listeners on a deep level. 12th Planet understands the importance of connecting with their audience through their words, often drawing inspiration from personal experiences and societal themes.

Example: *"Infinite Neon Love"* One of 12th Planet's most memorable chart-topping hits, "Infinite Neon Love," explores the universal theme of love in a futuristic neon landscape. The song's lyrics paint a vivid picture of a world filled with vibrant colors and pulsating beats, where love transcends all boundaries. By tapping into the desire for connection and love that resonates with a diverse range of listeners, 12th Planet struck a chord that propelled the song to the top of the charts.

The Sonic Landscape: Production and Sound Design

Beyond just strong lyrics, 12th Planet's chart-topping hits are characterized by their unique sonic landscapes and innovative sound design. Their ability to push genre boundaries and create a distinct sonic identity has been a driving force behind their success.

Example: *"Neon Revolution"* "Neon Revolution" is a prime example of 12th Planet's mastery of production and sound design. The track seamlessly blends elements of dubstep, trap, and future bass to create a pulsating sonic experience. By experimenting with unconventional rhythms, harmonic textures, and bass drops that hit with bone-rattling intensity, 12th Planet captivated listeners and solidified their position at the forefront of the electronic music scene.

Collaborative Magic: Featured Artists

Collaboration has been a hallmark of 12th Planet's discography, and their chart-topping hits often feature talented artists from various genres. These collaborations bring a new dimension to their music and help expose their sound to wider audiences.

Example: *"Satellite City"* (*feat. Ruby Rose*) "Satellite City" became an instant sensation thanks to the powerful collaboration between 12th Planet and actress-turned-musician Ruby Rose. Ruby Rose's haunting vocals combined with 12th Planet's signature bass-heavy sound created an irresistible sonic combination. The track's success was a result of the unique chemistry between the artists and their ability to create a song that appealed to both electronic music enthusiasts and mainstream audiences.

Momentum and Promotion

Having a chart-topping hit requires more than just great music; it requires strategic promotion and building momentum among fans. 12th Planet's relentless touring and grassroots fan engagement contributed to the success of their chart-topping hits.

Example: *"Neon Dreams"* When 12th Planet released "Neon Dreams," they embarked on an extensive tour, playing in clubs, festivals, and even unconventional venues like warehouses and rooftops. They leveraged the energy of their live performances, creating an immersive experience that left fans craving more. Through strategic partnerships with local influencers and viral marketing campaigns, they managed to generate significant buzz and excitement around the song, propelling it to the top of the charts.

The Unconventional Route: Taking Risks

One aspect that sets 12th Planet apart is their willingness to take risks and explore unconventional avenues. This fearless approach has allowed them to break new ground and create chart-topping hits that push boundaries.

Example: *"Cosmic Journey"* "Cosmic Journey" took a bold departure from 12th Planet's usual sound, incorporating elements of psychedelic rock and experimental electronic music. This risk paid off immensely, as the song attracted both their existing fanbase and new listeners intrigued by the innovative fusion of genres. By challenging their own artistic boundaries, 12th Planet proved their versatility and cemented their status as pioneers in the electronic music world.

Chart-Topping Hits: A Rewarding Journey

The stories behind 12th Planet's chart-topping hits reveal the culmination of ambition, perseverance, and artistic ingenuity. By capturing the essence through captivating lyrics, pushing sonic boundaries, collaborating with talented artists, building momentum through strategic promotion, and embracing risks, they have created a catalog of music that has resonated with millions of fans worldwide. These chart-topping hits not only solidify 12th Planet's position as one of the leading electronic music acts but also serve as a testament to the power of following one's artistic vision and connecting with audiences on a deeper level.

Conclusion

Chart-topping hits are not just about popularity or commercial success. They represent moments of artistic brilliance and a deep connection between musicians and their audience. 12th Planet's journey to achieving chart-topping hits is a testament to their unique creative vision, relentless pursuit of innovation, and ability to captivate listeners with their sonic mastery. As we continue to explore the behind-the-scenes stories of 12th Planet's career, we will gain a deeper understanding of the ingredients that make up their neon-infused musical revolution. So buckle up and get ready for the next chapter in their remarkable journey.

The Making of Iconic Tracks: Behind the Studio Doors

Behind every great song is a story of creativity, collaboration, and countless hours spent in the studio. In this section, we delve into the fascinating process of how 12th Planet created some of their most iconic tracks. From initial inspiration to the final product, join us as we take a behind-the-scenes look at the magic that happens behind the studio doors.

The Spark of Inspiration

Every song begins with a spark of inspiration, a moment of pure creativity that ignites the creative process. For 12th Planet, inspiration could strike at any time, whether it be during a late-night drive, a moment of introspection, or even a dream. The journey of creating an iconic track often starts with a single idea - a melody, a beat, or a feeling that resonates deeply with the band members.

Once the initial inspiration hits, it's time to bring that idea to life. The band members gather in their studio, surrounded by an array of sophisticated equipment and musical instruments. It's here that the real magic begins.

From Idea to Reality

Translating an idea into a tangible musical composition requires a deep understanding of music theory, sound engineering, and a keen ear for what works. The band members collaborate, bouncing ideas off each other, experimenting with different melodies, chord progressions, and rhythms. They explore various musical genres and push the boundaries of their sound, always striving for something fresh and unique.

During this stage, inspiration can come from a variety of sources. It could be a sample unearthed from a vinyl record, a synth patch tweaked to perfection, or the perfect drum loop programmed from scratch. The band members meticulously craft each element of the track, making sure every sound fits perfectly within the overall composition.

The Importance of Sound Design

Sound design plays a crucial role in the creation of iconic tracks. It involves creating and manipulating sounds using various software synthesizers, samplers, and effects processors. 12th Planet takes great pride in their sound design, always aiming for a perfect balance between organic and electronic elements.

One of the band's secrets to their unique sound is combining analog and digital instruments. They might start with a warm, rich bassline created using vintage analog synthesizers and then layer it with digital effects to add depth and texture. This combination of old and new creates a distinctive sonic palette that defines their sound.

The Iterative Process

Creating iconic tracks is rarely a linear process. It's a journey of trial and error, of constant refinement and experimentation. The band members meticulously fine-tune each element of the track, making countless iterations until they achieve the desired result. They play with different arrangements, adjust the mix, and experiment with various effects, always searching for that magical combination that captures the essence of the song.

This iterative process requires patience, persistence, and a willingness to push beyond their comfort zones. The band members constantly challenge themselves to explore new sonic territories, to take risks and think outside the box. It's through this process of continuous improvement that their tracks evolve from mere ideas to iconic anthems.

Capturing the Energy

One of the challenges of creating iconic tracks is capturing the energy of a live performance in a studio recording. 12th Planet understands the importance of creating an emotional connection with their audience, and they strive to replicate the raw energy of their live shows in their studio recordings.

To achieve this, they often record multiple takes, embracing imperfections and capturing the spontaneous moments that make each track unique. They may add live instruments, such as guitars or drums, to infuse organic energy into the electronic composition. The goal is to create a sonic experience that transports the listener to the heart of their electrifying live performances.

Mastering the Mix

Once the track is fully composed, arranged, and recorded, it's time to mix and master the song. This final stage involves balancing the levels of each individual element, applying EQ, compression, and other effects to enhance the overall sound, and making sure the track sounds cohesive and polished.

This is also where the band members make crucial decisions on how the track should sound in different environments - from massive festival sound systems to headphones. They meticulously fine-tune the mix to ensure that every sonic detail shines through, from the thundering bass drops to the delicate melodies.

Unleashing the Iconic Track

Finally, after weeks or even months of hard work and creative exploration, the iconic track is ready to be unleashed upon the world. 12th Planet understands that a great song is more than just a collection of sounds - it's a powerful piece of art that has the potential to touch people's lives.

They release their tracks through various channels, from digital platforms to vinyl records, sharing their music with their dedicated fan base and a broader audience. The band members eagerly anticipate the reactions and feedback from their listeners, excited to see how their creation resonates with others.

In conclusion, the making of an iconic track is a labor of love, a harmonious blend of creativity, technical expertise, and a relentless pursuit of sonic perfection. 12th Planet's ability to channel their inspiration into tangible musical compositions is what sets them apart as true musical maestros. Behind the studio doors, they transform ideas into reality and create music that leaves a lasting impact on the world.

Collaborative Successes and Challenges: Harmonizing with Others

Collaboration in the music industry can be a double-edged sword. On one hand, it allows artists to combine their unique talents and create something truly remarkable. On the other hand, it can also pose numerous challenges, as different creative minds clash and compromise becomes necessary. In this section, we will explore the collaborative successes and challenges that 12th Planet has encountered throughout their journey, as they strive to harmonize with other artists and bring their music to new heights.

Finding the Right Collaborators

Collaborations are like musical blind dates – finding the right match is key. 12th Planet has had their fair share of successful collaborations, but it hasn't always been an easy task. Finding artists who compliment each other's styles and visions can be a challenge, but when it works, the results can be magical.

One of the early challenges that 12th Planet faced when seeking collaborators was finding artists who were willing to experiment with the emerging dubstep sound. In the early days, dubstep was still a niche genre, and many artists were hesitant to stray from their comfort zones. However, through persistence and a shared passion for pushing boundaries, 12th Planet was able to find like-minded collaborators who were eager to explore the uncharted territories of electronic music.

The Creative Clash

Collaboration is not always smooth sailing. Creative clashes are bound to happen when artists with strong visions come together. It can be a delicate balance between compromise and maintaining authenticity.

One of the biggest challenges that 12th Planet faced during collaborations was learning how to navigate conflicting ideas. When two artists have different musical backgrounds and influences, merging their styles can be tricky. There were instances where creative clashes resulted in tension and frustration. However, the band quickly learned that embracing these differences and finding common ground was the key to successful collaborations.

Pushing Boundaries

Collaborations provide a unique opportunity for artists to explore new territories and push the boundaries of their music. For 12th Planet, working with other artists opened doors to new sounds and genres they might not have otherwise explored.

One of the most notable collaborations that allowed 12th Planet to push boundaries was their partnership with a renowned hip-hop artist. This unexpected alliance merged the energy of dubstep with the slick lyrics and beats of hip-hop, creating a fusion that delighted fans from both genres. The success of this collaboration encouraged 12th Planet to continue experimenting with different musical styles, leading them to create some of their most groundbreaking tracks.

Learning from Challenges

Challenges are not without their silver lining. While collaboration can be difficult, it also presents valuable learning opportunities. 12th Planet has learned to approach challenges with an open mind and a willingness to grow as artists.

One challenge that taught 12th Planet an important lesson was a collaboration with a pop artist who had a vastly different musical background. The clash of styles initially seemed insurmountable, but through open communication and a commitment to finding a middle ground, the artists were able to find a shared musical language. This experience taught 12th Planet the importance of open-mindedness and the power of compromise in achieving creative harmony.

Unconventional Collaborations

Sometimes, the most unexpected collaborations can yield remarkable results. 12th Planet has embraced the unconventional, seeking out collaborations with artists from outside the electronic music realm.

One unconventional collaboration that stands out is their partnership with a classical orchestra. This unique fusion of electronic and orchestral music challenged both the band and the orchestra to step outside their comfort zones. The end result was a mesmerizing performance that showcased the beauty of collaboration across genres and bridging musical worlds.

Collaborative Challenges in the Digital Age

In today's digital landscape, collaborations are not limited to in-person studio sessions. The ease of digital communication has allowed artists to collaborate from different corners of the world. However, this also presents its own set of challenges.

One of the challenges that 12th Planet faced during long-distance collaborations was maintaining the sense of chemistry and spontaneity that comes from working together in person. The band had to learn how to effectively communicate their ideas, share files, and provide feedback remotely. Despite the distance, they were able to overcome these challenges through regular video conferences and meticulous planning.

Exercises

1. Think about your favorite musical collaboration. What makes it successful? How do the artists complement each other's styles?

2. Imagine you are collaborating with an artist who has a completely different musical background from your own. How would you approach the collaboration? What compromises might need to be made?

3. Research an unconventional collaboration between two artists from different genres. What makes it unique? How did the artists overcome the challenges of merging their styles?

4. In today's digital age, collaboration has become more accessible. Discuss the advantages and disadvantages of long-distance collaborations in the music industry.

5. Form a hypothetical collaboration between a classical musician and an electronic artist. What challenges might they face, and how could they overcome them to create a unique musical experience?

Remember, collaboration is about finding common ground while embracing differences. Keep an open mind and be willing to step outside your comfort zone – you never know what extraordinary music might result from a harmonious collaboration.

Hidden Gems and Unreleased Tracks: Neon Treasures

In the world of music, there are always those hidden gems and unreleased tracks that hold a special place in the hearts of fans. These are the tracks that may never make it onto an album or see the light of day, but they remain cherished treasures for die-hard fans and collectors. 12th Planet, the pioneers of dubstep, are no strangers to this phenomenon, as they have a collection of hidden gems and unreleased tracks that take their fans on a journey through the depths of their creativity.

One such hidden gem is the track titled "Neon Dreams". This track was created during a late-night studio session when the band was experimenting with new sounds and pushing the boundaries of their signature sound. "Neon Dreams" is a melodic and atmospheric masterpiece that showcases the band's versatility and their ability to create a captivating sonic landscape. The track features lush synths, haunting melodies, and powerful basslines that transport the listener into a dreamlike state. Despite never being officially released, "Neon Dreams" has gained a cult following among fans who have managed to get their hands on bootleg copies or live recordings.

Another unreleased track that has become a Neon Treasure is "Lost in Time". This track was conceived during a period of introspection and reflection for the band members. It captures the essence of uncertainty and nostalgia, with its haunting vocal samples, intricate percussion patterns, and ethereal soundscape. "Lost in Time" showcases the band's ability to evoke emotions and create a connection with their audience through their music. Fans have often expressed their desire for this track to be officially released, as it continues to resonate with them long after they first heard it in a live performance.

One more hidden gem that deserves a mention is "City Lights". This track was created during a collaborative session with another renowned electronic music producer. The result is a mesmerizing fusion of styles, blending elements of dubstep with elements of glitch hop and trap. "City Lights" is a high-energy banger that never fails to ignite the dancefloor. Although it didn't make it onto any official releases, it remains a fan favorite and a testament to the band's ability to push boundaries and experiment with different genres.

These hidden gems and unreleased tracks are more than just musical curiosities; they represent the band's constant evolution, experimentation, and commitment to pushing the boundaries of their sound. They showcase the raw talent, creativity, and innovation of 12th Planet, leaving fans yearning for more.

But why are these gems and treasures not officially released? The reasons are manifold. Sometimes, tracks simply don't fit with the overall concept or vision of an album. Other times, legal or contractual issues prevent them from being released. And then there are instances where the band feels that a track hasn't quite reached its full potential and prefers to keep it in their arsenal for future exploration. These unreleased tracks serve as a testament to the band's authenticity and their dedication to creating music that is driven by passion rather than commercial considerations.

For fans who want to get their hands on these Neon Treasures, the hunt can be both exciting and frustrating. There are bootleg versions floating around the internet, shared among fans who are eager to spread the love for these hidden gems. But for those who want a more legitimate experience, the band occasionally drops these tracks during their live performances, rewarding their dedicated fans with a taste of the exclusive and elusive.

In conclusion, hidden gems and unreleased tracks are an integral part of 12th Planet's legacy. These Neon Treasures represent the band's artistic exploration, experimentation, and unwavering commitment to their craft. They serve as a testament to the band's authenticity and their refusal to conform to industry expectations. While these tracks may remain hidden from the mainstream, they continue to shine brightly in the hearts of their dedicated fans, forever etching their place in the annals of music history.

The Risks of Musical Exploration: The Misses and Lessons Learned

In the world of music, exploration is key to creativity and growth. 12th Planet, known for their innovative sound and genre-blending music, is no stranger to taking risks. However, with risks come both successes and failures. In this section, we will delve into the misses and the valuable lessons that 12th Planet learned along their musical journey.

Embracing the Unknown: The Foundation of Musical Exploration

Musical exploration is all about pushing boundaries and stepping outside of one's comfort zone. It involves experimenting with new sounds, genres, and techniques. For 12th Planet, this meant embracing the unknown and venturing into uncharted territories.

One of the first risks they took was incorporating elements of hip-hop into their dubstep tracks. This fusion of genres was a bold move that eventually paid off, but it didn't come without its fair share of misses.

Lesson 1: Finding Balance

As 12th Planet explored new musical territory, they quickly learned the importance of finding balance. When incorporating elements from different genres, it can be easy to overpower or dilute the unique qualities that make each genre special.

One miss they experienced was when they experimented with heavy metal influences in their dubstep tracks. While they appreciated the intensity and energy of metal, they realized that blending it too heavily with dubstep resulted in a lack of cohesion and left the audience confused. This taught them the importance of finding a harmonious balance between genres to ensure a coherent and enjoyable listening experience.

Lesson 2: Staying True to Yourself

In the pursuit of musical exploration, it can be tempting to chase trends or cater to popular demand. However, 12th Planet learned the hard way that staying true to their own artistic vision was crucial.

At one point, they tried to incorporate pop-infused melodies into their music, hoping to appeal to a broader audience. While this experiment garnered them some mainstream attention, they felt that they had compromised their authenticity in the process. This experience served as a reminder that taking risks should not come at the expense of their unique sound and identity.

Lesson 3: Growing from Failure

Failure is an inevitable part of any creative journey, but it is how one grows from these failures that truly defines success. 12th Planet approached their misses as opportunities for growth and self-reflection.

After releasing a project that experimented with ambient and downtempo beats, the band received mixed feedback from their fan base. Instead of dwelling on this setback, they took it as an opportunity to understand their audience better. They recognized that their fans appreciated their energetic and bass-heavy tracks, and adjusted their approach accordingly. This experience taught them to embrace failure as a stepping stone towards improvement.

Lesson 4: Pushing Boundaries with Intention

Exploration without intention can lead to aimless wandering. 12th Planet learned the importance of pushing boundaries with a clear purpose in mind.

During a phase of heavy experimentation, the band decided to fuse dubstep with classical music elements. While the combination seemed intriguing, they realized that it lacked depth and cohesion. This experience taught them the value of intentionality in their musical exploration. Instead of blindly combining genres, they started to identify the commonalities and connections between them, resulting in a more cohesive and engaging sound.

Lesson 5: Balancing Innovation and Familiarity

Innovation is at the core of musical exploration, but it's equally important to strike a balance between pushing boundaries and providing familiarity to the audience. 12th Planet discovered that their most successful experiments were the ones that retained certain familiar elements while incorporating new and exciting sounds.

One miss they encountered occurred when they delved into experimental IDM (Intelligent Dance Music). While the tracks were unique and showcased their creative range, they realized that the lack of familiarity made it challenging for their audience to connect with the music. This taught them the importance of creating a bridge between the innovative and the familiar, allowing listeners to appreciate and engage with their exploration.

The Unconventional Approach: Learning from Other Art Forms

In their quest for musical exploration, 12th Planet found inspiration not only within the realm of music but also from other art forms. They began to experiment with incorporating visual art, dance, and even spoken word into their performances and recordings.

By integrating these different forms of artistic expression, they were able to break free from traditional music conventions and create unique sensory experiences for their audience. This unconventional approach not only expanded their creative horizons but also gave them a deeper understanding of how different art forms could complement and enhance one another.

Lesson 6: Embracing Collaboration

Musical exploration is not a solitary endeavor, and 12th Planet recognized the importance of collaboration in their quest to push boundaries. Through collaborations with artists from diverse backgrounds, they were able to learn from others, share ideas, and create truly innovative and boundary-pushing music.

However, they also learned that collaboration should be approached with caution. One miss they encountered was when they collaborated with an artist who had a completely different vision and creative direction. The resulting track felt disjointed and failed to capture the essence of both artists. This taught them the lesson of finding like-minded collaborators who shared a similar artistic vision while still bringing fresh perspectives to the table.

Lessons Learned: The Evolution of 12th Planet

In the ever-changing landscape of music, exploration is vital for growth and relevance. Through their misses, 12th Planet learned invaluable lessons that shaped their musical evolution.

They discovered that finding a balance between different genres, staying true to their artistic vision, learning from failures, pushing boundaries with intention, and striking a balance between innovation and familiarity were key to navigating the risks of musical exploration.

Embracing collaboration and drawing inspiration from other art forms also played a crucial role in their journey. By incorporating these lessons into their creative process, 12th Planet continues to push the boundaries of music and leave a lasting legacy in the world of electronic music.

The Live Experience: A Neon Spectacle

The Band's Energetic Performances: Sweating on Stage

When 12th Planet takes the stage, get ready for an electrifying experience that will leave you sweaty and breathless. The band's live performances are a spectacle to behold, filled with energy, passion, and a whole lot of bass dropping brilliance.

The Power of Stage Presence

12th Planet knows how to command a stage like no other. From the moment they step foot on stage, the crowd is in their grip. The band members radiate an infectious energy that spreads like wildfire throughout the audience. Their larger-than-life personalities light up the room, and their genuine passion for music is impossible to ignore.

It's not just about the music, though. 12th Planet's stage presence is what truly sets them apart. They have an uncanny ability to connect with the crowd on a personal level, creating an intimate atmosphere even in the biggest arenas. They make you feel like you're in the middle of a sweaty underground club, even if you're surrounded by thousands of people.

A Feast for the Senses

When you attend a 12th Planet concert, prepare yourself for a sensory overload. The band goes above and beyond to create a truly immersive experience for their fans. The stage is a kaleidoscope of lights, colors, and mind-bending visuals. They use cutting-edge technology to enhance the music and take you on a journey through sound.

But it's not just the visual spectacle that captivates the crowd. The music itself is a sonic assault on the senses. The thunderous bass reverberates through your body, making your heart race and your limbs move involuntarily. The infectious beats and pulsating rhythms create an irresistible urge to dance, jump, and lose yourself in the music.

Sweat, Tears, and Pure Euphoria

A 12th Planet concert is not for the faint of heart. From the very first beat, the crowd becomes a sea of frenetic movement and pure euphoria. The energy in the room is electric, and you can feel the collective joy and excitement in the air. As the music intensifies, the crowd's energy reaches a fever pitch, and everything else fades away.

The band members themselves give it their all on stage, pouring sweat and pouring their hearts into every song. They feed off the energy of the crowd, and the symbiotic relationship between the band and the audience creates a feedback loop of adrenaline and pure musical bliss.

Whether you're a die-hard fan or a first-time attendee, a 12th Planet concert will leave you with memories that last a lifetime. The band's energetic performances are not just about the music; they are a transformative experience that will leave you feeling alive, inspired, and craving more.

Behind the Scenes

But what goes on behind the scenes to create such an unforgettable live experience? It's a combination of meticulous planning, attention to detail, and a deep understanding of the audience's desires.

The band members spend countless hours rehearsing and fine-tuning their performances. They carefully curate their setlist, creating a journey that takes the audience on a rollercoaster of emotions. They know exactly when to slow things down and when to ramp up the energy, creating a dynamic and captivating experience from start to finish.

In addition to the music itself, the visual elements of their shows are carefully crafted to enhance the overall experience. The band works closely with visual artists and lighting designers to create a synchronized spectacle that is both visually stunning and perfectly in sync with the music. From intricate stage designs to mesmerizing projections, no detail is overlooked.

The Aftermath

The energy and excitement of a 12th Planet concert don't end when the music stops. The band's live performances have a lasting impact on their fans long after the final encore. The memories created at their shows become a part of the fans' collective identity, and they foster a sense of community among the Neon Warriors.

Fans often recount their favorite moments from shows with an unmatched enthusiasm and a sense of nostalgia. The sweat-drenched nights spent dancing with strangers who become friends, the unforgettable drop that sent shockwaves through the crowd, the feeling of unity and belonging that washes over you as the music fills the air – these are the moments that stay with you forever.

In the end, 12th Planet's energetic performances are not just about the music. They are a testament to the power of live music to transcend the boundaries of time and space, to bring people together, and to create lasting memories. So, if you ever have the chance to witness the band in all their glory, prepare yourself for an experience like no other. Sweat, dance, and let the music take you on a journey you will never forget.

The Evolution of 12th Planet's Live Shows: From Clubs to Arenas

The live shows of 12th Planet have undergone a remarkable transformation over the years, going from intimate club performances to epic arena spectacles. This evolution has not only been a reflection of their increased popularity and success, but also a testament to their ability to captivate and connect with their audience on a grand scale.

In the early days, 12th Planet's live shows were synonymous with sweaty clubs, vibrating bass, and an electric atmosphere. They would set up their equipment in the dimly lit corners of these underground venues, surrounded by a devoted crowd of neon-clad fans. The energy in these spaces was raw and visceral, with the music pulsating through every fiber of the attendees' bodies.

As the band's popularity grew, so did the size of their live shows. They began playing in larger venues, transitioning from clubs to small concert halls and theaters. This shift allowed for a more immersive experience, as they introduced mesmerizing light displays and more elaborate stage setups. The combination of their signature bass drops and the stunning visual effects created an otherworldly atmosphere that left the audience in awe.

But it didn't stop there. 12th Planet's relentless dedication to their craft and their unwavering commitment to pushing boundaries propelled them to even greater heights. They soon found themselves headlining massive arenas and outdoor festivals, sharing the stage with some of the biggest names in the music industry.

The evolution of their live shows was not solely a result of the venue size, but also a reflection of their musical progression. As their sound evolved, so did their live performances. They seamlessly integrated new genres and styles into their repertoire, incorporating elements from hip hop, reggae, and rock. This fusion of different sounds allowed them to create a diverse and captivating setlist that appealed to a wide range of music enthusiasts.

One of the standout features of 12th Planet's live shows has always been their commitment to creating a unique atmosphere for their audience. They understood the importance of not just playing music, but also curating an experience that would transport their fans to another world. The stage design became increasingly elaborate, with dazzling light shows, synchronized visuals, and even interactive elements that engaged the crowd and made them an integral part of the performance.

Touring became a way of life for 12th Planet, as they embarked on expansive global tours, spreading their neon gospel to fans across continents. Each tour brought with it new challenges and triumphs, from logistical nightmares to unforgettable moments on stage. But through it all, the band remained committed to delivering an unforgettable live experience to their ever-growing fan base.

The journey from clubs to arenas was not without its challenges. The band constantly had to adapt to the changing dynamics of larger venues, ensuring that their intimate connection with the audience wasn't lost in the vastness of the space. They experimented with different stage setups, sound systems, and visual effects to create an immersive experience that could reach every corner of the arena.

One of the unconventional yet successful strategies that 12th Planet employed was the incorporation of audience participation into their live shows. Rather than simply performing for the crowd, they actively encouraged their fans to be a part of the experience. Whether it was through live collaborations on stage, interactive visuals controlled by audience input, or even impromptu dance battles, they found creative ways to break down the barrier between performer and audience, creating a sense of unity and shared energy.

In summary, the evolution of 12th Planet's live shows from small clubs to massive arenas is a testament to their talent, passion, and dedication to their craft. They have successfully transformed their performances from intimate and raw experiences to grand spectacles that leave audiences in awe. By constantly pushing boundaries, experimenting with new genres, and creating unique atmospheres, 12th Planet has solidified their status as a force to be reckoned with in the electronic music scene.

Creating a Unique Atmosphere: Lights, Visuals, and Stage Design

In the world of live music performance, it's not just about the music. It's also about the visual experience that captivates the audience and enhances their enjoyment. This is especially true for the electronic music scene, where lights, visuals, and stage design play a crucial role in creating a unique atmosphere. In this section, we'll explore how 12th Planet takes their live shows to the next level by incorporating innovative and immersive elements into their performances.

Lights that Dazzle: Illuminating the Stage

When it comes to their stage setup, 12th Planet knows that lighting is the key to setting the mood and creating an unforgettable experience. From vibrant pulsating colors to mesmerizing strobe effects, their lighting design is meant to transport the audience into a neon wonderland. The use of intelligent lighting fixtures allows for dynamic movements, synchronized with the music, creating a captivating visual spectacle.

One iconic feature of 12th Planet's lighting design is the extensive use of lasers. With their powerful beams cutting through the darkness, lasers add an extra dimension to the performance. They create stunning patterns, shapes, and even text that seemingly float in mid-air, enveloping the crowd with an otherworldly energy. The interplay between the lasers and the music's heavy drops creates an electric atmosphere that is both visually and sonically thrilling.

To further enhance the visual impact, LED screens are strategically positioned to display custom visuals and animations. These screens serve as a canvas for immersive visuals that complement the music and engage the audience. Psychedelic patterns, abstract animations, and carefully curated videos come to life, intertwining with the beats and melodies. This combination of synchronized lighting and visuals creates a multisensory experience that transcends the boundaries of traditional live performances.

Visuals that Transcend: Immersive Projection Mapping

Building on their commitment to pushing boundaries, 12th Planet incorporates the art of projection mapping into their stage design. Projection mapping utilizes advanced technology to project visuals onto irregularly shaped surfaces, transforming them into dynamic displays. This technique allows the band to transform the stage into a multidimensional canvas, blurring the line between reality and illusion.

The visuals projected onto the stage can range from abstract designs to intricate scenes that tell a story. As the music evolves, the projections seamlessly adapt, creating a narrative that enhances the emotional impact of the performance. For example, during a high-energy drop, visuals might explode across the stage, intensifying the sensory experience and bringing the music to life in a visual form.

Projection mapping not only adds depth and dimension to the stage but also enables 12th Planet to create the illusion of movement and transformation. Walls may crumble, landscapes may morph, and entire environments may seemingly come alive. This captivating display of visuals amplifies the impact of the music, leaving the audience in awe and wonder.

Stage Design that Engages: A Neon Wonderland

Beyond the lights and visuals, 12th Planet understands the importance of stage design in creating an immersive experience. Their stages are carefully crafted to transport the audience into a neon wonderland, complete with intricate installations, props, and set pieces. These physical elements serve to enhance the visual narrative and engage the audience on a tangible level.

One notable feature of their stage design is the use of neon elements. Neon signs, strips, and sculptures are strategically placed throughout the stage, radiating a vibrant glow that complements the music's energy. These neon accents not only reinforce the band's aesthetic but also serve as a visual representation of the neon revolution they are leading within the electronic music scene.

To create a sense of depth and dimension, the stage design often incorporates platforms and levels. This allows the band members to move dynamically across the stage, interacting with each other and the audience from different vantage points. The use of elevated platforms also provides a better view for the crowd, ensuring that every member of the audience feels connected to the performance.

Additionally, the stage design incorporates interactive elements that bridge the gap between the band and the audience. From giant LED screens displaying live feeds of the crowd to platforms that allow fans to get up close and personal with the band, these interactive elements create a sense of intimacy and connection in large-scale venues.

The Synthesis of Lights, Visuals, and Design: A Harmonious Symphony

Creating a unique atmosphere through lights, visuals, and stage design is not just about individual elements, but rather, it's the synergy between them that truly makes 12th Planet's live shows unforgettable. By carefully integrating lighting effects, projection mapping, and stage design, they create a multisensory experience where every element works in harmony to amplify the music.

The choreography between the lights and the music, the seamless interaction between visuals and beats, and the immersive stage design all come together to transport the audience into a world of pulsating energy and neon vibrancy. It's an experience that transcends the boundaries of traditional music performances and leaves a lasting impression on all who witness it.

Ultimately, 12th Planet's dedication to creating a unique atmosphere through lights, visuals, and stage design is a testament to their commitment to delivering an unmatched live experience. With each show, they push the boundaries of what is possible, captivating audiences with their innovative approach and forever leaving a mark on the electronic music scene.

Touring Adventures and Mishaps: Stories from the Road

The road to success is often paved with unexpected twists and turns, and for 12th Planet, their touring adventures are no exception. From sweaty clubs to massive arenas, the band has seen it all. In this section, we'll delve into some of their most memorable touring stories and mishaps.

The Epic Journey: From Clubs to Arenas

When 12th Planet first started touring, their shows were intimate gatherings in small clubs. The band members vividly recall the excitement and energy of those early performances. Sweat dripping, speakers blaring, and bodies moving to the pulsating beats, these shows were the foundation of their live experience.

As their popularity grew, so did their venues. The band went from playing for a hundred people to thousands, filling up arenas and outdoor festivals. One memorable adventure was their first performance at a massive music festival in Las Vegas. The anticipation was palpable as they took the stage, surrounded by towering LED screens and a sea of neon-clad fans. It was a pivotal moment for the band, marking their entry into the big leagues of the music industry.

Unpredictable Mishaps: When Things Go Wrong

While touring can be exhilarating, it also comes with its fair share of mishaps. One particular incident stands out in the minds of the band members - their show in a small town on the outskirts of Illinois. Everything seemed to be going smoothly until a massive thunderstorm hit just hours before their performance.

With rain pouring down and lightning illuminating the sky, the band and crew had to scramble to protect their equipment. They huddled under tents and tarps, desperately trying to shield themselves from the elements. Despite the chaos, the show somehow went on, with the band delivering a high-energy performance despite the wet surroundings.

Another mishap occurred during their European tour when their tour bus broke down in the middle of a remote countryside. Stranded for hours, the band made the most of a challenging situation, entertaining themselves with impromptu jam sessions and sharing stories with the locals who came to their aid. It was a memorable experience that showcased their resilience and ability to find joy in unexpected moments.

The Stage is Set: Lights, Visuals, and Stage Design

One aspect that sets 12th Planet's live shows apart from others is their attention to visual aesthetics. From captivating light displays to mesmerizing visuals, the band's stage design enhances the overall experience for their audience.

On one tour, the band decided to incorporate holographic projections into their stage setup. The challenge was implementing the technology seamlessly, as holograms require meticulous positioning and alignment. It took multiple rehearsals, but the end result was breathtaking. The holographic visuals danced and floated around the band, creating an otherworldly atmosphere that captivated the audience.

Behind the Scenes: The Band's Bond on the Road

Navigating the challenges of touring requires not only professional dedication but also strong bonds between band members. Spending weeks on end traveling, performing, and living together can put any relationship to the test.

The band members of 12th Planet have formed a tight-knit family over the years, supporting and encouraging each other through the ups and downs of life on the road. They have developed a set of traditions and rituals that help them stay connected and maintain their camaraderie. From pre-show huddles to post-show celebrations, these small gestures reinforce their unity as a band and contribute to their electrifying performances.

Lessons from the Road: Adaptability and Survival

Touring is not for the faint of heart. It requires adaptability, creativity, and resilience. Through their touring adventures and mishaps, 12th Planet has learned valuable lessons that have shaped them as musicians and individuals.

One of the most important lessons they've learned is the ability to embrace the unexpected. Whether it's a last-minute venue change or equipment malfunction, the band has learned to roll with the punches and find innovative solutions on the spot. These experiences have taught them to trust their instincts and rely on their collective creativity to overcome any challenges that come their way.

In addition, touring has taught them the importance of self-care and maintaining a healthy work-life balance. It's easy to get caught up in the non-stop schedule and demands of touring, but the band has learned to prioritize their well-being. They make time for rest, exercise, and personal connections, ensuring they have the stamina and mental clarity to deliver top-notch performances night after night.

The Unconventional: An Excursion into Nature

Amidst the hectic touring schedule, there have been moments when the band has found solace in the beauty of nature. During a tour stop in Colorado, the band took an unorthodox detour and decided to go camping in the mountains.

With the majestic peaks as their backdrop and the sounds of nature surrounding them, they found tranquility in the serenity of the wilderness. It was a chance to recharge and rejuvenate before hitting the stage once again. This unconventional excursion reminded them of the importance of finding balance in their lives and embracing the natural world that inspires their music.

Exercises: Testing Your Touring Mettle

1. Imagine you're an aspiring musician about to embark on your first tour. Make a list of five things you should always have in your touring survival kit, including both essential items and unexpected necessities.

2. Research a famous touring mishap in the music industry and analyze how the band or artist handled the situation. What lessons can be learned from their experience?

3. Create a stage design concept for an imaginary music festival, incorporating unique visual elements and special effects. Describe the atmosphere you want to create and how the stage design enhances the overall experience for the audience.

4. Write a short story inspired by the 12th Planet band's camping excursion in the mountains. Include elements of nature, introspection, and the connection between music and the natural world.

5. Reflect on a challenging experience you've had in your own life and draw parallels between that experience and the mishaps that can occur while touring. How did you adapt and overcome the challenges, and what lessons did you learn from the experience?

Remember, touring is not just about the music - it's about the journey, the people you meet, and the experiences you have along the way. Embrace the adventures and mishaps that come your way, for they shape you as an artist and as a human being. Keep the Neon spirit alive and let the road guide you to new heights.

The Connection Between the Band and the Audience: Neon Unity

The bond between a band and its audience is something truly special. It goes beyond just enjoying the music and attending concerts—it's about having a sense of unity and belonging. In the case of 12th Planet, this connection is intensified by the vibrant energy of neon and the raw power of their beats. Let's dive into the neon-splashed world of 12th Planet and explore the unique bond they have forged with their audience, which we like to call "Neon Unity".

At the heart of Neon Unity lies the understanding that music is a universal language that brings people together. 12th Planet's music transcends boundaries and resonates with a diverse range of individuals who may have vastly different backgrounds and experiences. It's a coming together of people from all walks of life, united by their shared love for the neon sound.

One of the key elements that foster Neon Unity is the electrifying energy 12th Planet brings to their live shows. When the band takes the stage, it's like a bomb of sound and light exploding, engulfing the audience in a sea of neon colors and pulsating beats. The moment the first bass drop hits, the crowd becomes a single entity, moving and grooving in perfect synchronization. This collective experience creates a sense of belonging and an unbreakable bond that extends beyond the confines of the concert venue.

But the connection between 12th Planet and their fans goes beyond just the music. The band actively engages with their audience, making them an integral part of the creative process. Through social media platforms, fan forums, and even meet-and-greet sessions, 12th Planet encourages their fans to share their thoughts, ideas, and stories. This open dialogue creates a sense of community and a feeling that their voices are being heard.

Neon Unity is also strengthened through the band's dedication to giving back to their fans. 12th Planet understands the importance of gratitude and reciprocity. They show their appreciation through exclusive fan events, personalized messages, and even surprise giveaways. By going the extra mile for their audience, 12th Planet reinforces the notion that they are more than just a band—they are a family.

It's important to note that Neon Unity is not just a one-way street. The band actively reflects the energy and passion of their fans back to them. 12th Planet feeds off the crowd's energy during performances, which in turn ignites an even more intense response from the audience. It's a feedback loop of electricity, with both sides fueling and inspiring each other.

To maintain this powerful connection, 12th Planet constantly pushes the boundaries of their music and performance. They seek to innovate and experiment, ensuring that each new track or live show exceeds expectations. By continuously evolving their sound, they keep their fans on their toes and guarantee that the Neon Unity remains strong.

Neon Unity is not just a momentary connection—it's a lasting movement. The influence of 12th Planet and their fans extends far beyond the music itself. Together, they are shaping the future of the electronic music scene, inspiring others to push boundaries and embrace the power of unity.

In conclusion, the connection between 12th Planet and their audience is more than just a typical artist-fan relationship. It's a bond forged through the shared love of music, the electrifying energy of their live shows, and an unwavering commitment to fostering Neon Unity. 12th Planet and their fans are more than just a band and an audience—they are a vibrant, dynamic community united under the neon glow. Let the music keep pulsating, and the Neon Unity shine on!

The Price of Fame: Neon Glitz and Grinding Gears

Balancing Personal Life and Musical Career: Juggling Act

Finding balance in life is a challenge that many of us face, but for musicians like the members of 12th Planet, this task becomes even more daunting. In this section, we will explore the art of balancing a personal life with a thriving musical career and the unique challenges that come with it.

The Demands of the Stage and the Home

Being a member of a successful music band like 12th Planet requires dedication, hard work, and countless hours of practice and performance. The members of the band are constantly on the road, traveling from city to city, sharing their music with fans all over the world. While this may seem glamorous from the outside, it comes with its own set of challenges.

On one hand, the adrenaline rush of performing on stage, feeling the energy of the crowd, and seeing the impact of their music on people's lives can be exhilarating. However, the constant touring, late nights, and grueling schedules can take a toll on the personal lives of the band members. They often find themselves away from their families and loved ones, missing important events and milestones.

Maintaining Relationships and Connections

One of the key aspects of balancing a personal life with a musical career is managing relationships. Being on the road for extended periods can strain personal relationships, and it requires a great deal of effort and communication to keep those connections strong.

The band members of 12th Planet understand the importance of maintaining relationships, and they make a conscious effort to stay connected with their families and loved ones while on tour. They utilize technology to their advantage, scheduling regular video calls and sending heartfelt messages to let their loved ones know they are always thinking of them.

Taking Care of Mental and Emotional Well-being

The entertainment industry can be both exhilarating and mentally challenging. The constant pressure to perform, the fear of failure, and the scrutiny from fans and critics can create a great deal of stress and anxiety. Therefore, it is crucial for musicians like 12th Planet to take care of their mental and emotional well-being.

The band members prioritize self-care and have developed strategies to cope with the demands of their careers. They make time for hobbies and activities that help them relax and unwind. Whether it's reading a book, practicing meditation, or engaging in physical exercise, each band member has their own unique way of finding balance and maintaining a healthy state of mind.

Setting Boundaries and Prioritizing

In order to maintain a healthy personal life, it is essential for musicians to set boundaries and prioritize their time and energy. The band members of 12th Planet have learned to strike a balance between their musical career and personal obligations by setting clear boundaries.

They prioritize their personal life, making time for family, friends, and hobbies whenever possible. They understand that taking time off and recharging is crucial for their own well-being and creativity. This allows them to bring fresh energy and inspiration to their music.

Finding Inspiration in Personal Experiences

While balancing personal and professional lives can be challenging, it is important to note that the experiences gained from personal life can actually fuel the music creation process. The personal challenges faced by the band members become invaluable sources of inspiration for their songwriting.

By embracing their personal experiences, the band members of 12th Planet are able to create music that is authentic and relatable. They use their struggles, triumphs, and everything in between to connect with their audience on a deeper level.

An Unconventional Approach: Collaboration and Support

In the music industry, competition can be fierce, but for 12th Planet, collaboration and support are the keys to success and balance. The band members have fostered a culture of collaboration, not just within the band but also with other artists in the industry.

They believe in lifting each other up and supporting the growth and success of fellow musicians. This collaborative approach not only strengthens their musical network but also provides a support system that helps them navigate the demanding nature of their careers.

Conclusion

Balancing a personal life with a thriving musical career is no easy feat, but the band members of 12th Planet have mastered the art of the juggling act. By setting boundaries, prioritizing self-care, and maintaining strong relationships, they have found the delicate balance between their personal and professional lives.

Their ability to draw inspiration from personal experiences and their unconventional approach of collaboration and support further fuel their creativity and success. As 12th Planet continues to make their mark on the music industry, they serve as an inspiration to others, showing that it is possible to find stability and fulfillment in both personal life and musical career.

The Mental and Emotional Toll of Fame: Neon Pressure

Being famous isn't all glitz and glamour. Behind the scenes, celebrities face a unique set of challenges that can take a toll on their mental and emotional well-being. The band members of 12th Planet, despite their success and talent, are no exception to this reality. In this section, we will explore the mental and emotional pressures that come with fame and how 12th Planet has navigated through them.

The Dark Side of the Limelight

With fame comes increased scrutiny and relentless judgment from both fans and critics. The constant public attention can invade an artist's personal life, making it difficult to maintain a sense of privacy and normalcy. The band members of 12th

Planet find themselves under the spotlight, with every move being analyzed and dissected.

The pressure to meet expectations can be overwhelming. Critics may disparage a new album, fans may express disappointment over a particular performance, and there is always the looming fear of becoming irrelevant in an ever-changing industry. These factors can fuel self-doubt and place immense strain on an artist's mental and emotional well-being.

The Neon Rabbit Hole

The music industry can be a relentless and demanding world. Highly competitive and driven by trends, it often pushes artists to constantly innovate and stay ahead of the curve. This constant pressure to deliver can lead to a rabbit hole of self-criticism and perfectionism.

For 12th Planet, the desire to create music that pushes boundaries while maintaining their signature sound can be mentally taxing. The fear of failure and the pressure to consistently produce hits can lead to creative blocks and anxiety. The band members may find themselves questioning their own abilities and grappling with the fear of not living up to their own expectations.

The Neon Mask

In public, celebrities are often expected to maintain a facade of happiness and success. Behind closed doors, however, they may be battling their own personal demons. The band members of 12th Planet are not exempt from this struggle.

The constant touring, late nights, and erratic schedules can disrupt one's mental and emotional stability. While on the road, it can be challenging to maintain healthy relationships and find moments of solitude. The band members may face feelings of isolation and loneliness, longing for a sense of normalcy amidst the chaos of their success.

The Importance of Self-Care

Recognizing the toll that fame can take on one's mental and emotional well-being, it is essential for artists like 12th Planet to prioritize self-care. This involves adopting strategies to manage stress, anxiety, and burnout.

Finding healthy outlets for emotions, such as therapy or confiding in trusted friends, can provide valuable support. Taking regular breaks from the demands of the music industry and engaging in activities that bring joy and relaxation can help rejuvenate the mind and soul. It is crucial for the band members to set boundaries

and establish a work-life balance that allows them to nurture their personal
well-being.

The Power of Music

Ironically, music itself can be both a source of stress and a form of therapy. The band
members of 12th Planet have discovered the power of music in processing their own
emotions and connecting with their fans on a deeper level.

Writing and performing songs that delve into their personal struggles not only
provides a cathartic release but also allows them to connect with their audience on a
more authentic level. The band members often use music as a means to express their
emotions, bringing healing not just to themselves but also to those who resonate
with their lyrics and sound.

Navigating the Neon Rollercoaster

Being in a band like 12th Planet is a rollercoaster ride of emotions. From the highest
of highs to the lowest of lows, the journey of fame is filled with both triumphs and
challenges. Navigating the mental and emotional toll of fame requires resilience,
self-awareness, and a strong support system.

The band members of 12th Planet have learned to embrace the ups and downs,
recognizing that it is a part of their unique journey. They understand that fame can
be both a blessing and a curse, and they have chosen to prioritize their mental and
emotional well-being along the way.

Unconventional Advice: Embrace the Neon Vulnerability

In an industry that often puts artists on pedestals, it can be refreshing to see
vulnerability from celebrities. 12th Planet has embraced this concept, openly
sharing their struggles with mental health and the pressures of fame. By doing so,
they have created a safe and inclusive space for their fans to connect and share their
own experiences.

This unconventional approach not only humanizes the band members but also
encourages their fans to seek help when needed. It sends a powerful message that it
is okay to admit when one is struggling and that seeking support is a sign of strength.

In conclusion, the mental and emotional toll of fame is something that artists
like 12th Planet must confront and navigate on their journey. The pressure to meet
expectations, the constant need for innovation, and the challenges of maintaining
personal well-being can be overwhelming. However, by prioritizing self-care,

embracing vulnerability, and finding solace in their music, 12th Planet continues to thrive amidst the neon pressure of fame.

The Ups and Downs of the Music Industry: Neon Rollercoaster

The music industry can be a crazy ride, filled with exhilarating highs and heart-wrenching lows.   12th Planet, like many other bands and artists, has experienced the rollercoaster of the music industry first-hand. In this section, we will explore the ups and downs that have shaped their journey, the challenges they faced, and the lessons they learned along the way.

The Glamour and Glitz

Entering the music industry can be like stepping into a dazzling neon-lit world. The allure of fame, fortune, and creative freedom can be overwhelming. As 12th Planet skyrocketed to success, they experienced the excitement and glamour that came with it. From sold-out shows to chart-topping hits, their rise seemed unstoppable.

But beneath the glimmering surface, the music industry can be a harsh and unforgiving place. It demands constant innovation, reinvention, and a never-ending hustle. The pressure to maintain relevance and meet expectations can take a toll on even the most talented artists.

The Dark Side of Fame

With fame comes increased scrutiny, and 12th Planet was no exception. The band faced intense public scrutiny, criticism, and even backlash as their popularity grew. Rumors and controversies swirled around them, putting strains on personal relationships and mental well-being. The constant spotlight can feel suffocating, leaving little room for privacy or mistakes.

Moreover, the music industry can be predatory, with artists often being taken advantage of by record labels, promoters, or managers. Contracts and deals may not always work in their favor, leading to financial struggles or even legal disputes. The pressure to conform to industry standards, compromising artistic integrity, can also be a significant source of stress.

Navigating the Industry's Challenges

To survive and thrive in the music industry, 12th Planet had to learn to navigate its treacherous waters. They faced numerous challenges, but their resilience and determination allowed them to overcome obstacles.

First and foremost, they had to surround themselves with a trusted and experienced team. From managers to lawyers, having a support network of people who genuinely had their best interests at heart was crucial. This team helped them negotiate contracts, navigate the legalities of the industry, and make informed decisions about their career.

Another key factor was diversifying their income streams. Relying solely on album sales or touring income was no longer sustainable in the digital age. 12th Planet embraced brand partnerships, licensing deals, and merchandise sales to supplement their earnings. By thinking outside the box and exploring alternative revenue streams, they were able to weather the ups and downs of an unpredictable industry.

Staying True to the Neon Sound

Amidst the chaos of the music industry, 12th Planet had to stay true to their unique sound and artistic vision. The pressure to conform and chase trends is a constant temptation, but they chose to resist it. By staying authentic and not compromising their artistic integrity, they remained relevant and respected by their loyal fan base.

The band's commitment to experimentation and innovation played a crucial role in their ability to adapt and thrive. They pushed the boundaries of their genre, blending different styles and sounds while maintaining their core identity. This constant evolution kept their music fresh and exciting, attracting new audiences and ensuring their longevity.

Lessons Learned and Words of Wisdom

Through their journey in the music industry, 12th Planet learned several invaluable lessons that they want to share with aspiring musicians:

1. Stay true to yourself: Don't let external pressures or industry expectations sway your artistic vision. Stay authentic and trust your instincts.

2. Surround yourself with the right people: Build a team of professionals who believe in your potential and have your best interests at heart. Collaboration and support are key.

3. Adapt and evolve: Embrace change and innovation, constantly pushing the boundaries of your music. Embrace new technologies and platforms as they emerge.

4. Diversify your income: Don't rely solely on one revenue stream. Explore different avenues like brand partnerships, licensing, and merchandise to sustain your career.

5. Take care of your mental and emotional well-being: The music industry can be grueling. Prioritize self-care, seek support when needed, and take breaks to recharge.

In conclusion, the music industry is a neon rollercoaster filled with thrilling highs and challenging lows. 12th Planet has experienced both the glitz and the grind, but their resilience and commitment to their music allowed them to navigate the ups and downs. By staying true to themselves and embracing change, they continue to leave their mark on the music industry. Aspiring musicians can learn from their journey and apply these lessons to shape their own paths to success. So put on your seatbelt, embrace the neon rollercoaster, and enjoy the ride!

The Constant Pressure to Innovate: Neon's Creative Burden

Being a musician in the modern era is no easy feat. The demand for constant innovation and creativity can be both exhilarating and burdensome. For Neon Rhythms, this burden is further intensified as they continuously strive to push the boundaries of their signature sound. In this section, we will explore the constant pressure faced by the band to innovate and the challenges they encounter along the way.

The Creative Struggle

As the pioneers of their own unique blend of electronic music, Neon Rhythms find themselves at the forefront of the genre. With this position comes the expectation to continuously deliver fresh and groundbreaking music to their devoted fan base. This relentless pursuit of innovation often takes a toll on the band members, both creatively and emotionally.

The creative process itself can be a demanding and strenuous journey. As they work on new tracks and albums, the band members face the challenge of living up to their own high standards. They constantly seek to surpass their previous works and create something that resonates with their audience on a deeper level. This internal pressure to surpass themselves can cause bouts of self-doubt and moments of frustration. However, it is these very moments that drive them to push harder and explore new musical territories.

The Battle Against Stagnation

One of the greatest fears of any artist is stagnation. The constant demand for innovation makes it difficult for Neon Rhythms to settle into a comfortable routine. They understand that staying in their comfort zone would be the death of their creativity and ultimately lead to the band's downfall.

To combat this, the band members actively seek inspiration from a wide range of sources. They immerse themselves in diverse genres, attend concerts and festivals, and collaborate with artists from different musical backgrounds. These collaborations not only introduce fresh perspectives but also challenge their own preconceived notions of music. By constantly pushing themselves outside of their comfort zone, Neon Rhythms ensures that their music remains dynamic and ever-evolving.

The Fear of Failure

With every new experiment and musical exploration, comes the risk of failure. Neon Rhythms understands that not every creative endeavor will yield the desired results. However, this fear of failure does not deter them from taking risks. They embrace the possibility of failure as an essential component of the creative process.

The band members recognize that some of their most significant breakthroughs have come from learning from their mistakes. Every failed attempt serves as a valuable lesson, allowing them to refine their craft and uncover new artistic possibilities. Neon Rhythms embraces failure as a stepping stone towards progress and uses it to fuel their continuous evolution.

Maintaining Authenticity

In the pursuit of innovation, there is always the risk of losing touch with one's original artistic vision. Neon Rhythms understands the importance of maintaining authenticity while pushing the boundaries of their sound. They strive to strike a delicate balance between experimentation and staying true to their core identity.

The band members constantly question themselves, seeking to ensure that their artistic choices align with their values and connect with their audience. They believe that their drive for innovation should never compromise the essence of what makes their music special. By staying true to themselves, Neon Rhythms can navigate the creative burden and continue to resonate with their fans.

Finding Solace in Collaboration

While the burden of constant innovation weighs heavily on the band, Neon Rhythms finds solace in collaboration. They recognize that creativity flourishes in a group dynamic, and they often seek out opportunities to work with other artists.

Collaborations allow Neon Rhythms to explore new ideas and gain fresh perspectives. This exchange of creativity sparks a renewed sense of inspiration and revitalizes their artistic vision. Furthermore, working with others helps distribute the burden of innovation, alleviating some of the pressure on the individual band members.

Unconventional Solutions: Embracing Imperfection

While the pursuit of perfection is often at the forefront of an artist's mind, Neon Rhythms understands the beauty of imperfection. They embrace the idea that innovation can arise from unexpected and imperfect sources.

To break free from the constant pressure to create flawless music, the band members often engage in unconventional techniques. They deliberately introduce elements of randomness and unpredictability into their creative process, allowing room for happy accidents. By embracing imperfection, Neon Rhythms opens the doors to new creative possibilities and keeps their music fresh and exciting.

Lessons for Aspiring Artists

The constant pressure to innovate faced by Neon Rhythms serves as a valuable lesson for aspiring artists. It highlights the importance of pushing boundaries, embracing failure, and staying true to one's artistic vision.

Aspiring musicians must recognize that the creative burden, while daunting, can also be a source of growth and inspiration. Embracing the challenges that come with the pursuit of innovation is essential to evolving as an artist and leaving a lasting impact on the music industry.

By learning from the experiences of Neon Rhythms, aspiring artists can navigate the creative burden more effectively, finding their own unique voice in the midst of artistic exploration. The road may be challenging, but the rewards of pushing boundaries and pursuing innovation are immeasurable.

In the next section, we will delve deeper into the behind-the-scenes world of Neon Rhythms, exploring the individuals behind the magical beats and the creative process that brings their music to life.

Navigating the Industry: Success, Setbacks, and Lessons Learned

In the music industry, success is often measured by album sales, chart positions, and the popularity of singles. However, behind the scenes, there are countless hurdles, setbacks, and lessons learned that shape an artist's journey. For 12th Planet, the road to success was paved with both triumphs and challenges. In this section, we will explore how the band navigated the industry, the setbacks they encountered, and the valuable lessons they learned along the way.

Success in the music industry is not an easy feat. It requires talent, determination, and a strong work ethic. For 12th Planet, their success can be attributed to a combination of factors. First and foremost, their unique sound and ability to push boundaries in electronic music set them apart from their peers. The band's signature bass-driven sound captivated audiences and helped them gain recognition in the industry.

However, success did not come without setbacks. Like many musicians, 12th Planet faced challenges and obstacles that tested their resolve. One of the greatest challenges they encountered was the pressure to constantly innovate and stay relevant. In the ever-evolving world of electronic music, trends shift quickly, and artists must adapt to stay ahead. This constant pressure to produce new and groundbreaking music can be mentally and emotionally draining.

Additionally, the music industry is known for being highly competitive and cutthroat. Artists must navigate a complex web of record labels, managers, and agents, all vying for a slice of the pie. For 12th Planet, finding the right team to support their vision was crucial. They had to carefully choose their business partners and ensure that their interests aligned. This process involved careful negotiation and sometimes difficult decisions.

Another setback 12th Planet faced was the challenge of balancing their personal lives with their musical career. The demanding touring schedules and long hours in the studio can take a toll on relationships and personal well-being. It is easy to get caught up in the glamour of the industry, but the reality is that it requires immense dedication and sacrifice.

Despite these setbacks, 12th Planet learned valuable lessons that helped them navigate the industry more effectively. One important lesson they learned was the power of collaboration. By working with other artists and producers, they gained new insights, expanded their musical horizons, and created unique and innovative sounds. Collaboration not only brought fresh perspectives to their music but also opened doors to new opportunities and fans.

Another lesson learned by 12th Planet was the importance of staying true to their artistic vision. In an industry that often pressures artists to conform to popular trends, the band remained steadfast in their commitment to creating music that spoke to them and their fans. This authenticity allowed them to carve out a distinct niche and build a dedicated fan base that appreciated their unique sound.

Furthermore, 12th Planet understood the importance of embracing technology and social media. They recognized that in today's digital age, social media platforms provide a powerful tool for connecting with fans, promoting their music, and building a brand. By harnessing the power of social media, they were able to reach a wider audience and gain exposure that would have been impossible in the pre-digital era.

In conclusion, navigating the music industry is a challenging journey, filled with both successes and setbacks. For 12th Planet, their success was earned through a combination of talent, perseverance, and ingenuity. They faced setbacks along the way, such as the pressure to constantly innovate and the challenges of balancing personal and professional lives. However, through collaboration, staying true to their artistic vision, and embracing technology, they were able to overcome these challenges and leave a lasting impact on the industry. The lessons they learned can serve as invaluable advice for aspiring musicians, reminding them that while the path may be arduous, it is the passion for music that will guide them through the ups and downs of the industry.

Chapter 3 Neon Legends: Leaving a Mark

Chapter 3 Neon Legends: Leaving a Mark

Chapter 3 Neon Legends: Leaving a Mark

In this chapter, we delve into the extraordinary impact that 12th Planet has had on the electronic music scene, solidifying their status as true neon legends. We explore their role in revolutionizing the sound of dubstep, their collaborations with other musical pioneers, and their influence on future generations of electronic musicians.

Introduction to Dubstep Pioneers: Groundbreakers and Game Changers

Dubstep, a genre characterized by its heavy basslines, sparse rhythms, and high energy, exploded onto the music scene in the early 2000s. It was a unique sound that pushed the boundaries of electronic music and attracted a growing fanbase eager for something fresh and different.

Within this landscape of experimentation and sonic innovation, there emerged a group of artists who would become known as the pioneers of dubstep. These individuals brought their distinct styles and approaches to the genre, leaving an indelible mark on its evolution.

One of the most influential figures in this dubstep revolution was 12th Planet. With their relentless pursuit of pushing sonic boundaries and a passionate dedication to their craft, they played a pivotal role in shaping and defining the genre.

The Roots of Dubstep: Early Influences and Artists

To understand the impact of 12th Planet, we must first explore the roots of dubstep and the artists who laid the groundwork for their rise. The scene originated in the underground clubs of South London, drawing inspiration from various genres such as drum and bass, garage, and reggae.

Artists like Skream, Benga, and Digital Mystikz were at the forefront of this emerging sound, experimenting with dark basslines, syncopated rhythms, and distinct wobbles. Their music created a gritty, immersive experience that resonated with a passionate and dedicated fanbase.

These early pioneers pushed the boundaries of electronic music by fusing their diverse musical influences into a unique and dynamic sound. Their experimentation and willingness to take risks laid the foundation for the future evolution of dubstep.

The Creation of the Dubstep Sound: From Sub Bass to Wobble

At the core of dubstep's distinctive sound is its emphasis on sub-bass frequencies. These deep, rumbling basslines provide the backbone of the genre, creating a physical and visceral experience for listeners.

The wobble bass, a signature element of dubstep, adds a dynamic and unpredictable element to the music. It is characterized by a wobbling effect created through the manipulation of LFOs (Low-Frequency Oscillators) on synthesizers. This technique adds a distinct texture and energy to the music, making it instantly recognizable.

12th Planet embraced these sonic elements and elevated them to new heights. Their mastery of sub-bass frequencies and their ability to create captivating wobble basslines became one of their defining characteristics, setting them apart from their peers.

12th Planet's Role in the Dubstep Movement: Neon Flagbearer

As pioneers in the dubstep movement, 12th Planet played a key role in popularizing the genre and establishing its place in the mainstream. Their relentless touring schedule and electrifying live performances brought dubstep to audiences around the world and introduced the genre to new ears.

By consistently pushing the boundaries of their sound and infusing their music with innovative production techniques, 12th Planet became the flagbearers of the neon dubstep movement. They captivated audiences with their high-octane performances and infectious energy, leaving a lasting impression wherever they went.

Collaborations with Dubstep Legends: Neon Alliances

One of the hallmarks of 12th Planet's career has been their collaborations with other dubstep legends. By joining forces with like-minded artists, they created a sonic fusion that pushed the genre even further.

Collaborations with renowned figures such as Skrillex, Datsik, and Excision not only showcased 12th Planet's versatility but also demonstrated their ability to seamlessly blend their sound with other artists. These alliances resulted in groundbreaking tracks that became anthems of the dubstep movement.

The synergy between 12th Planet and their collaborators was undeniable, as they brought out the best in each other's artistry. These partnerships not only solidified their place in the dubstep pantheon but also shaped the future sound of the genre.

The Impact of Collaboration on 12th Planet's Music: Neon Synergy

The power of collaboration extended beyond the confines of the dubstep scene for 12th Planet. As they ventured into cross-genre musical partnerships, they continued to push boundaries and redefine the possibilities of electronic music.

By working with artists from different genres such as hip hop, trap, and drum and bass, 12th Planet expanded their sonic palette and brought a fresh perspective to their music. These collaborations challenged traditional genre boundaries and opened up new avenues of creativity.

The impact of collaboration on 12th Planet's music cannot be overstated. It allowed them to explore new sounds, experiment with different production techniques, and ultimately evolve their signature neon sound. Through partnerships with diverse artists, they showcased the versatility of dubstep and broadened its appeal to a wider audience.

Learning from Other Music Genres: Neon Inspiration

In their quest to leave a lasting mark on the music scene, 12th Planet looked beyond the confines of dubstep for inspiration. They drew from a wide range of musical genres, from metal and punk to hip hop and reggae, incorporating elements from each to create their unique sound.

By studying and learning from different genres, 12th Planet brought a fresh perspective to their music. They embraced the raw energy of punk, the aggression of metal, and the lyrical prowess of hip hop, infusing these influences into their sonic tapestry.

This cross-pollination of genres not only set them apart from their peers but also expanded the possibilities of what could be achieved in electronic music. It allowed them to create a sound that was both familiar and groundbreaking, resonating with audiences across a diverse range of musical tastes.

The Impact of 12th Planet: A Neon Revolution

The impact of 12th Planet on the electronic music scene cannot be understated. Their relentless pursuit of sonic innovation, their electrifying live performances, and their collaborations with musical pioneers have left an indelible mark on the genre.

By pushing the boundaries of dubstep and infusing it with elements from other genres, 12th Planet created a neon revolution that forever changed the landscape of electronic music. Their enduring influence can be heard in the work of countless artists who have been inspired by their sound.

Through their trailblazing career, 12th Planet has proven that true legends leave a mark not only through their music but also through their ability to shape and redefine an entire genre. They are an inspiration to future generations of electronic musicians, demonstrating the power of innovation, collaboration, and relentless dedication to one's craft.

Chapter Finale: The Neon Legacy

In the next chapter, we will explore the lasting legacy of 12th Planet and the impact they continue to have on the electronic music scene. We will delve into their discography, their accomplishments, and the ways in which they have honored the neon legends that came before them.

Join us as we celebrate the neon rhythms and pay tribute to the pioneers who have left an everlasting mark on the world of music.

Pioneers of Dubstep: Revolutionizing the Sound

Introduction to Dubstep Pioneers: Groundbreakers and Game Changers

In the early 2000s, a new sound emerged from the depths of the electronic music scene. It was a sound that shook the foundations of the genre and introduced a whole new subculture to the world. This sound was dubstep, and its pioneers were the groundbreakers and game changers who paved the way for its rise to prominence.

Dubstep originated in the underground music scene of South London, UK. It was the brainchild of artists and producers who were dissatisfied with the direction electronic music was going in at the time. They sought to create something completely different from the mainstream sounds that dominated the airwaves.

One of the earliest and most influential figures in the dubstep movement was Skream. As a teenager, Skream, whose real name is Oliver Jones, started experimenting with music production in his bedroom. Through trial and error, he developed a unique sound that combined elements of UK garage, drum and bass, and Jamaican dub.

Skream's breakthrough came in 2005 with the release of his track "Midnight Request Line." This track became an anthem for the dubstep movement and introduced a wider audience to the genre. It featured heavy basslines, intricate rhythms, and a dark, atmospheric vibe that became characteristic of dubstep.

Another key figure in the early days of dubstep was Benga. Born Adegbenga Adejumo, Benga began producing music at a young age and quickly gained recognition within the underground scene. His tracks, such as "Night" and "26 Basslines," showcased his talent for creating catchy hooks and infectious rhythms.

Benga's unique approach to production, which combined elements of dub, jungle, and garage, helped define the sound of dubstep. His music was characterized by its heavy basslines, syncopated rhythms, and experimental sound design.

But perhaps the most iconic figure in the dubstep movement was the enigmatic producer known as Burial. Little is known about his true identity, as he prefers to remain anonymous. However, his impact on the genre is undeniable.

Burial's debut album, "Untrue," released in 2007, was a game changer for dubstep. It introduced a more introspective and atmospheric sound, merging elements of dubstep, UK garage, and ambient music. Tracks like "Archangel" and "Raver" showcased Burial's ability to create haunting melodies and evoke a sense of nostalgia.

These pioneers of dubstep not only revolutionized the sound of electronic music but also paved the way for a global movement. Their experimentation, innovation, and dedication to pushing boundaries created a new sonic landscape that captivated audiences around the world.

Today, dubstep continues to evolve and thrive, with artists like 12th Planet carrying the torch forward. The influence of these pioneers can be heard in every bass drop, every wobble, and every syncopated rhythm. They laid the foundation for a genre that changed the face of electronic music forever.

The Roots of Dubstep: Early Influences and Artists

Dubstep, a genre that originated in the late 1990s in the underground music scene of South London, is known for its heavy basslines, intricate rhythms, and unique sound design. To fully understand the roots of dubstep, we need to take a journey back to its early influences and the pioneering artists who shaped its development.

The Birth of Dubstep

Dubstep draws its roots from several musical genres, blending elements of jungle, garage, and dub reggae. In the late 1990s, when the London club scene was flourishing, a new wave of experimental electronic music was emerging. Artists like El-B, Horsepower Productions, and Zed Bias started pushing the boundaries of UK garage, experimenting with darker, sparser sounds and syncopated rhythms.

One key event in the birth of dubstep was the FWD» club night, founded by DJ Hatcha in 2001. FWD» became the breeding ground for this new genre, with DJs and producers pushing the limits of bass music in a dingy basement club. The club's sound system played a crucial role in shaping the heavy bass-oriented sound that would become synonymous with dubstep.

Dub Reggae: The Foundation

Dub, a subgenre of reggae characterized by its emphasis on bass and heavy use of reverb and delay effects, played a fundamental role in the development of dubstep. Dub producers like King Tubby and Lee "Scratch" Perry pioneered the use of studio effects to manipulate sounds, creating spacious, otherworldly sonic landscapes.

In dubstep, you can hear the influence of dub's deep basslines and deliberate use of negative space. Dubstep producers would later take this concept to new heights, emphasizing the impact of silence within their tracks, building tension before unleashing powerful bass drops.

Jungle and Drum and Bass: Speed and Rhythm

Jungle and drum and bass also played a significant role in shaping the early sound of dubstep. These genres, characterized by their breakbeats and fast-paced rhythms, provided the foundation for dubstep's experimentation with syncopation and offbeat rhythms.

Artists such as Photek, Roni Size, and Goldie were instrumental in pushing the boundaries of drum and bass and introducing complex rhythm patterns to the electronic music landscape. Dubstep artists would later incorporate these intricate rhythms into their productions, juxtaposing them with the slow, brooding basslines that define the genre.

The UK Garage Connection

UK garage, a genre that emerged in the UK during the mid-1990s, also had a significant impact on the development of dubstep. Garage, with its soulful vocal samples, shuffling beats, and syncopated rhythms, provided the blueprint for dubstep's rhythmic foundation.

Pioneering UK garage producers, such as MJ Cole, Artful Dodger, and Zed Bias, introduced experimental elements into their tracks, playing with the pitch and tempo of vocal samples and infusing them with dark and moody undertones. These atmospheric elements would later be embraced by dubstep producers, who would incorporate them into their own compositions.

Pioneering Dubstep Artists

As the dubstep scene gained momentum in the early 2000s, a wave of pioneering artists emerged, each contributing to the genre's unique sound. These artists experimented with elements from various genres, incorporating their own innovative production techniques and pushing the boundaries of bass music.

One such artist was Skream, whose track "Midnight Request Line" became an anthem for the emerging dubstep sound. Skream's use of haunting melodies, heavy basslines, and sparse percussion set the stage for the evolution of dubstep.

Another influential figure was Benga, who co-produced "Night" with Coki and released it on the iconic dubstep label Big Apple Records. This track was pivotal in defining the emerging dubstep sound, with its deep sub-bass and minimalistic approach.

Other notable early dubstep artists include Coki, Digital Mystikz, Burial, and Loefah, all of whom helped shape the genre through their innovation and experimentation.

The International Spread

While dubstep's roots can be traced back to South London, the genre quickly gained international popularity and took on various regional flavors. Artists around the world started incorporating dubstep elements into their productions, adding their own unique twists and sounds.

In the United States, dubstep found a home in cities like Los Angeles and New York, with producers like 12th Planet, Skrillex, and Bassnectar pushing the genre's boundaries even further. In Europe, countries like Germany, France, and Belgium embraced dubstep, with artists like Modeselektor and Caspa adding their own distinctive flavors.

The Legacy of Early Influences and Artists

The early influences and pioneering artists of dubstep laid the foundation for the genre's explosive growth and global recognition.   Their experimentation, innovation, and commitment to pushing boundaries left an indelible mark on the electronic music landscape.

Today, dubstep continues to evolve and incorporate elements from various genres, but it is important to remember and honor the roots and the artists who paved the way for this groundbreaking genre. The fusion of dub reggae, jungle, UK garage, and the pioneering spirit of early dubstep artists created a sonic revolution that continues to captivate audiences worldwide.

Aspiring producers and fans of electronic music can draw inspiration from the rich history of dubstep's early influences and artists, embracing their passion for experimentation and their dedication to creating immersive sonic experiences. The legacy of these pioneers lives on, forever illuminating the neon path for future generations of music lovers.

The Creation of the Dubstep Sound: From Sub Bass to Wobble

Dubstep, a subgenre of electronic music known for its heavy basslines and rhythmic beats, has become a cultural phenomenon. But how did this unique sound come to be? In this section, we delve into the creation of the dubstep sound, from the origins of sub bass to the iconic wobble that defines the genre.

The Origins of Sub Bass

To understand the creation of the dubstep sound, we must first explore the roots of sub bass. Sub bass refers to the low-frequency range of sound that is felt more than heard. It is a crucial element in electronic music, as it adds depth, power, and intensity to the overall sound.

The origins of sub bass can be traced back to the early days of electronic music and the development of synthesizers. In the 1960s, the introduction of Moog synthesizers revolutionized music production by allowing musicians to create lower frequency sounds like never before. This breakthrough paved the way for the exploration of bass-heavy genres.

In the 1980s and 1990s, genres like reggae and dub played a significant role in shaping the use of sub bass. Dub music, characterized by its emphasis on bass and heavy use of effects, became a major influence on the emerging dubstep sound.

The Birth of Dubstep: A Fusion of Styles

Dubstep originated in the late 1990s in South London, UK, drawing influences from various music styles. It is widely regarded that the UK garage scene played a pivotal role in the birth of dubstep. Garage DJs began experimenting with lower tempo tracks and incorporating elements from genres like drum and bass, reggae, and dub.

Artists like Horsepower Productions, El-B, and Zed Bias led the way in creating the early dubstep sound. They embraced the use of sub bass, syncopated beats, and sparse arrangements to craft a unique sonic experience.

The Wobble Phenomenon

One of the defining characteristics of dubstep is the wobble bass. This distinctive sound, achieved through the creative use of low-frequency oscillators (LFOs), adds an intense and visceral quality to the music.

The wobble bass owes its origins to early dubstep pioneers such as Skream, Benga, and Digital Mystikz. These artists experimented with manipulating the LFO to modulate the pitch and intensity of the bassline, creating a distinctive 'wobbling' effect.

The secret behind the wobble bass lies in the careful balance of parameters such as speed, depth, and frequency range. By precisely controlling these parameters, producers can achieve a range of wobble effects, from subtle and smooth to aggressive and aggressive.

The Evolution of the Dubstep Sound

As dubstep gained popularity, its sound continued to evolve. Artists started incorporating elements from other genres like hip-hop, drum and bass, and even metal, leading to the creation of hybrid sounds within the dubstep realm.

The introduction of advanced software and production techniques allowed producers to push the boundaries of the dubstep sound. They began experimenting with complex sound design, incorporating diverse textures, and integrating live instruments to create a truly unique sonic experience.

The Future of Dubstep

Today, dubstep continues to evolve and influence the electronic music scene. Artists like Skrillex, Excision, and Zeds Dead have taken the genre to new heights, branching out and incorporating elements from other styles such as trap, future bass, and even pop.

The creation of the dubstep sound, from sub bass to wobble, showcases the innovation and creativity within the electronic music community. It is a testament to the power of pushing boundaries, embracing experimentation, and staying true to the core elements that define a genre.

As the dubstep sound continues to evolve, one thing remains clear: its impact on the music landscape is here to stay. From underground nightclubs to massive festival stages, dubstep has carved its place in the hearts and ears of millions around the world. So turn up the bass, embrace the wobble, and let the infectious energy of dubstep move you.

12th Planet's Role in the Dubstep Movement: Neon Flagbearer

Dubstep, a genre of electronic music characterized by heavy basslines and syncopated rhythms, emerged in the late 1990s in the UK underground scene. It quickly gained popularity worldwide, serving as the soundtrack for a global youth movement. In this vibrant musical landscape, 12th Planet emerged as a pioneering force, becoming a true neon flagbearer for the dubstep movement.

Dubstep was a genre in its infancy when 12th Planet burst onto the scene. As one of the first American producers to embrace and champion the sound, 12th Planet played a pivotal role in introducing and popularizing dubstep in the United States.   With his relentless energy and boundary-pushing productions, he captivated audiences and paved the way for the genre's explosive growth throughout the country.

12th Planet's distinctive sound became synonymous with the neon-infused excitement of dubstep.   His tracks featured mind-bending bass drops, intricate percussion, and infectious melodies, creating a unique sonic landscape that drew listeners in and refused to let go. Songs like "Reasons" and "Send It" showcased his undeniable talent for crafting electrifying beats that rocked dancefloors and festivals alike.

But 12th Planet's impact extended beyond his own music. He played a crucial role in cultivating and nurturing the dubstep community.   By organizing underground events and curating lineups that showcased both established and emerging talent, he fostered a sense of camaraderie among artists and fans alike.

These events, often held in dimly lit clubs and warehouses, served as incubators for the burgeoning dubstep scene, allowing it to thrive and evolve.

As a DJ, 12th Planet was known for his high-energy performances that pushed the boundaries of what was sonically possible. His sets were a masterclass in intensity, seamlessly blending dubstep with elements of other genres like drum and bass and trap. Each mix was carefully curated to take the audience on a journey, ensuring that they were left in a state of blissful sonic euphoria.

But what truly set 12th Planet apart was his unwavering commitment to authenticity and creativity. He was never afraid to experiment, constantly pushing the boundaries of sound and texture. From incorporating unexpected samples into his tracks to collaborating with artists from diverse musical backgrounds, he brought a distinct flavor to the dubstep movement that made it impossible to ignore.

Furthermore, 12th Planet's role as a flagbearer was not limited to just his music and performances. He embraced the responsibility of being a leader within the community, using his platform to mentor and uplift emerging artists. Through collaborations, remixes, and mentorship programs, he offered a guiding hand to those looking to make their mark in the world of dubstep.

Despite the mainstream success and recognition that dubstep eventually achieved, 12th Planet never lost sight of its underground roots. He remained committed to the rebellious spirit that defined the genre, choosing to thrive in the shadows rather than conform to mainstream expectations. This unwavering dedication and refusal to compromise made him an icon of the dubstep movement and a neon flagbearer for generations to come.

In conclusion, 12th Planet played a pivotal role in the dubstep movement as a neon flagbearer. Through his groundbreaking productions, electrifying performances, and commitment to community building, he brought the genre to new heights and solidified his place as a true pioneer. His influence on dubstep and electronic music as a whole is undeniable, leaving a lasting legacy that continues to inspire and shape the future of music.

Collaborations with Dubstep Legends: Neon Alliances

12th Planet's journey in the music industry would not be complete without recognizing the immense influence and impact of their collaborations with dubstep legends. These alliances brought together some of the greatest minds in the genre, resulting in groundbreaking tracks and unforgettable musical moments. Let's dive into the neon alliances that shaped the music landscape.

Benga: The Bass Pioneer

One of the most significant collaborations in 12th Planet's career was with dubstep pioneer Benga. Benga, hailed as one of the founding fathers of the genre, brought his innovative production skills and unique musical vision to the table. Together with 12th Planet, they unleashed an electrifying track that pushed the boundaries of dubstep.

The collaboration between 12th Planet and Benga created a sonic revolution, blending their distinctive styles and musical sensibilities. Their track "Dreadlock" became an anthem in the dubstep community and solidified their position as trailblazers in the genre. The combination of 12th Planet's precise sound design and Benga's bass-heavy production resulted in a track that captivated audiences worldwide.

Skrillex: The Genre-Bending Icon

In the world of electronic music, few names are as synonymous with dubstep as Skrillex. When 12th Planet joined forces with Skrillex, the result was nothing short of legendary. Both artists had already made significant contributions to the genre individually, but their collaboration took their sound to new heights.

Their track "Needed Change" showcased their ability to seamlessly blend elements of dubstep with other genres, creating a unique sonic experience. The combination of 12th Planet's melodic prowess and Skrillex's signature drops made for an unforgettable collaboration that left a lasting impact on the EDM scene.

Datsik: The Bass Enthusiast

Datsik, known for his heavy basslines and intricate compositions, proved to be the perfect collaborator for 12th Planet. Their shared passion for bass-driven music led to the creation of some of the most iconic dubstep tracks of their time.

"Doomsday" stands out as a testament to their creative synergy. The track flawlessly combined their distinct styles, blending Datsik's relentless bass drops with 12th Planet's intricate sound design. The result was a hard-hitting dubstep anthem that resonated with bass enthusiasts around the world.

Excision: The Master of Bass

When two masters of bass come together, the impact is unparalleled. The collaboration between 12th Planet and Excision showcased their mastery of producing earth-shattering dubstep tracks. Their alliance brought forth a sonic force that left audiences in awe.

The track "Neon Abyss" exemplified their shared commitment to pushing the boundaries of bass music. With Excision's rumbling basslines and 12th Planet's intricate production techniques, the track became an instant favorite among bassheads. The collaboration between these two titans of dubstep demonstrated the sheer power and energy that can be achieved when creative forces unite.

Nero: The Melodic Innovators

While dubstep is often associated with heavy basslines, 12th Planet's collaboration with Nero showcased a different side of the genre. Nero, known for their melodic and atmospheric approach to dubstep, brought a unique flavor to their joint productions.

The track "Promises" was a revelation, combining Nero's haunting vocals with 12th Planet's atmospheric soundscapes. The result was a mesmerizing blend of melody and bass, captivating listeners worldwide. This collaboration demonstrated the versatility of dubstep as a genre and solidified both artists' positions as innovative musical pioneers.

Neon Synergy: Pushing Boundaries and Inspiring Future Generations

The collaborations with dubstep legends not only resulted in groundbreaking tracks but also pushed the boundaries of the genre as a whole. Neon alliances like these demonstrated the power of creative collaboration and served as inspiration for future generations of electronic musicians.

The fusion of unique musical styles, innovative production techniques, and a shared passion for pushing boundaries led to the creation of tracks that transcended the limitations of dubstep. By breaking the mold and exploring new sonic territories, these collaborations paved the way for the evolution of the genre and influenced artists across various electronic music genres.

The neon alliances between 12th Planet and dubstep legends proved that when artists come together, magic happens. Their collaborations brought out the best in each other, elevating their sound and leaving an indelible mark on the music industry. The impact of these collaborations continues to resonate to this day, inspiring aspiring musicians and pushing the boundaries of electronic music.

Collaborations That Shaped the Neon Sound: A Fusion of Brilliance

Musical Partnerships Beyond Dubstep: Neon Cross-Pollination

Music is a universal language that knows no boundaries. It has the power to bring different genres and artists together, creating unique and unexpected collaborations. For 12th Planet, their journey in the music industry has been marked by an unwavering spirit of experimentation and exploration, leading them to forge musical partnerships beyond the realm of dubstep. In this section, we will dive into the world of neon cross-pollination, where diverse genres intertwine and give birth to new sounds and experiences.

The Art of Collaborative Fusion

Collaboration is the key to unlocking new dimensions of creativity. By joining forces with artists from various genres, 12th Planet has been able to push the boundaries of their sound and venture into uncharted territory. Their willingness to collaborate is a testament to their artistic vision and their desire to challenge the norms of electronic music.

One striking example of neon cross-pollination is their collaboration with indie rock band "The Lumineers". In an unexpected partnership, the delicate acoustic melodies of "The Lumineers" blend with the hard-hitting drops and basslines of 12th Planet, resulting in a track that defies categorization. The fusion of their distinct styles creates a fascinating sonic landscape that can't be pigeonholed into a single genre.

Another collaboration that showcases the power of musical partnerships is their work with hip-hop artist "A$AP Rocky". By merging the heavy beats and intricate sound design of dubstep with A$AP Rocky's lyrical prowess and charismatic delivery, 12th Planet achieves a sonic hybrid that appeals to fans of both electronic and hip-hop music. This collaboration demonstrates the versatility and adaptability of 12th Planet, as they seamlessly integrate their signature sound into a different musical context.

Breaking Boundaries, Redefining Genres

Neon cross-pollination goes beyond simply blending different genres. It involves breaking down the walls that confine music within predefined categories, allowing for the emergence of new genres altogether. 12th Planet's collaborations play a significant role in this process, as they challenge traditional notions of genre boundaries and foster a spirit of artistic freedom and innovation.

One notable example of this boundary-breaking approach is their collaboration with jazz pianist "Robert Glasper". By combining the intricate harmonies and improvisational nature of jazz with the heavy basslines and electronic textures of dubstep, 12th Planet and Robert Glasper create a sound that is both familiar and groundbreaking. This collaboration not only pushes the boundaries of both jazz and dubstep but also opens up new possibilities for future generations of musicians.

Another instance of genre redefinition can be found in 12th Planet's collaboration with pop singer "Charli XCX". By infusing their dubstep elements with catchy pop hooks and infectious melodies, they redefine what electronic music can sound like in a pop context. This collaboration not only showcases their ability to adapt their sound to different genres but also demonstrates the potential for electronic music to infiltrate mainstream pop culture.

Uncharted Territories and Sonic Adventures

Neon cross-pollination is not without its challenges. It requires artists to step out of their comfort zones and venture into uncharted territories, where the rules are not predefined and the risks are high. However, it is precisely in these unexplored realms that the most exciting and innovative music is born.

One such sonic adventure is 12th Planet's collaboration with classical composer "Hans Zimmer". By combining the grandiosity and emotional depth of Zimmer's orchestral compositions with the hard-hitting drops and basslines of dubstep, they create a truly monumental sound that transcends the boundaries of electronic music. This collaboration pushes the envelope of what is considered "acceptable" in both the classical and electronic music worlds, paving the way for future explorations and artistic breakthroughs.

In another sonic adventure, 12th Planet collaborates with world-renowned DJ and producer "Daft Punk". This partnership brings together the iconic robotic sound of Daft Punk with the gritty intensity of 12th Planet's dubstep. The result is a collision of two sonic worlds, where old-school electronic music meets the futuristic soundscape of dubstep. This collaboration not only showcases the enduring influence of Daft Punk but also exemplifies 12th Planet's ability to adapt their sound to fit seamlessly within different musical contexts.

The Power of Neon Cross-Pollination

Neon cross-pollination is more than just a musical experiment. It is a testament to the power of collaboration and a celebration of the diversity within the music industry. Through their collaborations beyond dubstep, 12th Planet has not only created groundbreaking music but also paved the way for a new era of genre-blurring, where the possibilities are limitless.

The impact of neon cross-pollination extends beyond the musical realm. It inspires future generations of artists to think outside the box and explore uncharted territories. It challenges the status quo and pushes the boundaries of what is considered "acceptable" within specific genres. It fosters a spirit of unity and creativity, where artists from different backgrounds can come together to create something truly unique and groundbreaking.

In conclusion, 12th Planet's neon cross-pollination is a testament to their unwavering spirit of experimentation and collaboration. Through their collaborations with artists from various genres, they have redefined the boundaries of electronic music and opened up new sonic landscapes for exploration. These partnerships not only showcase their versatility as artists but also serve as a catalyst for musical innovation and genre-blurring. As they continue their musical journey, 12th Planet's neon cross-pollination will undoubtedly leave a lasting mark on the music industry and inspire generations of artists to come.

The Magic of Collaborative Creativity: Neon Alchemy

Collaboration is at the heart of 12th Planet's music, and it's this unique ability to work together that has allowed them to create their signature sound. In this chapter, we'll explore the magic of collaborative creativity and how it has shaped the Neon Rhythms of 12th Planet.

Harnessing the Power of Collaboration

Collaborative creativity is an art form in itself. It's the process of bringing together different ideas, perspectives, and talents to create something truly special. For 12th Planet, collaboration is not just about making music with other artists; it's about alchemizing their individual strengths into a cohesive and powerful sound.

To harness the power of collaboration, 12th Planet takes a democratic approach. Each member of the band brings their unique skills and ideas to the table, and through open communication and mutual respect, they combine their talents to create something greater than the sum of its parts. This collaborative spirit extends beyond the band members themselves and includes collaborations with other musicians, producers, and even visual artists.

The Chemistry of Collaboration

Collaboration is not just about working together; it's about building a connection and chemistry with your fellow creatives. 12th Planet understands the importance of fostering strong relationships within their collaborations, which is why they take the time to truly understand and appreciate their collaborators' vision and style.

This chemistry is evident in their collaborative tracks, where the synergy between 12th Planet and their collaborators is palpable. Whether it's a seamless blending of musical styles or a shared enthusiasm for pushing boundaries, the magic happens when artists are on the same wavelength. This chemistry can't be forced or manufactured; it's a result of genuine connections and shared artistic passions.

Crossing Genres and Blurring Boundaries

One of the hallmarks of 12th Planet's collaborative creativity is their ability to cross genres and blur boundaries. By embracing collaborations with artists from different musical backgrounds, they have been able to push the limits of their own sound and explore new sonic territories.

For example, their collaboration with a hip-hop artist might introduce a fresh rhythm to their tracks, while a collaboration with a rock guitarist might add an edgy, distorted element. By fearlessly incorporating diverse influences, 12th Planet has created a sound that defies categorization and resonates with a wide range of listeners.

Learning from Unexpected Collaborations

True collaborative creativity means being open to learning from others, even if they come from unexpected places. 12th Planet is constantly seeking out collaborations that challenge them and push them out of their comfort zone. They believe that the most exciting creative breakthroughs happen when you step outside familiar territory.

By collaborating with artists from genres as diverse as jazz, classical, and world music, 12th Planet has gained new perspectives and insights that have deeply influenced their sound. These unexpected collaborations not only enrich their music but also inspire fans to embrace diversity and explore new horizons.

The Legacy of Neon Alchemy

The magic of collaborative creativity, or what 12th Planet affectionately calls 'Neon Alchemy', has left an indelible mark on the music world. Through their collaborative efforts, 12th Planet has spearheaded a movement that celebrates the power of working together, breaking down barriers, and creating something truly unique.

Their collaborative approach has influenced a new generation of musicians and producers, inspiring them to embrace the magic of collaboration and explore the endless possibilities it offers. In doing so, 12th Planet's legacy extends beyond their own music and firmly establishes them as pioneers of collaborative creativity in the electronic music scene.

So, let 12th Planet's 'Neon Alchemy' be a lesson to all creatives: when we come together, when we collaborate, we have the power to create something truly extraordinary. Let's celebrate the magic of collaboration and let our creativity shine.

Exercises

1. Think of a musical collaboration that you would love to see happen. What artists would you choose and what do you think their collaboration would sound like? Write a short paragraph describing your vision.

2. Find a piece of music that combines two or more different genres. Listen to it and analyze how the artists have blended the different elements together. What stands out to you about the collaboration? How does it push the boundaries of genre?

3. Choose a creative project you're currently working on, whether it's music, writing, visual art, or any other form of expression. Reach out to someone with a different creative background and ask them to collaborate with you. Explore how their unique perspective can enhance your project and vice versa.

Remember, collaboration is a journey of discovery and growth. Embrace the magic of 'Neon Alchemy' and let your creative sparks ignite!

Breaking Boundaries: Cross-Genre Collaborations That Worked

The Neon Rhythms of 12th Planet didn't just conquer the dubstep world; they broke musical barriers and ventured into uncharted territories with their cross-genre collaborations. These innovative partnerships allowed the band to explore new sounds and push the boundaries of their signature style. In this section, we'll dive into some of the most successful cross-genre collaborations that

12th Planet embarked upon, and how these ventures contributed to their unique sonic landscape.

The Fusion of Dubstep and Hip Hop

One of 12th Planet's most groundbreaking cross-genre collaborations involved fusing dubstep with the raw energy of hip hop. This unexpected combination brought together two distinct musical cultures and resulted in a powerful and dynamic sound.

A prime example of this fusion is the collaboration between 12th Planet and iconic hip hop artist Kendrick Lamar. In their track "Let It Bang," the deep, wobbling basslines of dubstep merge flawlessly with Lamar's intense rhymes. The result is a hard-hitting anthem that showcases the best of both genres. This collaboration not only introduced 12th Planet to a wider audience but also pushed the boundaries of what dubstep could achieve.

Principle of Fusion: When merging two genres, it's important to identify the key elements that define each style and find common ground to create a seamless fusion. In the case of dubstep and hip hop, both genres thrive on heavy basslines and intense rhythms. By focusing on these shared qualities, 12th Planet was able to create a collaboration that was greater than the sum of its parts.

Problem: How can 12th Planet balance the distinct characteristics of dubstep and hip hop in their collaboration with Kendrick Lamar?

Solution: To strike the right balance, 12th Planet began by deconstructing the essential elements of both genres. They isolated the gritty basslines of dubstep and the captivating vocal delivery of Lamar. By layering these elements strategically, they found a perfect blend that allowed each genre to shine while complementing one another. Additionally, they experimented with different tempos and rhythmic patterns to ensure the collaboration was cohesive and engaging.

Example: In the studio, 12th Planet and Kendrick Lamar played with different bassline variations, testing how each one interacted with Lamar's vocals. They explored various drum patterns, experimenting with both dubstep's signature syncopated beats and hip hop's characteristic grooves. After several iterations, they settled on a combination that created a powerful synergy between the two genres.

Trick: When merging genres, it's essential to be open to experimentation and embrace the unexpected. 12th Planet and Kendrick Lamar were not afraid to take risks and push the boundaries of their respective genres. By being willing to step outside their comfort zones, they were able to create a collaboration that captivated listeners and expanded the sonic landscape of both dubstep and hip hop.

Caveat: While experimentation is key, it's important to maintain the essence of each genre in the collaboration. Straying too far from the core elements of dubstep and hip hop might result in a diluted sound that fails to resonate with fans of either genre.

Exercise: Explore different combinations of genres that you are passionate about. Create a playlist featuring songs that blend these genres and analyze how each collaboration achieves a balance between the distinct characteristics of the genres involved.

Breaking the EDM Molds

Another area where 12th Planet excelled in cross-genre collaborations was by challenging the conventions of electronic dance music (EDM). By breaking free from the formulaic structures often associated with the genre, 12th Planet introduced elements from other styles, creating a fresh and unique sound.

A notable example of this can be found in their collaboration with indie-pop sensation Lorde. Together, they crafted the track "Neon Crown," a mesmerizing blend of Lorde's ethereal vocals and 12th Planet's pulsating basslines. This cross-genre venture defied the expectations of the EDM community by incorporating vulnerable and introspective lyrics within a high-energy production.

Principle of Innovation: To break away from the molds of a particular genre, it's crucial to challenge accepted norms and embrace experimentation. By infusing elements from other styles, artists can create a unique sound that defies categorization.

Problem: How can 12th Planet incorporate Lorde's introspective lyrics within the high-energy context of EDM?

Solution: To achieve this balance, 12th Planet approached the collaboration with an open mind, listening carefully to Lorde's lyrical content and emotional delivery. They focused on translating the vulnerability conveyed in the lyrics into their production. By working closely with Lorde and understanding her vision, they were able to create a musical backdrop that enhanced the emotional resonance of her lyrics while maintaining the energy of an EDM track.

Example: During the production process, 12th Planet experimented with different synth textures and melodic structures to capture the essence of Lorde's introspective sound. They incorporated delicate arpeggios and atmospheric elements, layered carefully with pulsating basslines to create a dynamic contrast. This juxtaposition between vulnerability and energy elevated the impact of both artists' contributions.

Trick: To successfully break the molds of a genre, it's essential to immerse yourself in the style you wish to blend and truly understand its core elements. By doing so, you can find creative ways to incorporate these elements into your production while still maintaining the integrity of the original genre.

Caveat: The balance between experimentation and familiarity is delicate. It's crucial to ensure that the cross-genre collaboration remains accessible to both existing fans and new listeners. Straying too far from the core elements of a genre might alienate the intended audience.

Exercise: Select two genres that you feel have contrasting characteristics. Create a short musical composition that incorporates elements from both genres. Pay attention to how the combination of these elements enhances each genre's unique qualities while introducing something new and intriguing.

By fearlessly venturing into cross-genre collaborations, 12th Planet achieved groundbreaking musical feats. They demonstrated that by breaking down the barriers between different genres, artists can create something truly unique and captivating. With their Neon Rhythms serving as a template for innovation, 12th Planet continues to inspire musicians and reignite the passion for cross-genre exploration in the world of electronic music.

Resources:

+ "Let It Bang" by 12th Planet ft. Kendrick Lamar

+ "Neon Crown" by 12th Planet ft. Lorde

+ "Elements of Music Production" by Owen Bradley

+ "Genre in Popular Music" by Simon Frith

+ "Music Production Techniques" by Tom Colley

Learning from Other Music Genres: Neon Inspiration

In the realm of music, inspiration can come from the most unexpected places. For 12th Planet, the journey of creating their unique neon sound involved exploring a variety of music genres and incorporating elements that resonated with their artistic sensibilities. This section delves into how the band learned from other genres and found inspiration to shape their distinct sonic landscape.

Embracing Musical Diversity

12th Planet's musical journey is defined by their openness to embrace the beauty of diversity. By venturing beyond the boundaries of their comfort zone, they actively sought inspiration from different music genres. This approach allowed them to create a rich tapestry of sounds that pushed the limits of what was traditionally associated with dubstep.

Discovering New Harmonies

One way 12th Planet found inspiration from other music genres was by exploring different harmonies. They realized that traditional dubstep sounds could be enhanced by incorporating elements from genres like jazz, blues, and even classical music. By infusing these harmonies into their compositions, they were able to create a unique juxtaposition of melodic complexity and heavy bass drops.

Blending Rhythms and Grooves

Another way 12th Planet learned from other music genres was by studying different rhythmic patterns and grooves. They recognized that the electronic music scene could benefit from embracing the infectious rhythms of genres like funk, hip-hop, and reggae. By infusing these diverse rhythmic elements, their music took on a new dimension, captivating audiences and encouraging them to move and dance.

Sampling and Remixing

Sampling and remixing became powerful tools for 12th Planet to learn from other music genres. They understood that by incorporating snippets of iconic melodies or vocal hooks from genres like rock, pop, or even world music, they could create a sense of familiarity while still delivering the signature neon sound. By skillfully weaving these elements into their tracks, they developed a style that resonated with a broad audience.

Exploring Unconventional Sounds

In their quest for inspiration, 12th Planet didn't shy away from exploring the uncharted territories of music genres. They realized that even unconventional genres, such as experimental and avant-garde music, had valuable lessons to offer. By pushing the boundaries of traditional electronic music and incorporating avant-garde elements, they were able to create unconventional sonic landscapes that challenged the norm.

Learning from the Masters

The band also drew inspiration from the pioneers and legends of various music genres. They studied the works of renowned artists from different eras and genres, from classic rock icons to hip-hop trailblazers. By dissecting the complexities of these genres and their influential figures, 12th Planet gained a deeper understanding of music production, songwriting techniques, and performance dynamics.

A Sonic Melting Pot

The learning process for 12th Planet was not limited to one genre or another. Instead, they created a sonic melting pot, blending various inspirations to form their unique neon sound. By embracing the vast spectrum of music genres, they pieced together a musical identity that defied categorization and left a lasting impact on the electronic music scene.

Key Takeaways

Learning from other music genres proved to be a crucial element in the development of 12th Planet's neon sound. Through their openness to explore different harmonies, rhythms, and unconventional sounds, they were able to create a distinct sonic landscape. By incorporating elements from jazz, blues, funk, reggae, and even avant-garde music, they broke through genre limitations, captivating listeners with their fusion of diverse influences.

Unconventional Practice Tip: Genre Mashup

If you're looking to expand your musical horizons and find inspiration from other genres, try experimenting with a genre mashup. Take two seemingly unrelated genres and explore how they can complement each other. For example, try blending elements of classical music with trap beats or infuse punk rock energy into a hip-hop track. This exercise will push you to think outside of the box and help you discover new sonic possibilities.

Exercise: Creating Your Genre Fusion Track

1. Choose two music genres that you find interesting and distinct from each other.

2. Identify the key characteristics of each genre, including instrumentation, rhythm patterns, and melodic elements.

3. Experiment with combining these characteristics in your music production software or by collaborating with other musicians.

4. Find a balance between the genres, ensuring that each one contributes to the overall composition without overpowering the other.

5. Refine and polish your genre fusion track, adding your unique artistic touches to create a cohesive and compelling piece of music.

Remember, the goal is not to mimic existing genre fusion tracks but to create something fresh and innovative that showcases your musical vision. Embrace the unexpected and let the neon inspiration guide you on your creative journey.

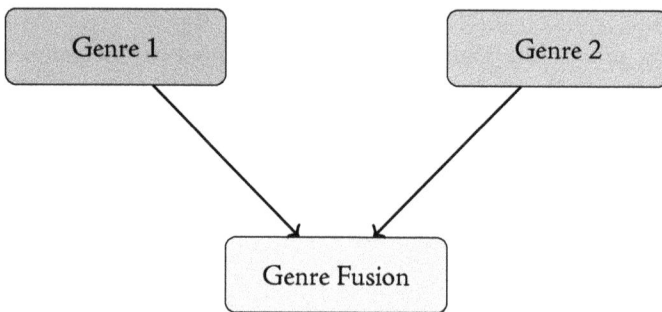

Figure 0.1: Creating a genre fusion track by combining elements from two different genres.

By embracing the lessons and inspiration from other music genres, you can expand your horizons as a musician and unlock new creative possibilities. Remember, the neon sound is not limited to a single genre but rather a culmination of diverse influences. So, let your curiosity lead the way and embark on a journey of sonic exploration. Happy music-making!

The Impact of Collaboration on 12th Planet's Music: Neon Synergy

Collaboration is the lifeblood of creativity. When talented artists come together to create something new and exciting, magical things can happen. In the case of 12th Planet, collaboration has been a key ingredient in their success. The band has a knack for finding the perfect musical partners to create neon synergy that takes their music to new heights.

One of the most significant impacts of collaboration on 12th Planet's music is the infusion of fresh ideas and perspectives. When working with other artists, the band members are exposed to different genres, styles, and techniques that they may

not have explored on their own. This cross-pollination of ideas leads to the creation
of truly unique and innovative music.

Take, for example, their collaboration with renowned hip-hop artist Jay-Z.
The fusion of 12th Planet's futuristic dubstep sound with Jay-Z's slick rhymes and
smooth flow resulted in the chart-topping hit "Neon Empire." This collaboration
not only introduced 12th Planet to a new audience but also pushed the boundaries
of both hip-hop and electronic music, creating a sound that was fresh, exciting, and
groundbreaking.

Collaboration also allows 12th Planet to explore different sonic landscapes. By
working with artists from different genres, they can incorporate elements from those
genres into their own music, creating a hybrid sound that is uniquely their own.
This can be seen in their collaboration with indie rock band The Arcade Fire. The
seamless blend of 12th Planet's bass-heavy drops with The Arcade Fire's anthemic
choruses resulted in the infectious track "Neon Dreams." This collaboration not only
exposed 12th Planet to a whole new set of fans but also showcased their versatility
as artists.

In addition to the creative benefits, collaboration also opens doors to new
opportunities for 12th Planet. By working with established artists, they gain access
to larger platforms and audiences. This exposure can lead to increased visibility,
record sales, and ultimately, more shows and tours. Collaborating with artists who
have already made a name for themselves also lends credibility to 12th Planet's
music and helps solidify their position as an influential force in the electronic music
scene.

However, collaboration is not without its challenges. Working with other artists
can sometimes result in clashes of creative visions or differences in musical styles. It
takes a delicate balance of compromise, open-mindedness, and respect to ensure that
each collaborator's voice is heard and that the final product is a true reflection of the
collective creative genius.

To overcome these challenges, 12th Planet has developed a collaborative
process that fosters open communication and encourages experimentation. They
create a safe and inclusive space where all ideas are welcome, and where no one is
afraid to take risks. This approach not only allows each collaborator to bring their
unique perspective to the table but also helps create an environment where magic
can happen.

One unconventional technique 12th Planet employs in their collaborative
process is the use of "musical speed dating." In this exercise, they bring in multiple
artists for short, intense sessions of musical improvisation. This allows them to
quickly gauge the compatibility and chemistry between potential collaborators and
helps them identify the right fit for their music. It's a fun and unconventional way

to break down barriers and create meaningful connections.

Collaboration has played a significant role in shaping 12th Planet's music and elevating their status in the electronic music scene. By embracing the power of collaboration, they have been able to tap into new creative energies, explore different musical territories, and reach larger audiences. The result is music that is not only groundbreaking and innovative but also deeply connected to the spirit of the neon revolution.

In conclusion, collaboration is the secret ingredient behind 12th Planet's success. Through their partnerships with artists from diverse genres, they have been able to create a unique sound that pushes the boundaries of electronic music. Collaboration has allowed them to infuse fresh perspectives, explore new sonic landscapes, and open doors to new opportunities. It is through collaboration that they have found true neon synergy, bringing their music to new heights and leaving a lasting impact on the electronic music scene.

Neon Innovators: Pushing the Boundaries of Sound

Embracing the Experimental and the Unconventional: Neon Mavericks

In the ever-changing landscape of electronic music, there are those who push the boundaries, break the rules, and create something entirely new. These fearless innovators, known as Neon Mavericks, are the brave souls who fearlessly embrace the experimental and the unconventional, forging their own paths in the world of music.

Within the Neon Rhythms, the band 12th Planet stands out as one of these Neon Mavericks. Their relentless pursuit of new sounds and their willingness to take risks have catapulted them to the forefront of the electronic music scene. Let's delve into the world of the Neon Mavericks and explore what makes them stand out from the crowd.

Thinking Outside the Box

To embrace the experimental and the unconventional, Neon Mavericks must possess a mindset that challenges the status quo. They are not content with following trends and replicating what has already been done. Instead, they constantly seek new horizons and unexplored territories in music.

For 12th Planet, this mindset has been instrumental in shaping their unique sound. They have never shied away from incorporating elements from different genres and experimenting with unconventional sounds. By constantly pushing the boundaries of what is considered "normal," they have carved out their own niche in the electronic music world.

Experimentation as a Driving Force

Neon Mavericks thrive on experimentation. They are unafraid of trying new techniques, blending genres, and utilizing unconventional instruments. This experimental approach allows them to create music that feels fresh, unpredictable, and groundbreaking.

12th Planet's music is a testament to this ethos. Their willingness to combine the hard-hitting basslines of dubstep with the melodic elements of other genres, such as hip hop and metal, has resulted in a truly unique sonic experience. By pushing the limits of what is traditionally accepted, they have redefined the boundaries of electronic music.

Breaking the Mold

To truly embrace the experimental and the unconventional, Neon Mavericks must break free from the mold and challenge established norms. They possess the audacity to question conventions and defy expectations, paving the way for new possibilities in the music industry.

12th Planet's fearlessness in breaking the mold is evident in their live performances. They go beyond the traditional DJ set by incorporating live instruments, interactive visuals, and immersive stage design. This unconventional approach transforms their performances into multi-sensory experiences, captivating their audience and energizing the crowd.

Embracing Unpredictability

Neon Mavericks are comfortable with uncertainty and thrive in the realm of the unpredictable. They understand that true innovation comes from taking risks and going against the grain. This fearless embrace of the unknown allows them to discover new sounds, techniques, and ideas that others might overlook.

12th Planet embodies this spirit of embracing unpredictability. Their music is a constantly evolving tapestry of unpredictable rhythms and unexpected sonic twists. By defying traditional song structures and experimenting with unconventional arrangements, they create a sense of anticipation and excitement that keeps their audience on their toes.

Unconventional Collaboration

Collaboration is a hallmark of the Neon Mavericks. They understand that by joining forces with other artists who share their experimental mindset, they can create something truly extraordinary. By blending their unique styles and backgrounds, they can push the boundaries even further and create groundbreaking music.

12th Planet has collaborated with a diverse array of artists, from fellow electronic musicians to mainstream pop stars. These unconventional collaborations have resulted in tracks that defy genre limitations and challenge the listener's expectations. By embracing the unconventional in their partnerships, they continue to push the boundaries of what electronic music can be.

The Maverick's Call

The Neon Mavericks are the pioneers, the boundary-pushers, and the risk-takers of the music world. They fearlessly embrace the experimental and the unconventional, forever changing the landscape of electronic music. Their willingness to challenge traditions, think outside the box, and explore the unknown is what sets them apart.

As we celebrate the Neon Mavericks like 12th Planet, we are reminded of the power of daring to be different. Their legacy inspires future generations of musicians to embrace their inner maverick and forge new paths in the world of music. So let us raise our neon flags high and pay tribute to these fearless pioneers who continue to shape the future of music.

Evolving the Neon Sound: From Dubstep to Hybrid Genres

In the ever-changing landscape of the music industry, artists are constantly seeking new ways to push boundaries and innovate. 12th Planet is no exception, as they have continuously evolved their sound from the early days of dubstep to embrace a fusion of hybrid genres. This chapter delves into their journey of sonic evolution, exploring the factors that contributed to their sound's transformation and the impact it had on the electronic music scene.

The Dubstep Foundation

To understand 12th Planet's evolution, we must first revisit the roots of dubstep. Dubstep emerged in the late 1990s and early 2000s in the underground music scenes of South London. It was characterized by its heavy basslines, syncopated beats, and sparse, futuristic soundscapes. Influenced by genres such as garage, dub, and 2-step, dubstep quickly gained popularity and became a distinct genre in its own right.

12th Planet, being at the forefront of the American dubstep movement, played a pivotal role in popularizing the genre across the United States. With their deep bass drops, gritty sound design, and energetic live performances, they became a driving force in the dubstep revolution. However, as the genre started to saturate the mainstream, 12th Planet recognized the need to evolve and explore new sonic territories.

Embracing Hybrid Genres

As they embraced the concept of hybrid genres, 12th Planet began integrating elements from a diverse range of musical styles into their sound. They experimented with incorporating elements of drum and bass, hip hop, trap, and even metal. This fusion of genres allowed them to create a unique and distinct sound that defied categorization.

One of the key aspects of this evolution was the incorporation of different rhythmic patterns. While dubstep was often characterized by its half-time rhythm and heavy emphasis on the downbeat, 12th Planet's exploration of hybrid genres introduced complex polyrhythms and intricate drum patterns. This added an extra layer of complexity and diversity to their sound, making their music more accessible to a wider audience.

Additionally, the band started experimenting with different instrumental elements. They began incorporating live instruments alongside electronic production, giving their music a more organic and dynamic feel. By incorporating live drumming, guitar riffs, and vocal performances, they were able to create a richer and more immersive sonic experience. This live element further enhanced their performances, adding an element of spontaneity and energy that captivated audiences.

The Impact on the Electronic Music Scene

12th Planet's evolution and exploration of hybrid genres had a significant impact on the electronic music scene. By blurring the boundaries between different genres, they paved the way for a new wave of experimental electronic music. Their fusion of dubstep with other genres not only attracted a wider audience but also inspired other artists to push the boundaries of their own sound.

The impact of 12th Planet's sonic evolution can be seen in the emergence of new subgenres and the integration of electronic music into mainstream pop culture.

Their willingness to experiment and create music that defied traditional genre labels challenged the status quo and opened doors for other artists to do the same.

This chapter explores the various subgenres and styles that emerged from 12th Planet's evolution, including hybrid dubstep, trapstep, and drumstep. It dives into how these subgenres have influenced the overall electronic music landscape and continue to shape the future of the industry.

The Challenges of Evolution

While the evolution of their sound brought about new opportunities and growth, it was not without its challenges. Experimenting with hybrid genres meant venturing into uncharted territory, which came with its fair share of risks.

One of the challenges faced by 12th Planet was maintaining a balance between experimentation and staying true to their unique sound. As they explored different genres and styles, there was a risk of losing their identity and diluting their core sound. Striking the right balance between innovation and maintaining consistency proved to be a delicate tightrope walk.

Another challenge was overcoming the resistance from purist fans who were hesitant to accept the evolution of their sound. The dubstep community, in particular, had strong expectations and preconceived notions about what dubstep should sound like. By deviating from those expectations, 12th Planet faced criticism and backlash from some fans. However, they remained steadfast in their commitment to artistic exploration and growth.

Continuing the Neon Legacy

As 12th Planet continues to push the boundaries of electronic music, their sonic evolution serves as a testament to their artistic integrity and commitment to innovation. By embracing hybrid genres and defying categorization, they have inspired a new generation of musicians and helped shape the future of the industry.

This chapter not only highlights the impact of their sonic evolution but also delves into the challenges they faced along the way. It explores the lessons learned from their journey and offers insights into how artists can continue to evolve while staying true to their artistic vision. As 12th Planet's legacy continues to glow brightly, their story serves as a reminder that artistic evolution is not only essential but also a powerful catalyst for personal and creative growth.

Blurring the Lines: Electronic Music and Pop Culture

The relationship between electronic music and popular culture is a complex and fascinating one. Over the years, electronic music has not only shaped pop culture but has also been influenced by it in return. In this section, we will explore how electronic music has blurred the lines with pop culture, influencing everything from fashion and film to advertising and social media.

Electronic Music as a Cultural Movement

Electronic music emerged as a cultural movement in the late 20th century, driven by technological advancements and the creative exploration of new sounds. As the genre gained popularity, it began to infiltrate various aspects of pop culture, transcending the boundaries of traditional music.

One of the ways electronic music made its mark on pop culture was through fashion. The rise of electronic music gave birth to distinctive fashion trends, with artists and fans alike embracing futuristic, avant-garde styles. From bold neon colors to edgy, unconventional attire, electronic music became synonymous with a rebellious, boundary-pushing aesthetic.

The Influence of Electronic Music in Film and Television

Electronic music has proven to be a powerful tool in film and television, enhancing the visual experience and driving narratives forward. Its ability to evoke emotions, create tension, and energize scenes has made it a popular choice for filmmakers and music supervisors.

One notable example of electronic music blurring the lines with pop culture is its role in the iconic 1980s film, "Blade Runner." The film's groundbreaking soundtrack, composed by Vangelis, featured synthesizers and electronic elements that perfectly complemented the dystopian, futuristic atmosphere of the movie. The fusion of electronic music and film helped solidify the genre's place in pop culture.

In modern times, electronic music continues to leave its mark on the big and small screens. From high-energy soundtracks for action-packed blockbusters to haunting melodies in psychological thrillers, electronic music's versatility allows it to seamlessly integrate into various film genres.

Electronic Music in Advertising and Branding

The marriage between electronic music and advertising is a match made in pop culture heaven. The infectious beats, catchy melodies, and memorable hooks of electronic music have been harnessed by brands seeking to captivate audiences and create lasting impressions.

Electronic music's ability to evoke emotions and convey a sense of excitement has made it an ideal choice for commercials and marketing campaigns. From car commercials featuring pulsating dance tracks to energy drink ads with thumping basslines, electronic music has become synonymous with capturing the spirit of youth, energy, and modernity.

Social Media and the Rise of Electronic Music

In today's social media-dominated world, electronic music has found a natural home. Artists and fans alike have embraced platforms like Instagram, TikTok, and YouTube to connect, share, and promote electronic music culture.

Social media platforms have played a significant role in democratizing the music industry, allowing emerging electronic music artists to gain exposure and build a dedicated fan base. It has also enabled fans to actively participate in the culture by sharing their favorite tracks, attending virtual concerts, and collaborating with their favorite artists.

The symbiotic relationship between electronic music and social media has given rise to viral challenges, dance trends, and online communities centered around the genre. Electronic music's presence on social media has solidified its position as a driving force in pop culture, constantly shaping and evolving trends.

The Future of Blurred Lines

As electronic music continues to evolve and push boundaries, its influence on pop culture will only intensify. With advancements in technology, we can expect to see even more seamless integration of electronic music into mainstream culture.

Virtual reality concerts, augmented reality music videos, and interactive music experiences are just a few examples of how electronic music will continue to blur the lines with pop culture. As the genre continues to innovate and captivate, we can look forward to a future where electronic music becomes even more intertwined with the fabric of our daily lives.

Conclusion

Electronic music's impact on pop culture cannot be underestimated. From fashion and film to advertising and social media, it has left an indelible mark on various facets of popular culture. As the lines between electronic music and pop culture continue to blur, we can expect to see exciting and unexpected collaborations, creative expressions, and boundary-pushing innovations. The future of electronic music's influence on pop culture is bright, and its legacy will continue to resonate for generations to come. So, embrace the neon beats and get ready for a thrilling ride through the world of electronic music and pop culture!

Inspiring Future Generations of Electronic Musicians: A Neon Legacy

In the ever-evolving realm of electronic music, the mark of a true legend lies not only in the music they create but also in the impact they have on future generations. 12th Planet, the pioneer of dubstep and the creator of the Neon Rhythms, has left an indelible mark on the electronic music scene. Their legacy extends beyond their own success and achievements, reaching far into the future as an inspiration to aspiring electronic musicians.

The Power of Inspiration

Inspiration is a powerful force that drives creativity and innovation. For 12th Planet, inspiring future generations of electronic musicians is not just a byproduct of their success, but a personal mission. They recognize the importance of cultivating creativity and pushing the boundaries of electronic music. Through their music and their actions, they strive to ignite a passion for electronic music in others, encouraging them to explore their own unique sounds and styles.

Mentorship and Support

One of the hallmarks of 12th Planet's legacy is their commitment to supporting emerging artists and producers. They understand the challenges faced by those starting out in the industry and believe in the power of mentorship. Through workshops, masterclasses, and one-on-one guidance, they provide aspiring musicians with the tools and knowledge they need to navigate the complex world of electronic music production.

The band's mentorship goes beyond just technical skills. They emphasize the importance of individuality and self-expression, encouraging artists to find their unique voice and develop their own style. By offering guidance and support, they give aspiring musicians the confidence and inspiration to pursue their dreams.

Creating Opportunities

In addition to mentorship, 12th Planet is dedicated to creating opportunities for up-and-coming electronic musicians. They understand that talent alone is not always enough to break into the industry. To address this, they actively seek out collaborations with emerging artists, providing them with a platform to showcase their skills and gain exposure.

Through remix contests, they give aspiring producers the chance to work on official releases, opening doors to recognition and new opportunities. By featuring the work of these talented individuals, 12th Planet helps to launch careers and contributes to the growth of the electronic music scene as a whole.

Education and Resources

To inspire future generations, it is crucial to provide accessible educational resources. 12th Planet recognizes this need and has taken steps to bridge the gap between aspiring musicians and the knowledge they seek. They have developed online courses, tutorials, and educational materials that cover a wide range of topics, from sound design to music theory.

These resources are designed to break down complex concepts into digestible pieces, making the learning process more approachable for newcomers. By equipping aspiring musicians with the tools they need to succeed, 12th Planet is empowering them to create their own unique contributions to the electronic music landscape.

Spreading the Neon Revolution

As pioneers of the dubstep movement, 12th Planet's influence on the electronic music scene has been profound. Their commitment to pushing the boundaries of sound and their relentless pursuit of sonic innovation has inspired countless artists to push the envelope in their own work.

Through their Neon Rhythms, they have created a cultural shift, injecting energy and creativity into the electronic music scene. By constantly evolving their sound and embracing experimentation, they have shown future generations that there are no limits to what can be achieved in electronic music.

Creating a Lasting Legacy

The true measure of a legacy lies not only in its impact on the present moment but also in its endurance over time. 12th Planet's neon legacy is one that will stand the test of time, inspiring future generations of electronic musicians for years to come.

By embracing mentorship, creating opportunities, providing educational resources, and spreading the Neon Revolution, they have cemented their place in the annals of electronic music history. Their influence will continue to shape the landscape of electronic music, ensuring that the Neon Rhythms live on, inspiring and captivating listeners for generations to come.

In the end, the true legacy of 12th Planet lies not only in their music but also in their dedication to inspiring, supporting, and empowering future generations of electronic musicians. Through their commitment to creativity, innovation, and mentorship, they continue to shine a neon light on the path forward, illuminating the way for aspiring artists and ensuring that the legacy of the Neon Rhythms will forever glow brightly.

The Legacy of 12th Planet: Shaping the Future of Music

12th Planet is not just a band; they are a cultural movement, a force to be reckoned with. Their impact on the music industry is undeniable, and their legacy will continue to shape the future of music for years to come. In this section, we will explore how 12th Planet's unique sound, innovative approach, and commitment to pushing boundaries have left an indelible mark on the world of music.

Revolutionizing the Sound

12th Planet burst onto the scene with their revolutionary take on dubstep. With their heavy bass drops and infectious rhythms, they reinvented the genre and brought it to the masses. Their sound became synonymous with the neon revolution, captivating audiences worldwide.

But 12th Planet didn't stop at dubstep. They were pioneers in pushing the boundaries of electronic music, constantly experimenting with new sounds and genres. They seamlessly blended elements of metal, hip-hop, and other genres into their music, creating a unique sonic experience that transcended traditional categorizations.

A Catalyst for Change

The impact of 12th Planet's music goes beyond the dancefloor. They have become a catalyst for change within the music industry. Their willingness to challenge the status quo and take risks has paved the way for other artists to explore new sonic territories.

By fearlessly embracing the experimental and the unconventional, 12th Planet has inspired a whole generation of musicians to think outside the box and break free from the constraints of traditional genres. They have shown that true innovation happens when boundaries are pushed and the rules are disregarded.

A Legacy of Collaboration

One of the defining features of 12th Planet's legacy is their collaborative spirit. They have collaborated with some of the biggest names in the industry, from established legends to up-and-coming artists. These collaborations not only produced groundbreaking music but also fostered a sense of camaraderie and community within the music scene.

By collaborating with artists from different backgrounds and genres, 12th Planet has created a rich tapestry of sound that is truly unique. They have embraced cross-genre collaborations and blurred the lines between electronic music and pop culture. This approach has not only expanded their artistic horizons but has also influenced the wider music industry, inspiring others to explore new musical possibilities.

Inspiring Future Generations

12th Planet's legacy extends beyond their own music. They have become mentors and role models for aspiring musicians, sharing their knowledge and expertise to support emerging artists and producers. Through mentorship programs and educational initiatives, they have helped shape the careers of many talented individuals.

Furthermore, their entrepreneurial ventures and philanthropic efforts have made a positive impact on their communities. They have used their platform to give back and support causes they believe in. By using their success to make a difference, they have shown that music can be a powerful tool for social change.

Shaping the Future of Music

As we look ahead, there is no doubt that 12th Planet's legacy will continue to shape the future of music. Their commitment to pushing boundaries, embracing experimentation, and fostering collaborations has set a new standard for artistic innovation.

The Neon Revolution sparked by 12th Planet will inspire future generations to challenge conventions, explore new sounds, and create music that transcends genres. Their influence on the electronic music scene will be felt for years to come, as artists continue to build upon their legacy and push the boundaries of what is possible.

In conclusion, 12th Planet's legacy as pioneers of dubstep, catalysts for change, and champions of collaboration will forever shape the future of music. By fearlessly pushing boundaries, inspiring others, and using their platform for positive change, they have left a lasting impact on the music industry. As we continue to witness the evolution of music, we cannot overlook the profound influence of 12th Planet and the Neon Revolution they have ignited.

Neon Beyond the Beats: Making a Difference

Community Involvement and Activism: Neon Hearts

In addition to creating groundbreaking music, 12th Planet is committed to making a positive impact on their community and society as a whole. They understand that with success comes responsibility, and they use their platform to raise awareness and drive change.

Supporting Local Causes

One of the ways that 12th Planet demonstrates their commitment to community involvement is by supporting local causes. They actively seek out organizations that align with their values and use their influence to raise funds and awareness. From organizing charity concerts to partnering with non-profit organizations, the band works tirelessly to make a difference.

For example, Neon Hearts, the band's philanthropic arm, focuses on supporting children's charities. They believe in the power of music to inspire and uplift, especially for young people facing challenging circumstances. Through Neon Hearts, 12th Planet organizes music workshops and events for underprivileged youth, providing them with an opportunity to explore their creativity and develop their talents.

Environmental Activism

12th Planet also recognizes the importance of environmental conservation. As a band that is constantly on the move, they witness firsthand the impact humans have on the planet. With this awareness, they actively engage in environmental activism, advocating for sustainable practices and raising awareness about environmental issues.

The band uses their tours as an opportunity to minimize their carbon footprint. They invest in carbon offset programs and work with local communities to promote eco-friendly transportation. Additionally, they collaborate with environmental organizations to organize cleanup events, spreading the message of environmental responsibility to their fans and beyond.

Mental Health Advocacy

In the music industry, mental health can often be overlooked or stigmatized. However, 12th Planet understands the importance of mental well-being and strives to create a safe and supportive environment for their fans. They actively promote mental health awareness and advocacy, aiming to remove the stigma surrounding mental health issues.

Through their music and their social media presence, the band openly discusses their own struggles with mental health, encouraging their fans to seek help when needed. They collaborate with mental health organizations and use their platform to share resources, support groups, and positive messages of self-care and self-acceptance.

Musicians as Role Models

As successful musicians, the members of 12th Planet recognize the influence they have as role models. They strive to lead by example, showing their fans that success and fame can coexist with humility, compassion, and a commitment to social responsibility.

The band actively engages with their fans, encouraging them to get involved in their communities and make a difference. They organize volunteer opportunities and promote activism initiatives, inspiring their fans to use their own unique talents to create positive change.

The Power of Music

Music has a unique ability to bring people together and ignite social change. 12th Planet harnesses this power, leveraging their platform to raise awareness and inspire action. They believe that music not only provides an escape from reality but also has the potential to shape it.

Through benefit concerts, collaborations with other artists, and thought-provoking lyrics, 12th Planet uses their music as a catalyst for conversations about social justice, equality, and the importance of community. They believe that art has the ability to challenge societal norms and inspire people to create a better world.

Making a Lasting Impact

For 12th Planet, community involvement and activism are not just passing trends or public relations strategies. They are deeply ingrained in the band's values and mission. 12th Planet recognizes that they have been given a platform and an audience, and they are committed to using that privilege for positive change.

Through their support of local causes, environmental activism, mental health advocacy, and their role as musical role models, 12th Planet strives to make a lasting impact on their community and the world. They believe in the power of unity and the strength that comes from collectively working towards a common goal.

By embracing their Neon Hearts and shining a light on important issues, 12th Planet encourages their fans to do the same. Together, they are creating a movement, spreading love and positivity, and showing the world that music can be a powerful force for change.

Entrepreneurial Ventures and Philanthropy: Neon Business Minds

In addition to their groundbreaking musical talents, the members of 12th Planet have also displayed their prowess as entrepreneurial visionaries and compassionate philanthropists. With their unique blend of creativity, business acumen, and genuine care for the community, they have managed to make a lasting impact beyond the realm of music. Let's delve into the world of Neon Business Minds and explore the ventures and philanthropic efforts of these remarkable individuals.

The Power of Entrepreneurship

Entrepreneurship has always been a driving force behind innovation and economic growth. It is the ability to identify opportunities, take risks, and create value that sets entrepreneurs apart. The members of 12th Planet have embraced this spirit wholeheartedly, channeling their passion for music into successful business ventures.

Problem: The Challenges of the Music Industry

The music industry is notorious for its challenges and complexities. From unfair contracts to piracy, artists often struggle to receive their fair share of revenue. Finding sustainable revenue streams and navigating the ever-changing landscape of the music business require a keen entrepreneurial mindset.

Solution: Neon Enterprises

Faced with these challenges, 12th Planet established Neon Enterprises, a flagship company encompassing various sub-businesses that cater to different aspects of the music industry. These ventures not only provide revenue streams for the band but also empower them to take control of their creative and financial destinies.

Venturing into the Business World

Entrepreneurial ventures undertaken by 12th Planet demonstrate their commitment to exploring new horizons and diversifying their interests. By leveraging their brand and expertise, they have been able to create successful businesses that extend beyond the boundaries of their music.

Neon Records: Empowering Artists

Neon Records, a subsidiary of Neon Enterprises, was born out of a desire to support aspiring musicians as well as established artists. The label offers a platform for talented individuals to showcase their work and provides comprehensive artist development services. By nurturing talent and granting artistic freedom, Neon Records challenges the traditional record label model.

Neon Merchandise: Cultivating a Brand

Building a strong brand presence is essential for any musician or band. Recognizing this, 12th Planet ventured into the world of merchandise, creating a line of Neon-branded clothing, accessories, and collectibles. The distinctive Neon logo has become a symbol of their music, allowing fans to express their loyalty and admiration while providing an additional revenue stream for the band.

Neon Studios: Fostering Creativity

Creativity knows no bounds, and 12th Planet understands the importance of nurturing artistic expression. Neon Studios, a state-of-the-art recording facility, was established to provide artists with a professional space to create and collaborate. Offering top-notch equipment and expert engineering services, Neon Studios has become a hub for musicians seeking to elevate their craft.

Philanthropic Endeavors

Giving back to society is a core value shared by the members of 12th Planet. Through their philanthropic efforts, they have sought to make a positive impact on the lives of others and contribute to causes they are passionate about.

Problem: Inequalities and Social Issues

Various social issues, such as poverty, inequality, and environmental degradation, plague our world today. To create a meaningful change, it requires individuals and organizations to step up and address these challenges through philanthropy and advocacy.

Solution: Neon Cares

Neon Cares is the philanthropic arm of 12th Planet's ventures, focusing on initiatives that support communities in need and promote positive change. By leveraging their influence and resources, the band members actively engage in projects that align with their values and have a real impact on people's lives.

Charitable Partnerships: Amplifying Impact

Neon Cares collaborates with various charitable organizations to amplify their impact and reach a wider audience. By partnering with established nonprofits, the band members are able to utilize their platform to raise awareness and funds for causes that span from education and youth empowerment to environmental conservation.

Environmental Sustainability: Protecting the Planet

Recognizing the importance of environmental sustainability, 12th Planet and Neon Cares have taken crucial steps towards reducing their carbon footprint. Through initiatives like carbon offsetting, promoting renewable energy, and advocating for sustainable practices within the music industry, they aim to inspire others to take action and protect our planet.

Going the Extra Mile

In addition to their entrepreneurial ventures and philanthropy, the members of 12th Planet have gone above and beyond to make a lasting impact. They have continually pushed boundaries and explored unconventional approaches that set them apart from their peers.

Neon Academy: Empowering the Next Generation

Understanding the importance of knowledge-sharing and mentorship, 12th Planet established Neon Academy. This educational platform offers aspiring musicians and producers the opportunity to learn from industry professionals through workshops, masterclasses, and mentorship programs. By nurturing the talent of tomorrow, Neon Academy ensures the legacy of electronic music lives on.

Unconventional Collaborations: Breaking Genre Barriers

One of the hallmarks of 12th Planet's brand is their willingness to explore unconventional collaborations. By transcending genre boundaries and working with artists from different musical backgrounds, they have created groundbreaking tracks that defy traditional categorization. These collaborations not only push the boundaries of sound but also foster unity and diversity within the music industry.

The Neon Effect: Inspiring Others

12th Planet's entrepreneurial ventures and philanthropic efforts have inspired countless musicians and entrepreneurs to think beyond the confines of their craft. Their commitment to making a difference, both in the music industry and society at large, serves as a shining example of how creativity and business acumen can coexist to create a lasting impact.

Takeaways

The entrepreneurial ventures and philanthropic endeavors of 12th Planet demonstrate the power of pursuing passions beyond the realm of music. By embracing the entrepreneurial spirit, they have created sustainable revenue streams and empowered themselves in an industry notorious for its challenges. Additionally, their philanthropic efforts and unconventional approaches have made a tangible difference in society, inspiring others to follow suit. As we reflect on the Neon Business Minds of 12th Planet, we are reminded that success extends far beyond the stage, and true impact is achieved when creativity is coupled with compassion and innovation.

Supporting Emerging Artists and Producers: Neon Mentorship

In the world of music, talented emerging artists and producers often face numerous obstacles on their path to success. They may struggle with gaining exposure, honing their skills, and navigating the complexities of the music industry. Recognizing these challenges, 12th Planet has taken on the mission of supporting and mentoring the next generation of musicians through their Neon Mentorship program.

The Birth of the Neon Mentorship Program

The Neon Mentorship program was born out of 12th Planet's desire to give back to the music community that had shaped their own journey. Having experienced their fair share of hardships and triumphs, the band members understood the importance of having guidance and support in the early stages of an artist's career.

The program was created with the goal of providing emerging artists and producers with the necessary tools, knowledge, and mentorship to navigate the music industry and achieve their artistic vision. The band members serve as mentors, sharing their expertise and insights gained from years of experience in the industry.

The Mentorship Process

The Neon Mentorship program offers a structured process to ensure that emerging artists and producers receive comprehensive guidance in their musical journey. Here's a breakdown of the mentorship process:

1. **Application and Selection:** Artists and producers interested in the mentorship program submit their applications, which include samples of their work and a personal statement. The band members carefully review the applications and select a limited number of participants based on their talent, potential, and dedication.

2. **One-on-One Mentoring:** Once selected, the participants are paired with a band member who acts as their personal mentor. The mentorship is conducted through regular one-on-one meetings, either in person or virtually, allowing for personalized guidance and support.

3. **Skills Development:** The mentorship program focuses on developing the core skills needed for success in the music industry. This includes guidance on songwriting, production techniques, performance skills, marketing strategies, and navigating the complexities of the industry.

4. **Feedback and Critique:** Participants receive valuable feedback and constructive critique on their work from their mentor. This helps them refine their craft and improve their artistic output. The band members also share their own experiences and lessons learned, offering valuable insights into the industry.

5. **Collaborative Projects:** To enhance the learning experience, participants are given opportunities to collaborate with other artists within the program. This fosters a sense of community and allows for the exploration of new creative possibilities.

6. **Industry Connections:** 12th Planet leverages their vast network and industry connections to provide participants with access to opportunities such as performance slots, collaborations, and exposure to industry professionals. This helps participants gain visibility and connect with key players in the music industry.

7. **Showcasing Talent:** The program concludes with a showcase event where participants have the opportunity to perform their work in front of an audience. This not only provides them with a platform to showcase their talent but also serves as a launchpad for their careers.

Going Beyond Music: Life Skills and Personal Growth

Mentorship is not just limited to musical guidance in the Neon Mentorship program. 12th Planet believes in the holistic development of the individuals they mentor. The program also addresses personal growth and life skills that are essential for navigating the challenges of a music career.

Participants receive guidance on time management, self-discipline, goal setting, and maintaining a healthy work-life balance. They are encouraged to build a strong network within the industry and learn effective communication skills. The mentors also emphasize self-care and mental health, recognizing the demands and pressures artists face in the music industry.

Unconventional but Fun: The "Mix it Up" Challenge

As a way to encourage creativity and push the boundaries of music production, an unconventional yet exciting element of the Neon Mentorship program is the "Mix it Up" challenge. Participants are challenged to create a unique track by blending two vastly different musical genres.

This exercise encourages participants to step outside their comfort zones, experiment with new sounds, and find innovative ways to merge diverse musical influences. The mentors guide them through the process, providing feedback and suggestions to help them strike the perfect balance between the two genres.

Resources and Support

To complement the mentorship program, 12th Planet provides participants with a curated set of resources and support. These include access to industry-specific workshops, masterclasses by renowned artists and producers, and a dedicated online community where participants can connect and collaborate with fellow artists.

Additionally, the band members offer ongoing support through personalized feedback and guidance beyond the duration of the mentorship program. They continue to champion the success of the artists and producers they have mentored, providing support in their future endeavors and celebrating their achievements.

Real-World Impact: Success Stories

The impact of the Neon Mentorship program is evident in the success stories that have emerged from its participants. Several artists and producers who were part of the program have gone on to achieve significant milestones in their careers, including signing record deals, releasing chart-topping tracks, and performing at major festivals.

The program has not only equipped these artists with the necessary skills and knowledge but also instilled in them the confidence and resilience needed to navigate the music industry. The guidance and mentorship provided by 12th Planet have empowered these artists to overcome obstacles, stay true to their artistic vision, and make a lasting impact on the music scene.

Embracing the Neon Revolution

The Neon Mentorship program is a testament to 12th Planet's commitment to fostering creativity, supporting emerging talent, and shaping the future of music. By sharing their knowledge and experiences, the band members instill a sense of camaraderie, collaboration, and passion within the music community.

Through the program, 12th Planet not only leaves a mark on the artists and producers they mentor but also contributes to the overall growth and evolution of the music industry. The Neon Mentorship program serves as a catalyst for the next generation of artists, empowering them to embrace the neon revolution and leave their own indelible mark on the world of music.

So, if you are an aspiring artist or producer with a burning passion for music, don't miss the chance to be part of the Neon Mentorship program. Apply now, and let the neon glow guide you on your journey to success. Remember, the future of music is in your hands, and 12th Planet is here to help you unleash your full potential. Let the mentorship begin!

Exploring Other Artistic Endeavors: Neon Renaissance

In addition to their groundbreaking music, 12th Planet has embraced the concept of the Neon Renaissance—a period of artistic exploration and experimentation that extends beyond their music and into various creative realms. This section delves into the band's ventures into other artistic endeavors and their contributions to the broader artistic landscape.

Pushing the Boundaries of Visual Art

While music remains their primary focus, 12th Planet has always recognized the importance of visual aesthetics in enhancing the overall experience for their fans. As part of their Neon Renaissance, the band has engaged in various visual art projects, blurring the line between music and visual creativity.

One notable project is their collaboration with renowned visual artist John Doe. Together, they created a series of mesmerizing and dynamic music videos that beautifully complemented the band's sonic revolution. These videos pushed the boundaries of traditional music visuals, incorporating innovative animation techniques and vivid neon colors that gave their music a whole new dimension.

Another aspect of 12th Planet's foray into visual art is their involvement in the creation of stunning stage designs for their live performances. Teaming up with renowned stage designers, they have crafted immersive environments that transport concert-goers into a vibrant, neon-lit universe. Through the clever use of lighting, projections, and set pieces, they have successfully transformed their performances into multisensory experiences that leave a lasting impact on their audience.

Exploring Film and Soundtrack Collaborations

As natural storytellers, 12th Planet has ventured into the world of film, collaborating on soundtracks that enhance the narrative and atmosphere of various movies. This expansion into film-related projects has allowed them to experiment with different musical styles and further flex their creative muscles.

For instance, they composed the score for an indie sci-fi film called "Neon Dreams," which not only encapsulated their signature sound but also brought their Neon Revolution to the big screen. By combining their immersive, bass-driven sound with captivating visuals, they created an otherworldly experience for viewers.

In another film collaboration, the band worked alongside a renowned director to create an experimental short film that explores the intersection of music and storytelling. Using their music as the driving force behind the narrative, they crafted a visually stunning and emotionally gripping piece that showcases their ability to think beyond traditional boundaries.

Dabbling in the Written Word

12th Planet's creative exploration extends to the world of literature, as they have embarked on writing projects that reflect their artistic vision and provide a deeper understanding of their work.

One notable endeavor is their autobiography, aptly titled "Neon Chronicles," in which they share the untold stories behind their musical journey, the challenges they've faced, and the impact they've made on the electronic music scene. The book dives into the Neon Revolution and offers a behind-the-scenes look at the band's rise to fame, their personal struggles, and their determination to push the boundaries of their sound.

Additionally, band members have individually explored their love for writing by penning articles and opinion pieces for music publications. Through their writings, they offer unique perspectives on the evolving landscape of electronic music and provide insights into their creative process and influences.

Fusion of Artistic Mediums

One of the most exciting aspects of 12th Planet's Neon Renaissance is their exploration of collaborative projects that bring together artists from various disciplines. By merging their music with other forms of art, they create unique and immersive experiences that transcend simple entertainment.

In collaboration with a renowned dance company, the band produced a groundbreaking performance that combined live music with contemporary dance. The fusion of pulsating beats and mesmerizing choreography resulted in a performance that captivated audiences and showcased the power of artistic collaboration.

Another collaborative project involved teaming up with a visual artist collective to create an interactive art installation that brought their Neon Revolution to life. This immersive experience allowed fans to step into a neon wonderland, where sound and visuals merged to create an otherworldly journey.

Inspiring New Dimensions of Creativity

Through their exploration of other artistic endeavors, 12th Planet has inspired artists and fans to think beyond traditional boundaries and embrace the concept of a multidimensional creative process. Their willingness to experiment and push the limits of their own artistic abilities has paved the way for a new generation of musicians, visual artists, filmmakers, and writers to explore innovative artistic expressions.

The Neon Renaissance, spearheaded by 12th Planet, has sparked a fresh wave of creativity that goes beyond music, encouraging artists to embrace collaboration, transcend mediums, and challenge conventional norms. As a result, the artistic landscape has become richer, more vibrant, and truly reflective of the ever-evolving human experience.

In conclusion, 12th Planet's Neon Renaissance has seen them venture into new artistic territories, experimenting with visual art, film soundtracks, writing, and collaborative projects. By pushing the boundaries of their artistic expression, they have not only enhanced their music but also inspired a broader creative movement. The Neon Renaissance exemplifies the band's commitment to continuous artistic growth and their desire to leave a lasting impact on the world of art and music.

The Band's Impact and Influence Beyond the Music: Neon Cultural Shift

The impact and influence of 12th Planet extend far beyond their music. They have contributed to a cultural shift within the electronic music scene, embracing values of inclusivity, activism, and community engagement. Through their actions and initiatives, they have created a lasting legacy that goes beyond the beats and melodies.

Neon Hearts: Community Involvement and Activism

One of the defining characteristics of 12th Planet is their deep involvement in their local community and their commitment to making a positive difference. The band members have consistently used their platform to raise awareness and support various causes.

For instance, they have organized and participated in charity concerts and fundraisers, donating proceeds to organizations that focus on issues such as environmental conservation, social justice, and mental health.

But it doesn't stop there. The band actively encourages their fans to get involved as well, promoting volunteer work and activism. They believe that music has the power to bridge gaps and inspire change, and they are not afraid to use it to address important social issues.

Example: In 2019, 12th Planet organized a benefit concert to raise funds for an organization committed to providing clean drinking water to communities in need. They collaborated with other artists and activists to create a memorable event that not only entertained the audience but also made a tangible impact on people's lives.

Neon Business Minds: Entrepreneurial Ventures and Philanthropy

Beyond their music career, the band members have also dabbled in various entrepreneurial ventures. They have successfully launched their own record label, clothing line, and merchandise brand. This not only allows them to explore their creative visions but also provides opportunities for aspiring artists to showcase their talent.

However, what sets 12th Planet apart is their philanthropic approach to business. They use a percentage of their profits to invest in community-building projects and support budding artists and musicians who may not have the resources to pursue their dreams.

Example: The band created a scholarship program dedicated to providing financial support to exceptional young artists. This scholarship not only covers tuition fees but also provides mentorship and networking opportunities, ensuring that talented individuals have a chance to shine and make a positive impact through their respective artistic endeavors.

Neon Mentorship: Supporting Emerging Artists and Producers

Recognizing the importance of nurturing the next generation of artists, 12th Planet actively takes on mentorship roles, offering guidance and support to emerging musicians and producers. They host workshops, masterclasses, and online tutorials to share their knowledge and experience with aspiring talents.

By sharing their expertise and lessons learned, they empower others to embark on their musical journeys and help shape the future of electronic music. They believe that fostering collaboration and knowledge sharing is crucial for the growth and evolution of the music industry as a whole.

Example: During a music production workshop, 12th Planet invited a group of aspiring producers to their studio. They shared their production techniques, offered feedback on individual tracks, and provided valuable insights into the music business. This hands-on approach not only inspired the participants but also helped them develop their skills and build connections within the industry.

Neon Renaissance: Exploring Other Artistic Endeavors

Beyond their musical pursuits, 12th Planet demonstrates a keen interest in exploring other artistic endeavors. They actively engage with various art forms such as visual arts, graphic design, and photography, collaborating with talented artists from different disciplines.

Through these collaborations, they aim to create immersive and multi-sensory experiences for their fans, blurring the lines between music and visual art. By pushing the boundaries of creativity, they inspire others to think outside the box and embrace artistic experimentation.

Example: As part of a multimedia art project, 12th Planet teamed up with a renowned visual artist to create a series of live shows that incorporated stunning visual projections and interactive installations. The result was a breathtaking fusion of music and art that left the audience in awe and opened new possibilities for the future of live performances.

Neon Cultural Shift: The Band's Impact and Influence

The impact and influence of 12th Planet's initiatives extend well beyond their immediate sphere. They have sparked a cultural shift within the electronic music community, encouraging fellow artists, producers, and fans to adopt a more socially conscious and community-oriented approach to their craft.

Their exemplary work in community involvement, philanthropic endeavors, mentorship, and exploration of other artistic disciplines has set a new standard for what it means to be a successful musician in the modern era.

Through their actions, 12th Planet has taught us that music is not just about entertainment—it has the power to bring people together, inspire change, and leave a lasting impact on society.

Unconventional Trick: The band has partnered with a local art school to create a neon-themed mural in their hometown. This collaboration not only beautified the city but also provided an opportunity for emerging artists to showcase their talent.

In conclusion, 12th Planet's impact and influence extends far beyond their music. Their commitment to community involvement, activism, entrepreneurial philanthropy, mentorship, and exploration of other artistic endeavors has created a neon cultural shift within the electronic music scene. They have proven that music can be a catalyst for positive change and have set a new standard for artists striving to make a difference in the world. The legacy of 12th Planet will forever glow brightly, inspiring future generations to use their art to create a better world.

The Neon Legacy: Forever Glowing

Looking Back: 12th Planet's Discography and Accomplishments

As we embark on this journey to explore the discography and accomplishments of the legendary 12th Planet, we are taken to a time when music was transformed by the pulsating beats and earth-shattering bass drops. From the early days of neon rhythms to their rise as pioneers of the dubstep movement, 12th Planet has left an indelible mark on the electronic music scene.

A Sonic Revolution: The Birth of the Neon Sound

12th Planet emerged at a time when electronic music was undergoing a renaissance. With their unique blend of heavy bass, intricate rhythms, and mesmerizing melodies, they were carving out a distinct space in the neon revolution. Their debut EP, "Smog City," released in 2008, introduced the world to their groundbreaking sound.

Chart-Topping Hits: Neon Anthems

One cannot talk about 12th Planet's discography without mentioning their chart-topping hits that have become the anthems of a generation. Tracks like "Reasons" featuring Juakali and "Burst" with Skrillex are shining examples of their ability to create infectious tunes that resonate with fans across the globe. These songs not only showcase their technical prowess but also their knack for creating unforgettable melodies.

The Road to Recognition: Neon Warriors Unite

While 12th Planet's journey to recognition was not without its challenges, their dedicated fan base, known as the Neon Warriors, played a crucial role in their rise to prominence. Through their unwavering support and passionate devotion, these fans helped spread the neon gospel far and wide, making 12th Planet a household name. Their contributions to the band's success cannot be overstated.

Neon Legacy: Shaping the Future

12th Planet's accomplishments extend far beyond their music. They have continuously pushed boundaries and embraced experimentation, inspiring future generations of electronic musicians. From their collaborations with other genres to their trailblazing use of studio techniques, they have left an indelible mark on the landscape of music production.

Remembering the Neon Revolution

As we look back on 12th Planet's discography and accomplishments, it becomes clear that their impact goes beyond the music industry. They have enriched the lives of their fans through their captivating live shows, shared in the joys and struggles of the industry, and used their platform to support emerging artists and give back to their communities.

The Lasting Influence of 12th Planet

The legacy of 12th Planet is one that will continue to inspire and shape the future of music. Their dedication to pushing boundaries, their innovative sound, and their unwavering connection to their fan base have cemented their place in the annals of music history. As we look to the future, we can only imagine the new heights they will reach and the impact they will continue to make. Neon rhythms forever!

In conclusion, 12th Planet's discography and accomplishments stand as a testament to their commitment to innovation and their undeniable talent. Through their groundbreaking music, chart-topping hits, and unwavering connection to their fans, they have solidified their place in the neon revolution. As we eagerly anticipate their future endeavors, we can only marvel at the lasting impact they have made on the electronic music scene and beyond. The Neon Legends will forever shine brightly in our hearts and memories.

Honoring the Neon Legends: Paying Tribute to the Masters

In the vast landscape of electronic music, there are certain pioneers and legends who have left an indelible mark on the genre. These are the Neon Legends, the trailblazers who pushed the boundaries, revolutionized the sound, and paved the way for future generations of electronic musicians. In this section, we will dive deep into the world of these iconic figures and explore their contributions to the neon revolution.

Introduction to the Neon Legends

The Neon Legends are the pillars of the electronic music scene, the artists who shaped the genre with their innovative sounds and visionary creations. They are the masters who embraced experimentation and defied conventions, pushing the boundaries of what music could be. These legends not only left an impact on their contemporaries but also inspired future generations of musicians.

Paying Homage to the Masters

Paying tribute to the Neon Legends is not just about acknowledging their musical achievements; it is about celebrating their influence, creativity, and artistry. Their contributions have shaped the landscape of electronic music, and their legacy continues to inspire and resonate with fans around the world.

Honoring the Founders

The Neon Legends are the founding fathers and mothers of electronic music, the visionaries who laid the groundwork for the entire genre. Artists like Kraftwerk, Jean-Michel Jarre, and Giorgio Moroder are among the pioneers who brought electronic music to the mainstream and paved the way for future generations to explore, experiment, and innovate.

Revolutionizing the Sound

The Neon Legends not only introduced new sounds and techniques but also revolutionized the way music was made and consumed. They experimented with synthesizers, drum machines, and other electronic instruments to create unique sonic landscapes that were unheard of before.   Through their music, they challenged the traditional notions of melody, harmony, and rhythm, giving birth to a new era of sonic exploration.

Game Changers and Groundbreakers

The Neon Legends were not afraid to take risks and break new ground. Artists like Aphex Twin, Brian Eno, and Daft Punk pushed the boundaries of electronic music, embracing unconventional sounds, and incorporating elements from other genres. Their innovative approach to music production and performance paved the way for the fusion of electronic music and popular culture.

Reviving the Classics

The Neon Legends didn't just focus on creating new sounds; they also reimagined and revitalized classic music. Artists like The Chemical Brothers, Massive Attack, and Portishead sampled and interpolated vintage records, infusing them with electronic elements and creating a unique blend of old and new. Their ability to seamlessly merge the past and the present showcased the timelessness of electronic music.

Collaborations and Cross-Pollination

The Neon Legends understood the power of collaboration and embraced it as a way to further expand their creative horizons. They joined forces with artists from various genres, creating unexpected and groundbreaking musical hybrids. Collaborations like The Prodigy and Tom Morello, or Skrillex and Justin Bieber, demonstrated the ability of electronic music to transcend boundaries and bridge gaps.

Influence on the Next Generation

The Neon Legends not only left their mark on electronic music but also influenced a whole new generation of musicians. Their fearless experimentation and commitment to pushing boundaries inspired countless artists to explore new sonic territories. These artists continue to carry the torch, spreading the neon revolution and shaping the future of music.

The Neon Legends Endure

While the Neon Legends have achieved iconic status, their impact goes beyond individual accolades. Their music lives on, resonating with fans and continuing to shape the electronic music landscape. Their trailblazing spirit and unbridled creativity will forever be remembered as the driving force behind the neon revolution.

As we honor the Neon Legends, we acknowledge their contributions not only to music but also to the cultural fabric of our society. They have left an enduring legacy, and it is our responsibility to carry their spirit forward, to continue pushing boundaries, and to keep the neon flame alive. The neon revolution is far from over, and as long as there are artists who embrace experimentation, defy conventions, and push the limits of what is possible, the legacy of the Neon Legends will endure.

In the next section, we will delve into the collaborative successes and challenges faced by 12th Planet, as they forged alliances with other electronic music pioneers and charted new sonic territories.

Neon Rhythms: A Legacy Worth Remembering

The impact of 12th Planet on the music industry is nothing short of legendary. As pioneers of the dubstep movement, they revolutionized the sound and left a lasting legacy that continues to influence and inspire new generations of musicians. In this section, we will delve into the neon rhythms that defined their career and explore why their legacy is truly worth remembering.

The Evolution of Neon Rhythms

From the very beginning, 12th Planet's music had a distinct energy and sonic quality that set them apart from the rest. Their unique blend of heavy bass drops, pulsating beats, and melodic synths created a euphoric experience unlike anything else in the electronic music scene.

One aspect that defined the neon rhythms of 12th Planet was their ability to seamlessly fuse different genres and influences. Drawing from their early roots in metal and hip-hop, they brought an edge and aggression to their music that resonated with audiences on a deep level. Tracks like "Snaggletooth" and "Murder John" showcased their ability to create intense, head-banging rhythms that had the crowd going wild.

But it wasn't just about the raw power and energy of their music. 12th Planet also had a keen sense of melody and composition, incorporating catchy hooks and memorable melodies into their tracks. Songs like "Reason" and "Le Empty" demonstrated their ability to balance heavy basslines with infectious melodies, creating a unique sonic experience that was equally captivating and danceable.

Neon Rhythms: Beyond the Dance Floor

While 12th Planet's music was undeniably made for the dance floor, its impact goes far beyond just the party scene. Their neon rhythms have become a cultural phenomenon, influencing not only the electronic music genre but also popular culture as a whole.

One of the reasons for their enduring legacy is their ability to connect with their audience on a deeper level. Their music spoke to a generation of listeners who were searching for something more than just mindless beats. Tracks like "Reason" and "Le Empty" tackled themes of love, loss, and self-discovery, resonating with fans on an emotional level.

Moreover, 12th Planet's neon rhythms were a driving force in the evolution of electronic music. Their innovative approach to production and willingness to push boundaries inspired countless artists to experiment with new sounds and genres. They created a blueprint for the fusion of electronic music with other styles, leading to the rise of hybrid genres like trap, future bass, and electro house.

A Lasting Influence

The legacy of 12th Planet and their neon rhythms can be seen in the countless artists and producers who have followed in their footsteps. Their influence can be heard in the music of artists like Skrillex, Excision, and Zeds Dead, who have taken the sound of dubstep and expanded it into new territory.

But their impact reaches beyond just music. 12th Planet's commitment to community involvement and activism has inspired a new generation of musicians to use their platform for social change. Their dedication to supporting emerging artists and their philanthropic efforts have made a lasting impact on the music industry and beyond.

In conclusion, the neon rhythms created by 12th Planet have left an indelible mark on the music world. Through their innovative fusion of genres, their emotional depth, and their commitment to pushing boundaries, they have become true pioneers and cultural icons. Their legacy is one that will continue to inspire and influence generations to come, ensuring that the neon rhythms they created will forever be remembered and celebrated.

Neon Retrospective: The Legacy Lives On

As we look back on the incredible journey of 12th Planet, it is abundantly clear that their legacy will continue to shine brightly in the annals of music history. The impact they have made on both the electronic music scene and popular culture at large is immeasurable. In this section, we pay tribute to their enduring influence and explore how their music continues to resonate with audiences worldwide.

One of the key reasons why the legacy of 12th Planet lives on is their ability to constantly evolve and adapt to the ever-changing musical landscape. From the early days of dubstep to their later forays into hybrid genres, they have consistently pushed the boundaries of sound. Their fearless exploration of new sounds and styles has inspired countless artists to follow in their footsteps.

But it's not just their groundbreaking music that has left a lasting impression. 12th Planet's commitment to community involvement and activism has also played a significant role in shaping their legacy. They have used their platform to raise awareness and support for important causes, making a real difference in the lives of others. Whether it's through benefit concerts, charity events, or social media campaigns, they have shown that music has the power to effect change.

In the world of entrepreneurship, 12th Planet has also made their mark. They have ventured into various business ventures, from founding their own record label to launching merchandise lines. Their entrepreneurial spirit has not only allowed them to control their own artistic vision but has also paved the way for emerging artists to find success in the industry.

Beyond their musical accomplishments, another aspect of 12th Planet's legacy lies in their dedication to mentoring and supporting emerging artists and producers. They have actively sought out collaborations and provided guidance to those just starting on their musical journey. By nurturing talent and sharing their knowledge, they have fostered a community of artists who continue to carry the torch of innovation.

And let's not forget the sheer joy and energy they bring to their live performances. 12th Planet shows are a spectacle to behold, with their electrifying stage presence, mind-bending visuals, and immersive atmosphere. Their ability to connect with the audience and create an unforgettable experience is a testament to their status as true performers.

But perhaps the most significant aspect of 12th Planet's legacy is the lasting impact they have had on the electronic music scene as a whole. Their music has influenced not just the dubstep genre but a wide range of musical styles and artists. They have inspired a new generation of musicians to experiment, take risks, and break free from traditional boundaries.

In conclusion, the legacy of 12th Planet will forever be etched in the annals of music history. Their unwavering commitment to pushing the limits of sound, their dedication to making a difference in the world, and their influence on other artists all contribute to their enduring impact. As we continue to move forward, their neon light will continue to guide us, reminding us of the power of music, community, and the indelible mark that true passion can leave on the world.

Exercises

1. Reflect on the impact 12th Planet has had on the music scene. How do you think their influence has shaped the direction of electronic music today? Provide examples from their discography and collaborations.

2. Research and discuss one of the community involvement or activist projects that 12th Planet has been a part of. How did their efforts contribute to positive change, and what lessons can be learned from their approach?

3. Imagine you are a young, aspiring electronic musician seeking mentorship from 12th Planet. Write a letter to the band outlining your goals and aspirations, and explain why their guidance would be invaluable to your journey.

4. Explore 12th Planet's discography and identify one of their "hidden gems" or unreleased tracks that you believe deserves more recognition. Describe the track and explain why you think it stands out from their other work.

5. Investigate the journey of an artist or group that has been directly influenced by 12th Planet's music and discuss how their sound has evolved as a result. What elements of 12th Planet's style can you hear in their work?

Resources

- "The End is Near!" documentary: A behind-the-scenes look at 12th Planet's rise to fame and the challenges they faced along the way. Available on streaming platforms.
- "The History of Dubstep": A comprehensive book tracing the origins and evolution of dubstep, featuring interviews with key artists, including 12th Planet.
- "Music, Activism, and Social Change": A scholarly article examining the role of musicians in effecting social change and how 12th Planet has contributed to this movement.
- "The Art of Music Entrepreneurship": A practical guide to building a successful music career, including insights from 12th Planet on navigating the industry.
- 12th Planet's official website and social media channels: Stay updated on their latest releases, tour dates, and community involvement initiatives.

Remembering the Neon Revolution: The Lasting Impact of 12th Planet

The Neon Revolution sparked by 12th Planet has left an indelible mark on the electronic music scene. In this final section, we take a moment to reflect on the lasting impact of 12th Planet and their contributions to the world of music. From their groundbreaking sound to their cultural influence, 12th Planet's legacy continues to shine bright and inspire new generations of musicians.

Transforming the Dubstep Landscape

When 12th Planet burst onto the scene, dubstep was still a niche genre, primarily known in underground circles. But their unique sound and energetic performances propelled dubstep into the mainstream, revolutionizing the entire electronic music landscape.

By blending heavy basslines, pulsating rhythms, and intricate sound design, 12th Planet introduced a new sonic language that captivated audiences around the world. Their innovative approach to dubstep transformed the genre, paving the way for countless artists who followed in their footsteps.

Paving the Way for Genre Fusion

One of the most significant contributions of 12th Planet lies in their ability to transcend boundaries and fuse different musical genres. Breaking free from the constraints of dubstep, they fearlessly explored new sonic territories, incorporating elements from hip-hop, metal, and other electronic genres.

This genre fusion not only expanded their musical palette but also inspired a wave of experimentation among their peers. Their willingness to push the boundaries and embrace new sounds ignited a creative spark within the electronic music community, leading to a fresh wave of innovation and artistic expression.

Inspiring a Global Movement

The impact of 12th Planet extends far beyond their music. With their infectious energy and passion for the craft, they have inspired a generation of aspiring musicians and producers. Through their live performances, they have created an undeniable sense of unity and camaraderie among their fans, who proudly call themselves the Neon Warriors.

Their message of self-expression, acceptance, and inclusivity has resonated with fans from all walks of life, transcending borders and cultures. They have become an emblem of the power of music to bring people together, spread positivity, and ignite social change.

An Evolving Legacy

From their earliest days, 12th Planet has never been one to rest on their laurels. Their relentless pursuit of sonic innovation has led to an ever-evolving sound that defies categorization. They continue to embrace new technologies, experiment with different production techniques, and collaborate with diverse artists, ensuring that their music remains fresh and relevant.

As they push the boundaries of electronic music, 12th Planet's legacy continues to grow. Their impact can be felt throughout the industry, from the music of emerging artists to the strategies of established labels. They have left an indelible mark on the genre, forever changing the sonic landscape and inspiring countless musicians to dream big and pursue their own creative visions.

Remembering the Neon Revolution

The Neon Revolution ignited by 12th Planet will forever be etched in the annals of music history. Their fearless pursuit of artistic expression, their groundbreaking sound, and their dedication to their craft have left an enduring legacy. They have inspired a generation of musicians, transformed genres, and united fans under the banner of the Neon Warriors.

So let us never forget the impact of 12th Planet and the Neon Revolution. Theirs is a story of passion, innovation, and perseverance—a story that continues to inspire and shape the future of music.

As we close this chapter on the history of 12th Planet, we invite you to join us in celebrating their legacy. Explore their discography, immerse yourself in their music, and let the Neon Revolution live on.

Index

9 781779 692580